Twelve Canadian Playwrights Talk about Their Lives and Work

edited by Geraldine Anthony

There seems little doubt that Canada has now achieved a theatre of real quality and variety and has produced a number of playwrights of international stature. *Stage Voices* celebrates this coming-of-age through the words of twelve of the country's best and most renowned dramatists.

The first voices to be heard are those of the old guard—John Coulter, Herman Voaden, Robertson Davies, and Gwen Pharis Ringwood—who fought and won the early battles, such as the one that led to the formation of the Canada Council. They speak with the wisdom of experience but with undiminished passion. These three are followed by the mature gladiators—Tom Grainger, James Reaney, and John Herbert—whose plays are reaching an ever-widening audience and have achieved some international success. The last voices belong to the young Turks—Michael Cook, David French, David Freeman, Michel Tremblay, and Michel Garneau. They have written many of the finest and most popular Canadian plays of the last decade and their names are increasingly known outside their own country.

These playwrights reveal the influences that formed them, the experiences that gave rise to their best works, and their often astringent but always lively views of the history of theatre in Canada and its present state. Their words are enriched by Geraldine Anthony's informative introductions, a chronology of each playwright's life, and selected bibliographies.

Stage Voices is both a modern history of theatre in Canada and a passionate and very personal statement by twelve of the men and women who made, and are making, that theatre happen.

About the Editor

Geraldine Anthony, S.C., Ph.D., teaches English at Mount Saint Vincent University in Halifax, Nova Scotia. In addition to one published book on Irish-Canadian playwright John Coulter she is the general editor of the Profiles in Canadian Drama Series and is the author of numerous scholarly articles. She has in progress books on Gwen Pharis Ringwood and John Herbert, and is co-author with Renate Usmiani of the forthcoming *Two Languages: The Canadian Theatre of Liberation*. Sister Anthony has travelled across the country and gotten to know many of the playwrights personally in the course of her researches.

Also by
Geraldine Anthony

John Coulter

STAGE VOICES

Twelve Canadian Playwrights Talk about Their Lives and Work

EDITED BY

Geraldine Anthony

Doubleday Canada Limited
TORONTO, ONTARIO

Doubleday & Company, Inc.
GARDEN CITY, NEW YORK

1978

ISBN: 0-385-12643-3 (cloth)
0-385-13540-8 (paper)

Library of Congress Catalog Card Number: 77-76223

Six lines from "The Passing Strange"
are reprinted with permission of Macmillan Publishing Co., Inc.
from *Poems* by John Masefield. Copyright 1920 by John Masefield
renewed 1948 by John Masefield.

Photograph Credits

John Coulter: Mario Geo, Toronto
Herman Voaden: V. Tony Hauser
Robertson Davies: Ashley & Crippen
Gwen Pharis Ringwood: Clive Stangoe
Tom Grainger: Vancouver Sun Photo
James Reaney: E. Hamilton
John Herbert: Milne Studios Limited
Michael Cook: Richard Stoker
David French: Arnaud Maggs
David Freeman: Rosemary O'Shaughnessy
Michel Tremblay: No Credit
Michel Garneau: André Cornellier

In memory of my parents
Agnes J. Anthony, 1888-1977
William Anthony, 1883-1950

Author's Note

This book grew out of an enthusiastic response to the excitement engendered today by Canadian playwrights and their work. A visit to the centres of Canadian theatre in the major cities of Canada during a sabbatical year, 1973-74, permitted me to meet and talk with actors, directors, and playwrights. Their modesty about their work and their intellectually stimulating conversations prompted me to consider the editing of a book that would present essays by outstanding Canadian playwrights about their works. As it turned out, what they say about their own work is often typical of their individual attitudes toward drama as an art form.

There are only twelve playwrights included in this volume. Some who were asked did not wish to contribute; others were excluded because their careers are still too embryonic or because of my personal critical judgment. This book is not intended to be the last word, but it is a representative gathering of some of the best living Canadian dramatists.

In preparing this volume, I sent each of the contributors a list of fifteen questions asking their reasons for writing, the influences on their work, their manner of developing a play, their opinions of their own plays, their comments on the future of Canadian drama. Because complete freedom was emphasized in the preparation of these chapters, no dramatist was obliged to use these questions unless he so desired. The result is therefore a wide variety of forms including scholarly essays, familiar essays, a short story, a creative play, and a long prose poem—all written specifically for this volume. My list of questions appears only in Chapter Three, by Robertson Davies.

The short critical prefaces to each chapter are intended to give the reader a capsule of information on the dramatist's themes, techniques, strengths, and weaknesses. Read as a continuous whole, the prefaces may also provide a summary of trends in Canadian drama for the past forty years. Bibliographies at the end of each chapter suggest further reading and the Chronologies give useful biographical details. The writers are treated chronologically, beginning with the oldest living English Canadian playwrights and ending with two of the most creative young Québécois writers, some of whose plays have been translated and produced in English Canadian theatres. To the reader unfamiliar with Canadian drama, *Stage Voices* should provide a telescopic view of the overall picture; to the specialist in Canadian drama, it may offer fresh insights, through the playwright's own words about his contribution, his personal opinions on drama as a whole, and his predictions of the ways in which Canadian drama may develop in the future.

I wish to thank the twelve dramatists represented in this book, many of whom are my good friends, for their patience and generosity in giving so liberally of their time in interviews, for answering my letters, and for trusting me with their manuscripts long before a publisher had committed himself to this project. My gratitude also to my editors, Betty Corson and Rick Archbold, for their advice and helpful criticisms of the manuscript. For the enthusiasm generated in me for theatre I acknowledge gratefully the memory of my father, William Anthony, and my Mother, Agnes J. Anthony, who brought me as a child to the plays and musicals on Broadway and who nurtured in me a love and respect for all those people dedicated to theatre.

Contents

Introduction

The history of the development of a national drama seems to follow a similar pattern in every country. It is a long, painful process of growth. Beginning with foreign importations and continuing with thin imitations of the masters, a national drama eventually evolves out of the frustrations of playwrights who refuse to be mere imitators. It is, in fact, born of the passion to create one's own art.

Although no exception in this evolutionary process, Canada has been confronted with more than the usual obstacles. Because of its enormous size of four million square miles (with a contrastingly small population of twenty-three million people in 1977) it is not a country that can speak with one dramatic voice. Canada is a land of ten provinces separated by the natural barriers of mountains, prairies, and water. Its drama, therefore, tends to be localized within each province. Added to this is the divisive bicultural aspect of English and French Canada, always a source of anxiety, and today threatening to split the country in two. Because theatre has traditionally expressed the unique character of a people, Canadian drama today, still in its early period of development, expresses its regional character in at least as many separate voices as there are provinces, and culturally in two distinct theatres — English and French. Montreal is the centre of theatre in French Canada; Toronto of English Canada in the east, Vancouver in the west, with Winnipeg, Regina and Edmonton increasingly active in the mid-west. The Atlantic provinces have seen some activity in Canadian drama, particularly in Newfoundland, while Nova Scotia, New Brunswick and Prince Edward Island have made their own unique contributions.

Canadians have always encouraged theatre. A glance at the history of theatre in Canada is highly revealing. From the first theatricals in New France at the beginning of the seventeenth Century to the more sophisticated productions of the present time, there has been a steady growth of theatres throughout this vast nation. If in the past Canadians did not create their own plays for these theatres, it was because the time was not ripe. All those fortuitous circumstances which combine to produce indigenous drama had not yet fallen into place. But Canadians always delighted in the plays of other countries. Now, after 350 years of foreign importations, we have at last begun consistently to dramatize our own unique characters, cultures, and backgrounds in plays that, as previously mentioned, are provincial rather than national in character, and experimental as well as traditional. A self-conscious and diffident people are suddenly, in this decade, finding the dramatic voices with which to express themselves on stage.

I   Brief History of Canadian Theatre

The history of Canadian drama reveals its roots in French garrison theatre as early as 1606 when Marc Lescarbot, a Parisian lawyer, in charge of the French habitation at Port. Royal (now Annapolis Royal, Nova Scotia), encouraged theatricals in order to boost the morale of the people. He himself wrote an original marine masque in verse, *Le Théâtre de Neptune*, which was performed on the beach and in a barge and canoes by Indians and voyageurs. Published in Paris in 1609, it was indeed the first Canadian play. There followed pageants and charades in the garrisons of Port Royal and Quebec, and an original tragedy played in Quebec in 1640 to celebrate the birthday of the Dauphin. Classical French plays were also performed in Quebec: Corneille's *Le Cid* in 1646, *Heraclitus* in 1651. Drama was encouraged in the military messes by the Governor Louis de Buade, Comte de Frontenac 1672-1698. Unfortunately the French Catholic clergy were prejudiced against what they considered profane theatrical entertainments, and in 1694 Bishop Joseph de St. Vallier forbade the presentation of Molière's *Tartuffe*. Although it has been noted that the Catholic missionaries wrote and produced plays among the Hurons, and the Jesuit colleges in Quebec continued to perform classical plays by Corneille, Racine, and Molière, the Church remained obdurate in its opposition to theatre in French Canada and was therefore partly responsible for the slowness of its development. Yet Quebec was the home of one of Canada's first playwrights in the person of Joseph Quesnel (1749-1809) one of whose works, *Colas et Colinette*, proved a great success.

It is interesting to note that the change from French to British rule in Canada resulted in a powerful revival of theatre. Because French classical plays were very popular in eighteenth century England, British officers sent to Montreal and Quebec City supported the revival of French plays, even those that the Catholic Church had banned.

Meanwhile, English Canada was beginning to introduce theatre in its garrisons. In 1749 the soldiers who assisted Lord Cornwallis in the founding of Halifax, Nova Scotia, also performed in plays. The first English Canadian play, *Acadius*, or *Love in a Calm*, was produced in Halifax in 1774. British officers doing garrison duty in Halifax were familiar with contemporary British plays and in 1788 the officers of the garrison and fleet presented Sheridan's *School for Scandal* and in 1789 Shakespeare's *Merchant of Venice*.

Around the same time professional English and American actors and stock companies were presenting plays in Montreal and Halifax. A group calling itself the American Company of Comedians performed in Halifax in 1768, after being refused permission to perform in Rhode Island, and by 1789 Halifax had its second Grand Theatre. A century later this small city could boast three theatres and an opera house. Quebec's permanent playhouse, Théâtre du Marché au Foin, opened in 1790 and the Théâtre Royal in Montreal in 1825. These Canadian theatres attracted famous actors to Montreal. John Durang of Hallam's New York Company performed in Quebec in 1797. His colourful diary describes the hazardous trip and the diverse theatrical performances. Edmund Kean came in 1826, Dion Boucicault in 1853, Horton Rhys in 1861, and the immortal Sarah Bernhardt in 1880. Charles Dickens, on a trip to Canada, was asked to select and stage three one-act plays for the Coldstream Guards at the Old Théâtre Royal in Montreal on May 25, 1842. Military theatricals were frequently given in the mid 1800s in Quebec City and Montreal. In the 1830s Pierre Petitclair, Quebec-born dramatist, wrote comedies in the style of Molière. They were anti-establishment satires of Quebec society. There followed a succession of plays written by French Canadian dramatists, stimulated by professional touring companies from other countries.

English Canadian plays written at this time were better read than acted. G. Simcoe Lee, a native Canadian, had plays produced in Toronto in the early 1850s. Charles Heavysege's *Saul* (1857) and Charles Mair's *Tecumseh* (1886) followed the tradition of the nineteenth-century British closet dramas. Other areas in English Canada were beginning to awaken to theatre. Toronto witnessed its first theatre in 1809, when a group of American comic gentry performed *School for Scandal*. Toronto also opened a theatre above Frank's Hotel before 1830. In 1857 the Garrick Club was begun in Hamilton, Ontario, and evolved into today's Players Guild. Brockville, Ontario, as early as 1877 had a dramatic club in old Victoria Hall and the Brock Opera House. Victoria, B.C., in 1848 presented plays first in a big tent, then in the Mess Hall and finally in the Star and Garter Hotel. Winnipeg produced plays as early as 1870 at Lower Fort Garry. Baskerville in the Cariboo, northern British Columbia, had a fine theatre housing the famous Hurdy Gurdy Girls. Companies of actors from Britain and Europe toured English and French Canada bringing to Canadians a taste for great plays. Yet there was no interest at this time in promoting an indigenous drama for Canada. Theatre for Canadians was simply a form of entertainment, not an original expression of one's own identity and culture. Indeed Canadians equated their identity with their European forebears. Hence they empathized with the characters in British and European plays.

The early years of the twentieth century saw little progress. Canadians seemed unaware of the revolution in style taking place in Europe, nor did they perceive with any comparable foresight the sudden growth of an indigenous American drama beginning with Eugene O'Neill and the Provincetown players in 1917.

However, one important event occurred that would have far-reaching effects on the development of theatre in Canada. In 1906 Governor General Lord Albert Henry George Grey decided to hold an annual competition in Music and Drama as an incentive for Canadian talent because professional theatre in Canada was being directed and performed almost entirely by outsiders. Thus for the first time the Canadian government became the patron of the arts. These competitions continued until 1911 when Earl Grey's tenure as Governor General ended and he departed for England. However he had succeeded in being the inspiration for the formation of several amateur theatre groups in Ottawa, Montreal, Toronto and Winnipeg. Some of these groups survived and continued to produce plays.

To serve and unite these amateur groups, the Dominion Drama Festival was established in 1932. It was the D.D.F. that was responsible for conditioning the Canadian people to the "play" instinct, for the growth of perhaps the largest number of amateur acting groups per capita of any country in the world, and for thus bringing drama to the rural communities of sparsely settled mountain and prairie lands. The first competition of the D.D.F. was held in Ottawa in 1933. Sponsored by the Earl of Bessborough, the Dominion Drama Festival was a federation of local drama groups divided into thirteen regions: British Columbia, Alberta, Saskatchewan, Manitoba, Western Ontario, Central Ontario, Eastern Ontario, Western Quebec, Eastern Quebec, Nova Scotia, New Brunswick, Prince Edward Island and Newfoundland. Annual regional festivals were held in which any amateur acting group could compete.

Adjudicators named the best play in each region. Then these winning plays were performed at the national competition. Judging at both the regional and national levels was by highly competent European directors. The young actors, Canadian amateur directors, and playwrights used the professional and constructive criticisms they received to improve their performances at the following year's festivals. The trophies and awards for these performances increased and multiplied with almost alarming rapidity. Beginning with the first trophy, the Bessborough Trophy, for the best performance of a play in either English or French, the list of awards included a prize for the best play performance in English and one for French, as well as diplomas for the actors. Sir Barry Jackson, founder and director of the Birmingham Repertory Theatre in England and frequent visitor to Canada, offered the Sir Barry Jackson Trophy for the best original play written by a Canadian. Playwrights destined to become important dramatists won this trophy as well as other awards at the Festival: John Coulter for *The House in the Quiet Glen* (1937); Gwen Pharis Ringwood for *Still Stands the House* (1939). Robertson Davies won a regional award for *Eros at Breakfast* (1948), and the play was sent to represent Canada at the Edinburgh Festival in 1949. Over the years many other awards were added. These encouraged every aspect of play performance and production and were usually accompanied by a cash prize.

The Dominion Drama Festival did not so much emphasize native drama as it did lively and artistic productions of outstanding British and European plays. It proved highly significant in the maturing of Canadian actors, actresses, theatre techniques, and critics. Balanced artistic judgement was emphasized in the selection of the plays. Not only did the participants profit but also the vast audiences across Canada who congregated on the local and regional levels to see sons, daughters, and neighbours perform in competitions. The D.D.F. proved a good substitute for a national theatre school, bringing small and struggling drama groups together from vast distances across the nation. "Nothing in Canada has done so much for the amateur theatre as the Dominion Drama Festivals," said the Royal Commission on Arts, Letters and Sciences in 1951.

After four decades of outstanding performances, the work of the D.D.F. was assessed by the government and it was decided to replace it in 1971 with the non-competitive

Theatre Canada, holding annual festivals in which participating groups came by invitation, not competition. Adjudicators were replaced by *animateurs* who discussed techniques of production with the cast. Provinces were thereafter encouraged to provide their own organizations and festivals. Obviously the Dominion Drama Festival had accomplished its purpose at a period in Canada's artistic growth when it was most needed. The sudden upsurge and proliferation of professional companies across Canada in the late 1960s and early '70s made it apparent that Canadian Drama had now established a firm foothold across the continent.

Another fortuitous circumstance in the development of Canadian drama was the birth of the little theatre movement across rural, urban, and suburban Canada in the 1920s and '30s. The Ottawa Drama League, the London Little Theatre, the Theatre Arts Guild of Halifax, and countless other little theatres in Vancouver, Winnipeg, and Montreal brought amateur and semi-professional actors together in a community effort to provide more opportunities for theatre. One of the finest of its kind was Hart House Theatre, established in 1919 and given by the Massey family to the University of Toronto in 1946. Many early Canadian plays were given production at Hart House Theatre as well as performances of British, American, and European plays. One of its leading lights, Dora Mavor Moore, founded the New Play Society in Toronto which made a considerable contribution by training young Canadians to be actors, directors, set designers, and playwrights. One of its pupils deserves mention: John Herbert Brundage, who eventually became a notable Canadian playwright and winner of the 1975 Chalmers Drama award, the annual award for the best Canadian play of the year, established by the Toronto Drama Bench in 1972. Indeed, so many graduates of The New Play Society achieved success in theatre that space does not permit the listing of all their names.

In French Canada one of the most vital influences on the development of drama in Montreal was the artistic leadership of Reverend Emile Legault of the Holy Cross Fathers. The same Church that had stifled theatre in the nineteenth century was to bring it back through Father Legault's efforts in 1937. Having studied drama in France under Henri Ghéon, the leader of the Christian Theatre revival, Father Legault then returned to Montreal where he developed a new, sophisticated, modern, highly professional theatre company with his college students at Collège de Saint Laurent, called les Compagnons de Saint-Laurent. The plays produced were not only classical French but new modern French dramas of Cocteau and Anouilh. Father Legault took his company on tour across Canada where they gave polished performances in both French and English. His pupils became the initiators, eventually, of practically all the later artistic innovations in Montreal. Their theatre, the Théâtre des Compagnons, was the most outstanding professional theatre in French Canada. From it developed that great venture, the Théâtre du Nouveau Monde, which is today responsible for some of the most original and experimental work in Montreal.

Before the depression one chain of theatres fared better than most, the Walker Theatres in Manitoba along "the Bread Basket Circuit"—towns along the Red River of the North. These theatres provided the stages for entertainment by touring companies. Actors and companies came from Stratford-on-Avon, the Abbey Theatre in Dublin, and Broadway and London theatres. Melodrama, opera, magic shows, as well as great classical plays were presented. During the depression the Walker Theatres operated as movie houses. They finally closed between the two world wars because of limited funds, competition from film and radio, and the soaring expenses of production and travel.

In the 1930s several worker theatres were founded in Canada in an attempt to create a proletarian drama. The Toronto Progressive Arts Club, formed in 1931, initiated the movement for a proletarian theatre that would emphasize Canadians' complaints against the forces that caused the depression of the '30s. A national socialist journal, *Masses*, in print from 1932 to 1934, published articles calling for a workers' theatre. In the winter of 1932 an amateur group of actors answered this call by forming the Workers Experimental Theatre, later called the Workers Theatre. It was dedicated to the presentation of drama exposing the exploitation of the

Canadian people by what they considered to be a Canadian bourgeois society. This group was similar to workers' drama groups in the U.S.A., England, Russia, and Germany. Determined to create its own Canadian plays rooted in Canada's sweat shops, mines, and farms, the leaders used social inequalities and a need for social awareness as their themes. They performed in labour halls, parks, and in any available place. In centres from Halifax to Vancouver, these plays consisted of mass recitations, doctrinaire repetitions, and stereotype characters. Such plays as *Eviction* by two Montreal writers, *Unity* by Oscar Ryan, *War in the East* by Stanley Ryerson, *Looking Forward* by H. Francis, provided the stimulation from which grew such theatres as Toronto's Canadian Theatre of Action. This theatre was less politically involved but committed instead to an alleviation through drama of the problems of poverty, labour, and war which threatened mankind. Their plays were produced at the Hart House Theatre. This movement ended with World War II. Not since then has there been such a concerted use of drama for political purposes in English Canada.

CBC Radio Drama played the most powerful role in the development of both English and French Canadian drama. Established in 1936, it provided the outlet for script writers to create original Canadian plays. Out of CBC were born great Canadian radio dramatists whose work has still not been properly assessed—people like Len Peterson, Eric Nicol, Lister Sinclair, Merrill Denison, Joseph Schull, Mavor Moore, Gratien Gélinas, and countless others. Under the dynamic leadership of Andrew Allan who inspired numerous writers to its drama department, the CBC Radio began a long and successful career in the production of original Canadian plays reaching such heights of masterful, original performances in the 1940s and '50s, (before the advent of television) that it utterly surpassed the early goals set for it. Allan's series of radio plays entitled *Stage* proved to be their most stimulating output. Almost all the plays in this series were original Canadian dramas. The CBC Wednesday Night program presented some excellent original Canadian plays as well as adaptations from world theatre. Meanwhile the CBC French

network, Radio-Canada, was producing highly educational
drama programs such as Radio Collège in a successful effort
to bring to French Canadians the best in theatre from France.
All the great classical French dramatists were represented in
productions deliberately planned to educate French Canadians in their cultural heritage. Without a doubt it was this
rich fare that prepared young potential writers in Quebec to
become such artistic innovators in theatre arts surpassing the
work of their English contemporaries.

It was the original intention of CBC to use radio to fuse this
vast country into one cultural whole. What it did instead and
unwittingly was to provide French Canada with the perfect
means to consolidate and strengthen its own cultural identity.

Through CBC Radio, both French and English, the
Canadian playwright was assured national recognition and
financial security. It reached out over millions of miles to
people in rural areas as well as those in populated cities,
enriching and broadening the cultural lives of Canadians from
British Columbia to Nova Scotia, from southern Alberta to the
far distant points of the Northwest Territories.

Many of these radio dramatists wrote two and three
versions of each of their original plays in the hope of
attracting stage and television performances. With the advent
of CBC-TV in 1952 (CBFT in Montreal and CBLT in Toronto)
CBC Radio dramatists were forced to choose to write either
for radio or for television but they were not permitted to write
for both. Many of the older writers preferred not to risk their
careers in such a new and untried medium. Freelance writers,
such as John Coulter, could exercise their talents in both.
Over the past twenty years English Canadian television
drama, though steadily improving, has not yet reached the
heights that radio drama achieved, possibly because so many
American and British importations have been easily available.
French television drama surpassed the English because
outside programs were not as available in French. Québécois
writers were forced to provide original material.

The final step in the development of Canadian drama came
with the sudden, almost explosive proliferation of small
theatres throughout Canada in the 1960s, offering radio and

television playwrights the great opportunity they had long awaited—the stage on which to produce their plays. This movement was the result of many factors on the cultural political scene. Perhaps the catalyst that set it all in motion was the Canadian Centennial celebration, calling for original Canadian drama, and the government's willingness to provide the funds to open a veritable chain of little theatres across Canada. Radio writers offered stage plays whose oral and imaginative content was remarkable. Several of these writers also developed organizational skills and political expertise, such as Gratien Gélinas who became President of the Canadian Film Development Corporation. Herman Voaden and John Coulter had earlier shown their leadership qualities when they had used radio, newspapers, magazines, and books to voice their plea for native Canadian drama and government support of theatre in Canada. Public agitation by these leaders forced the Canadian government eventually to pass legislation to support the organization and financing of Canadian theatre. The Canadian Arts Council, now the Canadian Conference of the Arts, was the result of pressure by leaders such as Voaden and Coulter.

On June 21, 1944, a delegation of Canadian artists and dramatists presented the artists' briefs to the Turgeon Committee of the House of Commons in Ottawa—a committee designed to expand recreational, educational, and cultural services throughout Canada. Herman Voaden wrote the brief which John Coulter read in dramatic, ringing tones to the parliamentarians. These artists' briefs were part of the movement which led to the formation of the Massey Commission and subsequent Massey Report, which in turn led to the founding of the Canada Council in 1957, that substantial funding base for the arts in Canada. The Canada Council serves the artist through individual awards and bursaries. Among other things, it subsidizes professional theatres and gives grants to the National Theatre School and other artistic institutions.

In the years following World War II the number of repertory theatres increased significantly in Toronto, Ottawa, Vancouver, and other cities. The now internationally famous

Shakespearean Festival at Stratford, Ontario, was opened in 1953 under the direction of Tyrone Guthrie. It presented performances by some of the greatest internationally known actors and developed Canadian talent and produced some of Canada's finest actors: Douglas Campbell, Eric House, Douglas Rain, William Hutt, Bruno Gerussi, Christopher Plummer, Jean Gascon, Jack Creeley, Tony Van Bridge, Frances Hyland, Kate Reid, and many others. Canadian plays were produced in the associated Avon Theatre and on the Third Stage.

There were other sources of theatre development in the schools and colleges across Canada. In the fall of 1945 Emrys M. Jones was appointed Chairman of the first department of drama at a university in the British Commonwealth—the University of Saskatchewan. The Banff School of Fine Arts was founded in 1933 and directed by Elizabeth Sterling Haines in Banff, Alberta. It proved a powerful source of education in drama and artistic expression. Begun as an extension department to the University of Alberta, it soon became a separate school. Eventually Canadian universities helped the growth of theatre by setting up well-equipped and professionally directed drama departments where young Canadians could learn the art of acting, directing, designing, playwriting, and criticism. The University of Toronto, McGill University, Dalhousie University, York University, the Universities of British Columbia, Alberta, Saskatchewan, Waterloo— these are but a few of the many institutions of higher learning with drama departments committed to the development of theatre.

Another significant movement in the production of major drama was the Regional Theatre Movement begun in 1958 and heavily subsidized by federal and provincial grants. It was a successful attempt to provide a network of professional theatres, one in each province. Each centre was to have its own company, theatre school, and touring company. The prototype for these was the Manitoba Theatre Centre in Winnipeg, founded by John Hirsch and Tom Hendry. Relating intimately to the community and region, it gradually opened a

Children's Theatre, a low-budget Studio Theatre, the outdoor Rainbow Theatre for musicals, a touring company, a school for actors, a lecture series, visits to neighbouring schools, workshops, and playwriting competitions. The Canada Council designated the Manitoba Theatre Centre in 1962 as a model for all future regional theatres. Subsequently, many fine regional theatres opened: the Playhouse Theatre Company in Vancouver in 1962; Theatre Calgary; Theatre New Brunswick; the Neptune Theatre in Halifax; Edmonton's Citadel Theatre; the St. Lawrence Centre in Toronto; the National Arts Centre in Ottawa; the Arts and Culture Centre at St. John's, Newfoundland; Charlottetown Confederation Centre in Prince Edward Island; Place des Arts in Montreal; the Globe Theatre in Regina, Saskatchewan. However, these regional theatres are committed to the performance of outstanding international drama and are in no way obliged to stage Canadian plays, although one Canadian play a season is usually a token nod to native drama.

Thus developed from all these varied sources theatre in Canada and subsequently an indigenous Canadian drama. Today one can attend performances of original Canadian plays in hundreds of small makeshift theatres in unused old churches and schools, over supermarkets, in abandoned fire halls—places closely resembling in physical structure the off-Broadway theatres. Now is an exciting time in this flowering of a national drama.

II   Present State of Canadian Drama

A brief survey of Canadian Drama at the present time reveals a lively and very active theatre in a state of flux. Canadian dramatists have moved with great rapidity through those normal stages of development that have traditionally taken other countries long periods of time to develop. The usual pattern of initial historical plays, followed by obvious identity plays, moving thence into that larger and broader field of contemporary problem plays related more closely to an international rather than a national theatre, has been the pattern too of Canadian drama development but it has been compressed into a very short period of time.

Both English and Québécois playwrights today, while not yet relinquishing traditional historical and identity plays, have simultaneously moved into decidedly contemporary themes, themes that are indigenous to Canada but that deal also with problems plaguing the world outside our borders. In French Canada plays are appearing concerned with separatism, and in English Canada plays on women's liberation, prison reform, homosexuality and lesbianism, dignity and independence for the elderly. These share the general theme of liberation—the Canadian theatre of liberation—and reflect the general spirit of peoples in countries throughout the eastern and western hemispheres.

A glance at drama in French Canada shows a marked spirit of rebellion against all taboos—political, social, moral, and verbal. Québécois dramatists are reminding Quebec of its past enslavement to church and government; they are deepening audience awareness of Quebec culture and language. *Joual*, the hybrid language of the lower class French Canadian, is being used seriously in plays by writers like Michel Tremblay and Michel Garneau who seek to reflect thereby the tone and quality of Québécois life. Plays for and against separatism and plays simply exploring the problem are being written and produced in Quebec. Drama there is vibrant with artistic creativity and originality. The many facets of Quebec life, in the city slums, in rural areas, among the upper class and the intellectuals, are being examined on stage. More original plays are being written and produced in Quebec than perhaps in any other one province. The arts flourish there.

Three companies in Montreal specialize in Québécois plays and four repertory companies offer plays in the French classical tradition, while in Quebec City three large theatres thrive. The architecturally handsome Place des Arts, which is city-government supported, presides over Montreal and its theatres. There is also in Montreal a reasonably healthy English language theatre orbiting around the Saidye Bronfman Centre and the Centaur Theatre. But by and large, English theatre in Montreal is minimal because the English minority do not produce much material for the stage. The bilingual National Theatre School founded in Montreal in 1960 offers a three-year course in acting technique and a two-year course in directing, designing, and stage-managing. In the summer the students move to Stratford for an English-oriented program. Other French areas in Canada have established professional theatre companies, such as Le Cercle Molière in Saint Boniface, Manitoba, and Théâtre des Lutins in Ottawa. In French Canada, theatre is today creative enough to take a modest place within the field of world drama.

In English Canada, drama is thriving in every province. Between 1971 and 1973 more than two hundred new English Canadian plays received full scale productions. These reflected English Canadian life styles, values, interests, problems, characters, and the rhythms of their lives. Unfortunately, a lack of critical judgment has been responsible for the production of much inferior work, causing audience dissatisfaction. Since 1974 there has been a more conscious effort to weed out the mediocre. Theatre directors of large regional theatres were opposed to risking box office receipts on such new Canadian ventures and, therefore, alternative theatres were established in all the provinces and subsidized in a limited way by provincial and municipal governments. In the last few years the proliferation of professional and semi-professional theatre companies has continued across Canada.

There have been stimulating developments in the Atlantic provinces. In Newfoundland three companies made their contributions: CODCO, the Mummers Troupe, and the Newfoundland Travelling Theatre Company. In Prince Edward Island the Charlottetown Festival at the Confederation Centre of the Arts has been responsible for the contribution of the P.E.I. musicals to Canadian theatre. Since 1963 Nova Scotia has had one live theatre, the Neptune, producing traditional and some Canadian drama, highlighted for a brief period in the early 1970s by Neptune's Second Stage—a group of young professional actors who produced English Canadian plays and a few Québécois plays in translation—and by John Dunsworth's Pier One Theatre, a highly experimental, semi-professional company courageously performing despite financial burdens. In Wolfville, Nova Scotia, the Mermaid Theatre offers Micmac Indian legends and other indigenous plays. The Writers Federation of Nova Scotia is now encouraging Nova Scotia writers to create original drama. Theatre New Brunswick in Fredericton, is promoting the writing of Canadian plays.

Toronto has always been the centre of English Canadian theatre in the east. Since the sudden flowering of English Canadian drama in the 1960s, there has been a simultaneous development of a large number of small theatres and companies in Toronto dedicated to the production of Canadian plays. The senior experimental theatre, Toronto Workshop Productions founded by George Luscombe in 1959, was an experiment in collective creativity. This was followed by another experimental group, Paul Thompson's Theatre Passe Muraille, emphasizing group writing and production of documentary drama involving the folklore and local history of various provinces. The Toronto Free Theatre, the Factory Theatre Lab, the Tarragon Theatre and theatre groups too numerous to mention—all have espoused the cause of the English Canadian drama movement and have introduced the plays of some of English Canada's most notable playwrights. Indeed they are responsible for the development of these young dramatists.

Western Canada has made significant contributions to Canadian drama. The Manitoba Theatre Centre is largely responsible for the original Canadian plays coming from that province. The Globe Theatre in Regina and the Twenty-Fifth Street House in Saskatoon have produced original Canadian plays. Edmonton's Citadel presents world drama but its Citadel II devotes three quarters of its season to Canadian plays, and Theatre Network's Studio Theatre has inaugurated the annual Clifford E. Lee Award for original Canadian plays. Calgary's Alberta Theatre Projects produces western Canadian drama in its Log Opera House at Heritage Park while the prestigious government-supported Theatre Calgary produces world drama and the Pleiades Theatre offers Canadian fare. Vancouver holds a strong position in the development of Canadian Drama in the west. During the past ten years at least forty companies of actors were formed in the city and survived for a while on small grants, doing experimental works. The annual Du Maurier One Act Play Festival encourages the production of plays by new and hitherto unknown young playwrights. The New Play Centre in Vancouver, directed by Pamela Hawthorne, is a strong supporter of Canadian drama, directing, criticizing, producing, and publishing the work of West Coast playwrights. The splendid government-supported Vancouver Playhouse Theatre Centre has produced some Canadian work, but, like its sister regional theatres across Canada, it focuses mainly on foreign importations.

Summer theatre festivals develop Canadian talent, particularly the Lennoxville Festival at Bishops University in Lennoxville, Quebec, which was founded in 1971 by David Rittenhouse and William Davis in an attempt to rediscover the Canadian theatrical past and produce original English Canadian plays and French Canadian plays in translation. Directors, playwrights, and actors collaborate to develop scripts and performances.

Canada's celebration of its Centennial Year in 1967, calling for artistic, dramatic talent to express its identity; the Canada Council's Meeting of Playwrights in 1971 resulting in the Gaspé Manifesto demanding fifty percent Canadian content in subsidized Canadian theatres; the founding of the Playwrights Circle and the Playwrights Co-op for the reading and publishing of Canadian scripts; the founding in 1972 of the Toronto Drama Bench for the encouragement of theatre criticism and its institution of the annual Chalmers Award Contest for the best Canadian play of the year; the initiation in 1976 of the Association for Canadian Theatre History Research—all are signs of the intense activity on the part of Canadians to support a solid Canadian theatre and a creative, original drama.

III   Conclusion

The twelve contributors to this book encompass in experience and accomplishment the modern history of theatre in

Canada. Beginning with John Coulter, an Irish Canadian whose arrival in Canada in 1936 coincided with a cultural awakening in English Canada, and closing with Michel Tremblay and Michel Garneau whose plays in *joual* have contributed to Quebec's recent political and cultural awakening, the twelve chapters as a whole constitute a remarkable insight into the evolution of this important art form in Canada.

The founding figures—John Coulter, Herman Voaden, Robertson Davies, and Gwen Pharis Ringwood—brought to Canadian Dramatists a sense of perfection in form, much needed government support of the arts, and an insight into Canada's identity both in the east and in the west. The middle-aged gladiators—James Reaney, John Herbert and Tom Grainger—added new perspectives, new themes and, new forms to creative drama. The young Turks—Michael Cook, David Freeman, David French, Michel Garneau, and Michel Tremblay offer fresh and sensitive insights into English and French Canadian contemporary problems, moving Canadian drama into the wider field of human life. Coulter and Voaden, Reaney and Ringwood are interested in the history and spirit of Canada, re-creating for us outstanding figures like Louis Riel, Emily Carr, Billy Barker, and the Donnelly family; Davies concentrates on national idiosyncrasies; Herbert and Freeman depict the outcasts of Canadian society; Cook and French, Tremblay and Garneau are preoccupied with the spirit and values, the emotional anguish of their English and Québécois characters; Grainger's plays, when not set in England, exist in some nameless country where man's inhumanity to man gives them universality.

The current state of drama in Canada is a very healthy one and will likely continue to flourish and grow. Regional theatres should now be willing to include more Canadian content in each season of plays. There is a need too, for more and finer critics such as we had in the late, great critic, Nathan Cohen. A combination of constructive reviewers and appreciative, perceptive audiences can provide the healthy climate needed for artistic creation.

Canadian drama has yet to become a truly popular art. Most theatre-goers in Canada are primarily entertainment seekers, and this is understandable in an age dominated by television. But perhaps when they discover that plays written by contemporary English Canadian and Québécois playwrights can provide meaningful, exciting and satisfying experiences, they will join the ever-increasing audiences who are recognizing that their country is at last producing plays of stature.

Selected Bibliography

Note: Throughout the book, both in the selected bibliographies and in the text, titles of all plays that have been previously published in book form, either independently or as part of a compilation, are italicized. All other plays, whether unpublished or published only in a periodical such as *The Canadian Theatre Review*, appear in quotation marks.

ANTHONY, GERALDINE. "Canadian Drama: A Major Literary Form?" *Canadian Library Journal* 32, No. 5 (1975), pp. 349-55.

————. "The Forgotten Man: John Coulter, Dean of Canadian Playwrights." *Canadian Drama/L'Art dramatique canadien* 1, No. 1 (1975), pp. 12-17.

————. *Gwen Pharis Ringwood.* Twayne World Authors Series. Boston: G. K. Hall & Co., forthcoming.

————. *John Coulter.* Twayne World Authors Series. Boston: G. K. Hall & Co., 1976.

————. "Similarities to Brechtian Techniques in John Coulter's Play, *Louis Riel.*" *Canadian Drama/L'Art dramatique canadien* 2, No. 2 (1976), pp. 228-33.

————. "Neptune's New Messiah." *The Canadian Theatre Review*, No. 5 (1975), pp. 143-44.

————. "Pier One: Dream Deferred." *The Canadian Theatre Review, No. 6 (1975), pp. 120-21.*

————. Ed.*Profiles in Canadian Drama*. Toronto: Gage Publishing Ltd., 1977.

ASHLEY, LEONARD R. N. "Canada." *History of the Theatre*. George Freedly and John A. Reeves. New York: Crown Publishers, Inc., 1968.

ATHERTON, W. H. *Montreal 1535-1914*. Montreal: Clarke, 1914.

BALL, J. L. "Theatre in Canada: A Bibliography." *Canadian Literature*, No. 14 (1962), pp. 85-100.

BERAUD, JEAN. *350 Ans de théâtre au Canada français*. Ottawa: Le Cercle du livre de France, 1958.

BLAKELY, PHYLLIS R. "The Theatre and Music in Halifax." *Dalhousie Review* 29, No. 1 (1949), 8-20.

BOOTH, MICHAEL. "Gold Rush Theatre." *Pacific Northwest Quarterly* 51, No. 3 (1960), pp. 97-102.

————. "Pioneer Entertainment: Theatrical Taste in the Early Canadian West." *Canadian Literature*, No. 4 (1960), pp. 52-58.

BULLOCK-WEBSTER, Major Llewellyn. "The Development of Canadian Drama." *Asides 1945-46*, No. 5, Stanford, California: Stanford University Dramatists Alliance, 1946, pp. 22-27.

CBC: A Brief History and Background. Ottawa: CBC Information Services, 1972.

Canadian Players Foundation. *On Stage with Canadian Players 1960-64*. Toronto: Canadian Players Foundation, 1965.

KLINCK, CARL F. and WATTERS, REGINALD E., Eds. *Canadian Anthology*. Toronto: Gage Publishing Ltd., 1966.

"Canadian Drama." In *Dictionary Catalog of the Harris Collection of American Poetry and Plays*, pp. 550-56. Boston: G. K. Hall &. Co., 1972. (Collection is at Brown University, Providence, Rhode Island.)

COHEN, NATHAN. "Theatre Today: English Canada." *Tamarack Review*, No. 13 (1959), pp. 24-37.

COVERT, CHRIS. "Saskatoon Vision," *The Canadian Theatre Review*, No. 7 (1975), pp. 128-31.

CRAIG, IRENE. "Grease Paint on the Prairies." *Historic and Scientific Society of Manitoba*, Winnipeg Papers, Series 3, No. 3 (1946-47), pp. 38-53.

DAFOE, CHRISTOPHER. "MTC: Past and Present, Theatre in Winnipeg," *The Canadian Theatre Review*, No. 4 (1974), pp. 6-12.

DAVIES, ROBERTSON and GUTHERIE, TYRONE. *Renown at Stratford*. Toronto: Clarke, Irwin &. Company Ltd., 1953.

————.*Twice Have the Trumpets Sounded*. Toronto: Clarke, Irwin &. Company Ltd., 1954.

DURANG, JOHN. *The Memoirs of John Durang, 1785-1816*. Edited by Alan S. Downer. Pittsburgh: University of Pittsburgh Press, 1966.

EAMER, CLAIRE. "Saskatoon's Twenty-Fifth Street House". *The*

Canadian Theatre Review, No. 13 (1977), pp. 111-13.

EDWARDS, MURRAY. *A Stage in Our Past: English Language Theatre in Eastern Canada from the 1790's to 1914*. Toronto: University of Toronto Press, 1969.

Encyclopedia Canadiana. Toronto: Grolier of Canada, 1970.

Encyclopedia of World Drama. New York: McGraw-Hill Book Co., 1972.

FERGUSON, C. BRUCE. "The Rise of the Theatre in Halifax." *Dalhousie Review* 29, No. 4 (1950), 419-27.

FIELDEN, CHARLOTTE. "Montreal's *Melanie*", *The Canadian Theatre Review*, No. 8 (1975), pp. 64-66.

FRAZER, ROBBIN. "D.D.F. — The First Forty Years." *Performing Arts* 9, No. 4 (1972), pp. 10-13.

FOORD, ISABELLA. "Edmonton Update, *The Canadian Theatre Review*, No. 8 (1975), pp. 67-69.

FREEDLEY, GEORGE. *The Theater in the U.S. and Canada*. New York: New York Public Library, 1955.

FULFORD, ROBERT. "The Yearning for Professionalism." *Tamarack Review*, No. 13 (1959), pp. 80-85.

GABORIAU, LINDA. "English Theatre Is Alive and Well in Canada . . . But How's It Doing in Montreal?" *The Saturday Gazette* (Montreal), December 14, 1974.

GAISFORD, JOHN. *Theatrical Thoughts*. Montreal: 1848.

GARNETT, GALE. "The Triple-headed Monster—Genius of Toronto Free Theatre." *Performing Arts* 9, No. 2 (1972), p. 50.

GERMAIN, JEAN-CLAUDE. "Théâtre Québécois or Théâtre Protestant?" *The Canadian Theatre Review*, No. 11 (1976), pp. 8-21.

GILBERT, EDWARD. "A Personal View," (Manitoba). *The Canadian Theatre Review*, No. 4 (1974), pp. 22-25.

GUSTAFSON, DAVID A. "The Canadian Regional Theatre Movement." Ph.D. dissertation, Michigan State University, 1971.

————."Manitoba Theatre Centre." *Performing Arts* 9, No. 1 (1972), pp.46-48.

HAMBLET, EDWIN C. *Marcel Dubé and French Canadian Drama*. New York: Exposition Press, 1970.

————."Quebec's Theatre of Liberation." *Comparative Drama*, No. 5, pp. 70-88.

HAMELIN, JEAN. "Theatre Today: French Canada." *Tamarack Review*, No. 13 (1959), pp. 38-47.

HARVEY, RUTH. *Curtain Time*. Boston: Houghton Mifflin Co., 1949.

HENDRY, TOM. "Theatre in Manitoba." *Theatre World* 57, No. 435 (1961), pp. 48-50.

————."A View From the Beginnings," (Manitoba). *The Canadian Theatre Review*, No. 4 (1974), pp. 13-21.

HICKS, R. K. "Le Théâtre de Neptune." *Queen's Quarterly* 34 (1926): 215-23.

HIRSCH, JOHN. "Healthy Disengagement," (Manitoba). *The Canadian Theatre Review*, No. 4 (1974), pp. 26-32.

HOULE, LEOPOLD. *L'Histoire du théâtre au Canada*. Montreal: Fides, 1945.

KURZ, HARRY. "Canada in French Plays of the 18th Century." *Queen's Quarterly* 31, (1924): 371-87.

LEE, BETTY. *Love and Whiskey: The Story of the Dominion Drama Festival*. Toronto: McClelland and Stewart Ltd., 1973.

LJUNGH, ESSE. "Curtain Going Up." *Performing Arts in Canada* (Summer, 1963), pp. 28-29.

LOGAN, JOHN DANIEL, and FRENCH, DANIEL B. *Highways of Canadian Literature 1760-1924*. Toronto: McClelland and Stewart Ltd., 1924.

MASSEY, VINCENT. *Canadian Plays from Hart House*. Toronto: Macmillan Company of Canada Ltd., 1926.

————."The Prospects of a Canadian Drama." *Queen's Quarterly* 30 (1926): 194-212.

MICHENER, WENDY. "Towards a Popular Theatre." *Tamarack Review*, No. 13 (1959), pp. 63-79.

MILNE, W. S. "Drama Festival Afterthoughts." *Canadian Forum* 30, No. 354 (1950), pp. 82, 83.

MOORE, MAVOR. "Theatre for Canada." *University of Toronto Quarterly* 26 (1956); 1-16.

————."Theatre in English-Speaking Canada." In *The Arts in Canada: A Stock-Taking at Mid Century*. Edited by Malcolm M. Ross. Toronto: Macmillan Company of Canada Ltd., 1958.

MORLEY, PATRICIA. *Robertson Davies*. Profiles in Canadian Drama Series. Toronto: Gage Publishing Ltd., 1977.

NEW, WILLIAM. *Dramatists in Canada*. Vancouver: University of British Columbia Press, 1972.

NOVICK, J. "Touring the Hinterland." *Nation* 202, No. 21 (1966): 626-29. (Manitoba Theatre Centre.)

O'NEILL, PATRICK B. "Theatrical Activity at York (Toronto), Canada, (1793-1834." *Canadian Speech Communication Journal* 6, No. 6 (1974), pp. 47-6l.

Ontario Council for the Arts. *The Awkward Stage: The Ontario Theatre Study Report*. Toronto: Methuen Publications, 1969.

Oxford Companion to the Theatre. Edited by Phyllis Hartnoll, pp. 150-55. London: Oxford University Press, 1967.

PARKHILL, FRANCES N. "The Dominion Drama Festival: Its History,

Organization and Influence." Master's thesis, Emerson College, 1952.

PHELPS, ARTHUR. "Canadian Drama." *University of Toronto Quarterly* 9 (1939): 82-94.

RABY, PETER, ED. *The Stratford Scene, 1958-1968.* Toronto: Clarke, Irwin & Company Ltd., 1968.

REANEY, JAMES STEWART. *James Reaney.* Profiles in Canadian Drama Series. Toronto: Gage Publishing Ltd., 1977.

SILVESTER, REG. "Prairie Profile: The Globe." *The Canadian Theatre Review,* No. 11 (1976), pp. 126-28.

SOUCHOTTE, SANDRA. "Canada's Workers' Theatre." *The Canadian Theatre Review,* Nos. 9, 10 (1976), pp. 169-72, 92-96.

SPENSLEY, PHILIP. "English Theatre in Montreal." *Performing Arts 9, No. 2 (1972), pp. 14-15.*

————."National Theatre School." *Performing Arts* 9, No. 1 (1972), pp. 10-14.

TAIT, MICHAEL. "Drama and Theatre." In *Literary History of Canada: Canadian Literature in English.* Edited by Carl F. Klinck, pp. 633-34. Toronto: University of Toronto Press, 1965.

USMIANI, RENATE. *Gratien Gélinas.* Profiles in Canadian Drama Series. Toronto: Gage Publishing Ltd., 1977.

WAGNER, ANTON. "Nationalism and the French Canadian Drama." *The Canadian Theatre Review,* No. 1 (1974), pp. 22-27.

WAISMAN, ALLAN H. "Building the Building," (Manitoba Theatre Centre). *The Canadian Theatre Review,* No. 4 (1974), pp. 32-37.

WHITTAKER, HERBERT. "Canada on Stage." *Queen's Quarterly* 60 (1954): 495-500.

————."The Theatre." In *The Culture of Contemporary Canada.* Edited by Julian Park. Ithaca, N.Y.: Cornell University Press, 1957.

WILLIAMS, NORMAN. "Prospects for the Canadian Dramatist." *University of Toronto Quarterly* 26 (1957): 273-83.

One

JOHN COULTER

(1888-   )

Preface

If one were to set a date when native Canadian stage plays were first regarded as possible Canadian theatre productions, and if one were to attempt to locate the playwright who initiated this movement, the name John Coulter springs immediately to mind, and the date — 1937. An immigrant from Northern Ireland, Coulter bridged the gap between, and defined the purposes of, the Canadian radio play (an already solid staple of entertainment in Canada) and the Canadian stage play (an art form seldom written because so rarely produced by theatres in Canada). Coulter did this through his controversial dialogue, "Radio Drama Is Not Theatre," with Ivor Lewis in 1937 on CBC radio in Toronto. It was subsequently published in book form by Macmillan, Toronto.

John Coulter had arrived in Canada in 1936, immediately assessed the state of theatre here, and then promptly used the media to protest with typical northern Irish vehemence, vigour, anger, and passionate appeal. Thus was the plight of Canadian dramatists brought to the notice of the public. This was the start of the battle he waged for the next twenty years via the press, radio, and public address, in sharp and ironic comment as a one-man lobby for a truly indigenous drama.

He was one of the playwrights responsible for an improved Dominion Drama Festival, the formation of the Canadian Conference of the Arts, the founding of Canada Council, the opening of the Stratford Festival and Theatre, the arousing of interest in Canadian opera, and finally, within the past decade, the proliferation of small theatres across Canada ready to produce Canadian drama, and the sudden response of young

Canadian dramatists with literally hundreds of Canadian plays. For all of these developments, John Coulter is either directly or indirectly responsible. His place in the history of Canadian drama is on the threshold between that prolific outpouring of radio drama that early constituted Canadian "theatre," and that point in time when young Canadians began seriously to write stage plays in the early 1960s.

In the actual writing of Canadian drama John Coulter's contribution is intangible. James Reaney, Mavor Moore, and other Canadian dramatists have said that Coulter inspired perfection of form in young Canadian writers. In other words, he demanded a careful structuring and an explicit use of traditional techniques. In his own plays, Coulter endeavoured to fit his subjects into vessels that would comfortably hold them. He thereby unwittingly initiated forms that would later, in the hands of major European, British, and American playwrights, become new and authoritative forms of world drama. Coulter wrote his play, Riel, in a form that is now recognized as Bertolt Brecht's epic theatre although it was written before the English-speaking world had been introduced to Brecht. Coulter's play, "Sleep My Pretty One," was created in a style now known as theatre-of-the-absurd, again before that style had reached the English-speaking theatre. Portions of Coulter's play, "François Bigot and the Fall of Quebec," resemble in style a later play of Arthur Miller — After the Fall. The late Nathan Cohen, that most perceptive of Canadian theatre critics, deeply appreciated Coulter's talent and was not only his strong supporter, particularly in advancing the production of Riel, but also the first to perceive his innovations.

Out of Coulter's total output of twenty-four stage plays, only seven were Canadian. He early discovered that an "immigrant-exile," as he termed himself, coming to Canada at the age of forty-eight, could hardly pick up the nuances of the Canadian tongue and adequately reproduce the Canadian voice in dialogue. He therefore turned to what he could do eminently well —historical Canadian drama. He could very dramatically create realistic productions of Canadian history. The type of character that appealed most to him as a Belfast man, was the freedom fighter, the victim of injustice, the man on trial for his ideals. As a result we have his most memorable characters: Louis Riel, the founder of Manitoba and one of the most controversial figures in Canadian history: François Bigot, the scoundrel and partial cause of the fall of Quebec; Joseph Howe, the fighter for freedom of the press in Nova Scotia. Coulter has contributed a trilogy of plays on Riel, a trilogy on Quebec, and the single play, "The Trial of Joseph Howe." The nationwide revival of interest in Riel happened as a result of Coulter's trilogy.

Coulter's remaining plays are devoted to Irish and other subjects, including lively Irish dramas on country peasants, urban labourers, wealthy gentry, creative artists, and single-minded revolutionaries. The characters he excels in creating are megalomaniacs; the dialogue he finds easiest to evoke is the dialogue of debate; the scene he is most adept at reproducing is the courtroom trial. His most memorable Irish and British characters are Edmund Kean, the famous actor; Winston Churchill about whom he has written a play and a biography; Denis Patterson, the fictitious I.R.A. leader in The Drums Are Out; and the Reverend Andrew McNeagh, an Ian Paisley type of character in "The Red Hand of Ulster." Coulter also provided the librettos for two successful operas in Canada: the Canadian opera, "Transit Through Fire," which celebrates Canadian youth in World War II, and the Irish opera, "Deirdre," which re-creates very poetically the Deirdre legend. Healey Willan composed the music for these librettos. Their collaboration was a happy and fruitful one.

Given more perspective on his total output in drama, one is able to draw the conclusion that John Coulter thoroughly understands the elements that combine to make up good theatre. Although his plays occasionally suffer from some rather pretentious language and melodramatic effects, on the whole they are solid and substantial contributions. From the early northern Irish peasant plays of racy dialogue and warmly evocative scene, to the dramatic and tragic stature of such Canadian plays as Riel, Coulter has traversed the field of drama, using romanticism, realism, folk drama, epic theatre, and theatre-of-the-absurd. Whatever best suited his purposes *he would use, and if the style did not exist, he invented one. He has provided Canadians with drama of the history of Canada in a style that combines dignity, vigour, and truth. To young Canadian playwrights he has bequeathed his adherence to perfection of form. But more than this, his greatest gift to Canada has been his long and successful campaign for an indigenous Canadian theatre.*

I am reluctant to talk about myself and my work because I find that writers in such circumstances are lured into a kind of vanity, self-esteem, mock-modesty, and general self-betrayal which is distasteful indeed. Although I have talked about myself in my unpublished book of memoirs, "In My Day," I wrote the memoirs less to put myself on public display than to portray people with whom my life was lived, and the world through which we went on together. I have always felt that the craftsman should practice his craft behind closed doors, producing for public inspection only his finished work. Craftsmen know that talk about their craft which has point, practical meaning, is for fellow craftsmen. In my confessional appendix to my book of poetry, *The Blossoming Thorn*, I point out that I have always believed my fellow craftsmen could tell *me* a thing or two—writers' wrinkles—far more than I could tell them. In fact I doubt that I can say anything that other writers don't know already. But apart from telling them what they know already—if they should find any comfort in learning that the commonplaces of one writer's experience, namely mine, especially the commonplace of failure and frustration, are parallel with their own, then I am ready.

The earliest recollections I have of feeling I could write—in the sense of having an aptitude—go back to the far-off years when I was just entering my teens. The occasion was the death of Queen Victoria. About this my class at school was required to write a "comp." I think there was some prize for the "comp" most worthy of the august subject. With some notion of achieving the appropriate note of pomp I had the ingenuity to trick out the few hundred laboriously engrossed noble words (they were a small island in the middle of the page) by placing all around them a wide band of sombre colour, royal mourning in black and purple crayon. My "comp" was best. I was proud of it, and kept it for a long time—or my parents did. Which perhaps is why I still can see it though almost eighty years have passed. So—that was *when* I started.

Now, as to *what* started me. It was the setting of that cosmic event as subject for a school "comp" and the feeling that

I could write it and write it better than anyone else in my class. The success of my juvenile piece gave me assurance—assurance which never failed to sustain me. It sustained me through all my schooldays and at all later times in the writing of exam papers when apart from ability to answer at all, I knew that ability to write the answer well counted toward success with examiners. I knew I could *write* the answer better than my fellows. At least in that one sense I was more than a match for them. That knowledge I enjoyed. And there you have the secret, the root of my long addiction to writing: enjoyment. It was always a private joy—ever since that schoolboy lament for the formidable-looking fat old lady on the backs of our pennies—ever since I discovered the pleasure to be had in writing.

But I was never for long free of questioning about the *point* of it all—of the sustained struggle to get something I wanted to make clear to myself clearly written down, and written in a manner that satisfied me. When not writing I have been uneasily aware of an emptiness, a lack of purpose—even, at its worst, lack of purpose other than the involuntary biological one which we share with all dumb animals—that of existing in order to exist. It was this existential view which was mine long before I ever heard of Kierkegaard or Sartre or that harsh, mechanical-sounding term, existentialism. For me it is less a pessimism than an irony, a fate—to be accepted but kept out of sight by the merciful necessity to work—work, work, work—in a writer's case, necessity to write.

Unconsciously I attempted to find a personal style. A verbal style is come by unawares, if what one is, if whatever element of uniqueness an individual may possess, is consistently reflected in the manner in which one's thoughts are ordered, in speech or in writing. A verbal style is the sound pattern made of submerged half-conscious rhythms and hinted melody—euphony of alliteration and assonance—the horns of elfland faintly heard in the flow of words one uses to convey one's feelings or thought. I should call anyone a poet whose speech or writing draws at all deeply on that dark well of the unconscious which holds all that is not reasoned, that is not of the light of day—all one's obscure heritage of submerged intuitions, insights, instincts—the hidden core of one's intellectual self.

A badly written play, an irritation with the ineptness of a piece in which two girls with whom I was half in love, were playing parts, led me to write plays. The play in which these fellow students at the Belfast School of Art were actresses was a short farce "My Kingdom for a Horse" by the headmaster R. A. Dawson. At easel or drawing board I greatly admired the deftness and talent of Mr. Dawson but as for writing—I felt that he should have known better. I have now forgotten all else about the play except that, as I stood in the wings as a member of the stage crew, I felt that I could do better at playwriting than at drawing or painting or design.

Unfortunately my parents were among those unworldly Wesleyans for whom the theatre was a place of sinful frivolity—a view I doubted and ceased to share when, unknown to them, I attended a matinée of *Romeo and Juliet*. Alone in the gods I crouched, watching, enchanted, entranced, utterly enthralled; and for weeks afterwards I was above myself—living in imagination with the Capulets and Montagues, moving among vivid scenes and people all by far more real to me than actual scenes and people—my family at home, passersby in the streets. The spell was on me. I had been touched by magic.

The next play for me was Shaw's *The Shewing-Up of Blanco Posnet*, sponsored in Ireland when the censor forbade production in England. I was stimulated and shocked; stimulated by the flaunting braggadocio and wit; shocked by the open public use of what I had been taught to think of as "bad language." After that, at every opportunity of which I could avail myself, I saw plays—particularly the plays of the Ulster Literary Theatre, the Abbey Theatre of the north. I was possessed by a deepening desire to try my own hand, to emulate them, and by a growing conviction that I could.

Having moved from Belfast to Dublin in the September of 1914, and having found a studio flat in what was then called Sackville (now O'Connell) Street, close to the Abbey Theatre, I attended almost every new production there and every revival of the Abbey masterpieces. My first was a matinee in which Sara Allgood—later to become my friend—Ireland's greatest actress, especially in the tragic roles of Irish plays—was Maurya in *The Riders to the Sea*.

I have told in my memoirs of the effect of that experience on me, and shall not retell it—or not beyond saying that from that heart-searing experience there could be no turning back. It had finally set my course. Come failure, come success, I must go on to be a playwright. I had the notion that the best chance of gaining a hearing as an Irish dramatist was to write a *Deirdre*. Had not they all—genius or journeyman—Yeats, Synge, AE (George Russell), Lady Gregory, James Stephens and so many others, written of Deirdre? And so I attempted seriously and persistently beginning in Dublin with five acts of blank verse and culminating in Toronto three decades later with the libretto for the opera *Deirdre of the Sorrows*, later *Deirdre*.

Every playwright whose work I have seen or even read with admiration and some degree of emotional involvement has influenced me. At first Synge and Yeats and Lady Gregory and to a lesser extent, perhaps, Rutherford Mayne. But after that, if the pen in my hand was ever pushed about by even the playwrights whose work excited and was a joy to me, I was unaware of it—or if aware of it I promptly tore up the evidence as thoroughly as I could and in secrecy disposed of it.

Yeats has told of his method of inducing sleep or trance by laying on his pillow certain emblems—writing for him being out of a sort of trance. Much of what I have written has been out of a sort of trance: but without recourse to trance-inducing emblems. All my life since adolescence, on going to bed, I have lain awake for a time going over in detail all the events of the day. Then I have fallen asleep, but have half-awakened and remained in that half-awake condition between sleep and total awareness for, frequently, several hours before dawn. Those middle-of-the-night hours of half-trance have been the time in which virtually everything I have written of a creative kind has taken shape. I think that little of any depth is achieved entirely on the surface of consciousness.

As I think of my own plays I cannot but recall the desperation of struggle in the writing of them, the miasma of doubt descending and darkening my day, those many sad days of contemplating unwarranted or largely unfulfilled hopes. But at other times I think of this or that play or scene or character as the best of which I am capable, and I even allow myself to believe that one day the life and truth in them may be seen and will please others, even to the point of persuading those myopic arbiters known as artistic directors into risking production. Intermittently this is true of that endearing and deeply wise old lazybones Elie Oblomov, the laziest man in literature, in the play "Oblomov," my only play adaptation, from the classic Russian novel of Ivan Goncharov. Or of those two old codgers, John and Robert, in *The House in the Quiet Glen*. Barry Fitzgerald claimed that their bit in that play was the funniest he knew in any play.

At other times it may be Samuel and Uncle Dick and Bella in *The Folks in Brickfield Street*, alias *The Family Portrait*. One of its productions—and it has had many—was by Lennox Robinson in the Abbey Theatre. He used it as a textbook for his Abbey Theatre School and mounted it as a school production. He was not satisfied with the second and third acts. Neither was I—though I never found our dissatisfaction shared by audiences whom I have observed. At various times I tried to find out what had gone wrong in the two acts following a first as perfect as I could make it. Where lay the fault? The problem defeated me. For forty years I turned away from thinking about it. It had been washed down, far down in the wake.

Then in Dun Laoghaire, Dublin, where my aging bones now take refuge at year's end from the severity of Canadian winter, during March or April of 1976, I was walking along the sea front when I was suddenly possessed as by a vision. In utter surprise I saw where the flaw lay concealed in those two acts. I stood still, amazed and wondering. Wondering that, when not even thinking about it and after four decades of not thinking about it, there it was.

I was at once alight to set about revision. Having with me in Ireland no copy of the original I hurried to Dublin to the National Library and found one. There, in that storied and once familiar reading room I, for the first time, studied one of my own works. The principal flaw was in an excess of stage "business"—comic "business," dramatically inessential but written in at the insistence of Molly (Marie) O'Neill for her then husband Arthur Sinclair, the Abbey's great broad comedian. They were planning a London production, Sinclair to play Samuel with Molly as Aunt Ellen and her sister Sara Allgood as Bella. Molly begged me to "give Arthur lots of 'material'" with which to set audiences aroar. I knew well how capable he was of doing so, though sometimes, when not under a firm director's control, he did it at the expense of the text. I wrote in the "material"—but at least I had had the integrity to see that all of the dramatically inessential comic "business" was not simply pasted on but did naturally arise from the action.

But how had I never seen that without Sinclair's talent it would weigh down and retard the action? So, it must now be ruthlessly cut. Cutting would, of course, reduce the playing time to less than was, in those years, regarded as obligatory for a full evening of theatre. I regretted that, for whatever reason, I had been lured into extending a play beyond its proper length. Seeing, now, that the proper length was two acts, I cut my second and third acts down to a single act of two scenes. I also eliminated the unconvincing introduction of Daffodil, the film star, at the play's end. At long last I felt confident that I had my comedy. Yet to fill an evening it would have to be part of a double bill.

To go with it I thought of *The House in the Quiet Glen*. The two have much in common. Both belong to my rapt early period of infatuation, of longing to lead the folk I knew and loved on to the stage. I linked the two together, a double bill under the title "When I Was Young." To the script I added a Foreword, observing that playwrights in 1976 were no longer interested in the portrayal of simple country or city folk; but that as a "period" piece of 1910 these two linked comedies might provide a welcome variation from the very different themes of playwriting today.

(This aside, to tell in parenthesis of work being found unsatisfactory by the playwright who yet permitted it to be published and produced; allowed it to lapse though remaining available for forty years; then, as by the unexpected drawing aside of a curtain saw it for the first time unflawed, I include here for whatever of hope or comfort it may hold for fellow playwrights uneasily aware that some script has been finished and allowed to pass with its writing problem still unsolved.)

Of my other plays, I am especially fond of "Sleep My Pretty One". The distraught girl, Anne Pearson, seeking solace for her wounded spirit in outbursts of fierce belligerence alternating with spells of lonely silence and melancholy, has all my love and sympathy. And in the civilized forbearance and wit of Flora Delahay, the stepmother whose proffered affection Anne bitterly rejects, I see what Laurence Olivier meant when he said that in Flora I had written a Frenchwoman whose role would be difficult to cast among English actresses. This play, of which Anne and Flora are the centre, gave me most pleasure in the writing. This was largely because of its verse form which set me free to use all the resources of language at my disposal—language unhampered by the crippling inhibitions imposed in the simulating of actual conversation, particularly in its restriction of thought and vocabulary to what can be decently spoken in the give-and-take of tea-table talk or during drinks before dinner. I consider the writing of "Sleep My Pretty One" the best I have done.

Deirdre, in the libretto for the opera of that name, and Sara, the grand old lady of Gregor Lodge in "While I Live," I think of with some pleasure, when I happen to think of them at all. With Jean and her father and Matt the pigeon-fancier in *The Drums Are Out* I am back in the "troubles" of Belfast and, as the play which fulfilled my ambition to be an Abbey Theatre playwright, I occasionally think of it with a touch of pride.

As for Louis Riel, in my play *Riel* and my other two plays in the trilogy about him, *The Trial of Louis Riel* and *The Crime of Louis Riel*—each about different aspects of his enigmatic character and of the symbolic relations in which he stands to the emerging Canadian nation of his time and the emerging Third World nations of today—I feel sympathy for him in his suffering, and admiration for his moral courage and integrity. He had these qualities, and with them a spark of political genius tragically complicated by mental instability. Riel is one of those unfortunates for whom the lid is frequently off that dark well of the unconscious, leaving them subject to illusions, madness, and the horrible and terrifying phantasms of nightmare which invade and persist in the waking consciousness. If he was fortunate in anything, I have believed it to be in the singular confluence of historic circumstances which combined to give him heroic stature.

In the libretto for the opera, *Transit through Fire*, I felt that the problem of transmuting passionate indignation about social iniquity into the scope and shape of a script for theatre, was solved. The particular object of indignation was the great Depression of the late twenties and early thirties and the demoralization of the young which it brought about. I would disown not a word of it, except what now seems the rather fatuous flamboyance of the preachy Preface, and the "resolution"—the joining up in the armed forces as a way of salvation for the divided self of the student hero, William Thompson. But that was *his* solution. Not mine. For the rest, and for what it implies, *Transit through Fire* is my social testament. I would have it known.

Propaganda may become the proper business of a playwright if what moves him is passionate desire to proclaim in public a point of view, a political principle, a philosophy— and to do so in the language of the stage—i.e., action. That is the sense in which dramatic literature differs from literature in general. Its vehicle is action. Of course to make it effective, to make it *work* as a play, the use of special techniques is required. That is, all the action and speeches of the characters must be set. They do and say what they do and say because of the way in which they are affected by the subject of the propaganda.

And I am one of those who think that in propaganda plays the characters can frequently be described, correctly, as not alive and rounded characters at all, but cardboard cut-outs whose sole function is to mouth the playwright's opinions. And the playwright has justification for making them so, because they must not divert or obscure the course of the argument.

There are, admittedly, severe limitations to the *scope* of any argument which even cardboard mouthpieces, undeflected in their flow, can bring to a conclusion on stage. Shaw got round this impediment by adding to his plays proper, lengthy prefaces in which he could explore and expand to his heart's content all elements of his argument excluded by those imitations from being dealt with on stage. But what Shaw could do, with his mental agility and mischievous sense of comedy, and his wit and buoyant verbal style, is desperately dangerous for playwrights of lesser talent to attempt.

It has also to be said that, as the years go by, propaganda plays—more than plays of any other kind—are by their nature likely to fade in importance as soon as the propaganda has achieved its aim of bringing about some change or adjustment in social behaviour. After that, only the vehicle remains—the structure, the style, the intellectual ingenuity.

There are also plays which have at least a secondary purpose of simply conveying information—the play which presents edited facts, perhaps facts of history, facts selected in the service of the playwright's interpretation of some historic event or persons who at some crucial moment in the life of a nation, helped to shape its destiny—for example the Louis Riel trilogy.

In addition to the Riel trilogy I have written another history-lesson-as-play: "François Bigot and the Fall of Quebec". For it, as for *Riel*, there was, preliminary to the writing, a search for appropriate technique. In neither could the conventional three-act form be used. *Riel* was a panorama of many successive scenes, and the uninterrupted flow of these could only be achieved by reverting to the methods of the Elizabethan stage, that of indicative props and scenery only. For "Bigot", after much scribbling of trial scenarios, I had to accept that even the Elizabethan fluid staging would not accommodate the story. To encompass it completely only the resources and method of a feature film on the most lavish scale could serve—and incidentally the Bigot story seems to me to cry aloud for such a film.

The play required such treatment because the teeming number of people in the cast and the multiplicity of scenes were beyond the resources of any production on any stage save that of a major opera house. In addition, it was necessary to confront personages who historically were not alive at the same time, or were never together in any given place. A seemingly insoluble problem. It was solved only by completely abandoning the illusion of the actual or real; by turning to abstraction; by adapting to the stage a technique which had proved its efficacy in television—that which is known through the programme called Man Alive. In making use of it the stage becomes a television studio—though without the paraphernalia of the cameras—with the customary raised dais on which is the Interrogator dressed in the clothes of today and speaking in the manner of today. The historic personages to be introduced, dressed in the costumes of their time, are announced, make their entrances, and are seated around the Interrogator's dais, to be called up and questioned, one after another. It means that the spectacular social phenomenon of Quebec under Bigot during the ten years of his—the last—intendancy can be presented in a theatre solely by means of evocative narration.

Fortunately, much of what helps to create dramatic life in the theatre of representation and illusion was available, if percipiently used. For instance, in the sharply dramatic counterpoint between the characteristics of the opposing generals—the "Monty"-like Wolfe, and the soldier-aristocrat and country gentleman, Montcalm. There was also available that stage tension created by searching cross-examination of witnesses notoriously successful in trial scenes of courthouse drama.

As far as I have been able to discover, Canadians generally know little if anything of that truly amazing decade, turning point of transcendent import in Canadian history, with its banquets, balls, gaming for high stakes—its sexual licence, its exploitation of the peasantry, its corrupt amassing of enormous fortunes by La Grande Society, Claverie and Company, its legendary Forty Millionaires, led by Bigot in their brazen robberies of the King of France; its boasted rivalry of the Court of Versailles in its pomps and splendours—till at last the siege of the Citadel by the English in the river, the ignominious collapse under sustained bombardment and sly treachery; the cunningly contrived capitulation providing for the escape to France of Bigot and his millionaires with their jollyboys and wives and mistresses, their banquetting plate and utensils and, supremely, their papers. The denouement—the carefully planned and surprise arrest of Bigot and the others, and after almost two years in the Bastille their prolonged trial by a court of twenty-seven magistrates who found them guilty of corrupt administration and punished them accordingly—what an ending forever of that chance, slight chance though it was, which might have changed drastically the entire course of human history, the chance that the laws and customs, language and religion of France, not of England, should henceforth be those of all but, perhaps, a few English-speaking enclaves in the North American continent! In the reputed opinion of Louis XV of France and his mistress La Pompadour, it was the most portentous event of the century.

This historic play about Bigot may take its place along with *Riel* in the literature of the theatre in Canada but not an equal place, though something of the kind was my original hope and intention.

I am sometimes asked what I think of Canadian drama now, and of its future. I know too little of Canadian drama's "now" or its future to offer an opinion. At the venturesome "growing tip" of Canadian theatre today, are not the directors and actors attempting to banish the playwright, to improvise their productions, each contributing whatever random idea comes into his head, all to be welded together into a sort of community comment, a theatrical "statement" on a selected subject preferably of a controversial nature and concerned with some aspect of contemporary social behaviour? Or the improvised "play" may take the form of mimic portrayal of the daily life in some occupation such as that of a farm (Passe Muraille Theatre's Farm Show). Or with a disinterring of some forgotten but once notorious event and the people involved in it (Passe Muraille's "1837"). A refleshing and dressing-up for stage parade of skeletons from the cupboard of history.

What we see in such parades is a company of actors interpreting, not a playwright, not a play conceived and shaped into unity and meaning and given momentum by a playwright, but their own notions of what a play might be—as it were a symphony without a score and without a conductor other than the director striving to keep together an orchestra of players, each of them busy following his own beat. Extemporized plays are merely theatrical "statements" or good experimental use of stage. One thinks of them as a theatrical camera picturing the Canadian social landscape, a sort of illustrative documentary of areas of our life not otherwise susceptible of dramatic treatment.

Extemporizing is an extension of a useful part of an actor's schooling; but I think the school classroom of a theatre school is where it is of most use. It may help an actor to discern and isolate for performance the spark which gives theatrical life to a character or situation. But I believe there is little difference in the skills which an actor uses to simulate a character imagined by himself or one imagined by a playwright. I also believe that imagining a character or situation and supplying the appropriate speeches is not the proper business of actors; and I know of sensitive and talented actors whose imagination is subject to blockage, with consequent painful and damaging humiliation, when they are required to be both playwright and actor. The feeling of frustration and fear of inadequacy which failure to be fluent in extemporizing inflicts can certainly not be said to help the actor master his trade. Quite, and sadly, the contrary.

Art is the imagination at work in the making of something, and such productions are the collective imagination at work in making what might perhaps be humorously called art by committee. But seriously, is there in imaginative work in any medium, any which has the power and intensity of art unless that of the lone artist? The lone artist in his private wilderness is wrestling with his angel—his artistic problem. I know of none. And in theatre that lone artist is the playwright—all others of the theatre being his interpreters, finding themselves in using their talents to display on stage the gift he has brought from his lonely struggle. These lone artists and the theatre companies who are their interpreters constitute the main-line theatre of Canada. Our Canadian extemporizers are minor only in relation to theatre as entertainment for the major public.

Our large heavily subsidized theatres, such as the Shakespearean Museum Theatre of Stratford, Ontario, and the commercial theatres such as the O'Keefe Centre and the Royal Alexandra Theatre in Toronto, I think of as major only in their capacity to provide traditional entertainment for the public who still regard theatre-going as no more than a night's fun: after-dinner fun with, preferably, nothing of a thought-provoking nature to disturb the digestive juices, souring the belly and spoiling the evening out. Of course it is a useful and needed capacity in a civilized society. It is worth the money. But is it more useful and—when made possible by subvention from Canada Council and other funding bodies—worth so very much more of public money than the now numerous and still proliferating little, under-subsidized or not-subsidized-at-all group theatres? Useful and needed as a way of helping people in Canada to discover themselves, and discover Canada?

Whatever the answer, I for one rejoice at the transfiguration of the theatrical scene in Canada from the stony ground—Dominion Drama Festival and commercial houses for visiting companies with second-run productions of West End or Broadway successes—the stony ground on which a few of us scattered seed nearly forty years ago.

The transfiguration of which I speak is not alone in the new and architecturally beautiful buildings which house modern theatre in Canada today, such as the Festival Theatre at Stratford, the National Arts Centre Theatre in Ottawa, the O'Keefe Centre, and the St. Lawrence Centre in Toronto, and many others on university campuses such as the Talbot Theatre at the University of Western Ontario. By far the more important aspect of this transfiguration is the evidence of new plays, the writing of new plays, Canadian plays; plays Canadian in the sense that they are the work of Canadians, written by, for, and about Canadians. And there is in this a sense of personal gratification to me because I had some part in helping to initiate it.

I believe it is at least in part a response to a plea I had the effrontery to offer at a time when I had been in Canada for a couple of years and was, as I thought, leaving it with no certainty that I should ever return. That plea—often quoted—was in an article written for Mrs. Isaacs, the percipient editor of the New York magazine, *Theater Arts Monthly*. The title was "Canadian Theatre and the Irish Exemplar" in the July, 1938, issue. Knowing how the Abbey Theatre and its playwrights had transfigured the Irish theatre scene in the first decade of the century, I pleaded with Canadians to emulate them. Here is part of it:

> It is as well to say at once that I speak of the theatre in Canada as a visiting Irishman . . . I confess, therefore, that my notion of values in the theatre was powerfully and permanently affected by years of regular attendance at the Abbey. Week by week I sat there, 'all mouth and eyes' watching with delight and wonder while the life I knew, the dreary, secular life of Irish parlours and kitchens and farms and pubs, was turned by the Abbey playwrights and players into parable . . . dramatic parable. Tragic plays there were, showing the Irish to themselves as noble persons of heroic breed; and plays full of extravagant fun and high spirits, revealing us to our surprised and flattered selves as a humorous and witty race; and plays of savage satire or irony at which we stared in angry astonishment—Irish mugs in Irish mirrors. In short nearly all the plays I saw were Irish, flowering from the soil of Ireland and deeply rooted in it.

And I was naive enough to assume that the plays of other countries were similarly rooted, that they were similarly a means, and a most potent means, for the imaginative criticism, portrayal, interpretation of national life and character."

The article concluded with these lines:

If playwrights, actors and producers north of Niagara would turn their eyes from Broadway and look around them at a place called Canada. . . . There is inviting subject matter for plays in prairie droughts and crop failure, in mining disasters, in the poverty of slum dwellers of city streets or country shacks, but accurate reporting . . . is not enough to make a play; and indeed what is dark and grievous in the actual circumstances of life has no rightful place on the stage till it is transmuted by art into . . . the tragic experience. A hundred Canadian plays are ready for Canadians who will write them."

I remembered these lines:

Old experience doth attain
To something of prophetic strain.

I added a premonitary:

But if there were a great Canadian play, would Canadians bother to stage it? Till someday Americans or British do it and tell them not to be ashamed.

The stony ground yielded and brought forth. Now Canadians have begun to look without shyness or shame at a place called Canada. In particular our playwrights have found it worth looking at; worth the grinding hard work of learning to write about it. Inevitably much of the writing should have placed on it a large red capital L—for Learner. But there has also been skilled writing—skilled to the point of deserving production in the first-rate manner possible only on the stages of those large new theatres. Yet they are all but never produced, to the shame of the managements—and equally to the shame of the people who support their productions—Canadian supporters if not the alien and indifferent patrons of the tourist trade—who could, if, as some of them would claim, they were genuinely interested in theatre arts, insistently demand and see to it that Canadian plays of merit, or even of sufficient promise, be included in every season's productions.

The greatest need of aspiring writers in Canada is a man of genius, whose authority they would respect and accept. For my own part, I would say: be sure that whatever you write is a flowering from your own roots. Be rigorous in self-criticism, and ruthless in acting on it. Be genuine.

Chronology

1888	Born in Belfast, Northern Ireland, son of Francis and Annie (Clements) Coulter.
1892-1911	Attended Belfast schools: Model Primary, School of Art and School of Technology from which he won scholarship to Manchester University, England.
1912-19	Teaching career at: School of Technology, Belfast; Coleraine Academical Institution, Northern Ireland, Wesley College, Dublin.
1917	*Conochar*, first stage play published by W. and G. Baird, Belfast.
1920-36	Worked for BBC, London, contributing programs.
1924	Editor of *The Ulster Review*, Belfast.
1925	First produced play, "Sally's Chance," BBC radio, Belfast.
1927-35	Wrote articles for John Middleton Murry's periodical, *The Adelphi*, and became Managing Editor of *The New Adelphi* in 1927.
1936	Moved to Canada and married Olive Clare Primrose, poet and author.
1937	Won almost all the awards for his play, *The House in the Quiet Glen*, at the Dominion Drama Festival. Participated with Ivor Lewis in the radio dialogue, "Radio Drama Is Not Theatre," CBC, Toronto.

1938	First child, Primrose, born in Toronto. Moved to New York, wrote for CBS radio station WABC, the program series, The Living History Series.
1940	"Holy Manhattan," stage play produced by the Arts and Letters Club, Toronto.
1942	Second daughter, Clare, born in Toronto. *Transit through Fire*, Canadian opera, produced on CBC radio.
1943	"Mr. Churchill of England," produced by CBC radio, Toronto.
1944	Co-founder of Canadian Arts Council (now Canadian Conference of the Arts). Presented the "Artists Brief" to Turgeon Committee, House of Commons, Ottawa, resulting in the Massey Commission and the formation of Canada Council.
1946	*Deirdre of the Sorrows*, opera, produced on CBC radio. "Oblomov," stage play, produced by Arts and Letters Club, Toronto.
1948	*The Drums Are Out*, stage play, produced by the Abbey Theatre, Dublin.
1950	*Riel*, stage play, produced by the New Play Society, Toronto.
1951	Moved with his family to London, England.
1954	"Sleep, My Pretty One," stage play option bought by Laurence Olivier Productions; reading at Royal Court Theatre and St. James Theatre, London, with Irene Worth in principal role. Première performance at Centre Stage, Toronto, 1961.
1960	*The Crime of Louis Riel* and *The Trial of Louis Riel* commissioned by Canada Council in a Senior Arts Fellowship. Later produced in Regina, Saskatchewan (*Trial*); *The Crime of Louis Riel* won an award at the Dominion Drama Festival and was revised for radio.
1967	"A Capful of Pennies," stage play produced by Central Library Theatre, Toronto. *The Trial of Louis Riel* commissioned by Regina, Saskatchewan, Chamber of Commerce, for annual production.
1968	Radio and television tribute to John Coulter on the celebration of his eightieth birthday, February 12, on CBC, Toronto. Returned with his wife to Ireland for an extended stay.

1973	Death of his wife, Olive Primrose Coulter, in Toronto.
1974	"Red Hand of Ulster," produced on CBC radio, Toronto, February 9.
1975	Triumphant revival of *Riel*, National Arts Centre, Ottawa.
1976	Engaged in writing his memoirs, "In My Day."
1977	Edited his wife's journals. Wrote an account of their love affair, "Prelude to a Marriage," which he completed in Dun Laoghaire, County Dublin, Ireland, where he spends his winters. His play, *The Trial of Louis Riel*, continues with its eleventh annual summer season of productions at the Regina, Saskatchewan, Chamber of Commerce's behest.

Selected Bibliography

The following list contains plays both published and unpublished with alternate titles in parenthesis. All Coulter's works are in the Coulter Archives, Mills Memorial Library, Special Collections, McMaster University, Hamilton, Ontario. "MS" signifies manuscript, "TS" typescript of radio broadcasts. All the plays have been produced with the exception of: "Grand Old Lady of Gregor Lodge," "Laugh, Yorick, Laugh," and "Sketch for a Portrait."

Primary Sources

CANADIAN PLAYS

Conochar. Belfast: W. and G. Baird, 1917. Later revised as "Conochar's Queen" for BBC radio. TS, Belfast, 1934.

The Crime of Louis Riel. Toronto: Playwrights Co-op, 1976.

"François Bigot and the Fall of Quebec." TS, CBC radio, Toronto, 1970.

"Quebec in 1670." TS, CBS radio, New York, 1940.

Riel. Hamilton: Cromlech Press, 1972.

"A Tale of Old Quebec." TS, BBC radio, London, England, 1935.

Transit through Fire. Toronto: Macmillan Company of Canada Ltd., 1942. (Libretto for an opera.)

The Trial of Louis Riel. Ottawa: Oberon Press, 1968.

"The Trial of Joseph Howe." TS, CBC radio, Toronto, 1942.

IRISH PLAYS

"Clogherbann Fair" ("Pigs") ("Father Brady's New Pig"). TS, CBC radio, Toronto, 1940.

Deirdre of the Sorrows. Toronto: Macmillan Company of Canada Ltd., 1944. Republished in 1965 as *Deirdre*. (Libretto for an opera.)

The Drums Are Out. Chicago: De Paul University Press, Irish Drama Series, 6, 1971.

The Family Portrait. Toronto: Macmillan Company of Canada Ltd., 1937.

"God's Ulsterman." In two Parts: 1. "Dark Days of Ancient Hate." 2. "Red Hand of Ulster." TS, CBC radio, Toronto, 1974.

"Grand Old Lady of Gregor Lodge" ("Green Lawns and Peacocks") ("While I Live"). MS, 1951.

"Holy Manhattan" ("This Is My Country"). TS, CBC radio, Toronto, 1941.

The House in the Quiet Glen and Family Portrait. Toronto: Macmillan Company of Canada Ltd., 1937.

"Sally's Chance." TS, BBC radio, Belfast, 1925.

OTHER PLAYS

"A Capful of Pennies" ("This Glittering Dust"). TS, CBC radio, Toronto, 1967.

"Christmas Comes But Once a Year." MS, 1942.

"Laugh, Yorick, Laugh." MS, 1956.

"Mr. Churchill of England." TS, CBC radio, Toronto, 1942.

"Oblomov." TS, BBC radio, 1946, CBC - TV, Toronto, 1962.

"Sketch for a Portrait" ("One Weekend in Spring"). MS, 1950.

"Sleep, My Pretty One." MS, 1954, revised 1975.

"Still There's Christmas." MS, 1942.

ARTICLES, ESSAYS, RADIO PROGRAMS ON CANADIAN THEATRE

"The Art of the Playwright." MS, lecture, Hart House Theatre, University of Toronto, 1938.

"Book Review of the Arts," *Canadian Review of Music and Art* 5, Nos. 6, 7, (1946), pp. 48.

"Books and Shows." TS, CBC radio, Toronto, June 16, 1942-March 30, 1943.

"Books for the Times." TS, CBC radio, Toronto, June 19-July 10, 1945.

"Canadian Drama and the Dominion Drama Festival." TS, CBC radio, Toronto, 1941.

"Canadian National Theatre and Theatre School." Manifesto, Arts and Letters Club, MS, 1945.

"The Canadian Theatre and the Irish Exemplar." *Theater Arts Monthly* 22, No. 7 (1938), 503-09.

"The Dominion Drama Festival in Retrospect." TS, CBC radio, Toronto, 1948.

"The Dominion Drama Festival Review." TS, CBC radio, Toronto, May, 1947.

"A Festival Adjudicator Should Wear Two Masks." *Saturday Night* 62, No. 34 (1947), pp. 18-19.

"Festival in Retrospect." *Saturday Night* 63, No. 32 (1948), pp. 25, 36.

"Fridolin in English." TS, CBC radio, Toronto, 1946.

"Fridolin Plans a Show With English Idiom." *Saturday Night* 62 No. 20 (1947), p. 3.

"Manifesto: The War and the Festival Theatre in Canada." MS, 1941.

"On the Art of the Playwright." *Curtain Call*, No. 9 (1938), p. 7.

Radio Drama Is Not Theatre. Toronto: Macmillan Company of Canada Ltd. 1937.

"Revival of the Dominion Drama Festival." *Saturday Night* 63, No. 32 (1948).

"So Canadians Can't Act." TS, CBC radio, Toronto, February 4, 1940.

"Some Festival Visions of National Theatre." *Saturday Night* 62, No. 37 (1947) pp. 20-21.

"Speaking As a Listener." TS, CBC radio, Toronto, March 12-May 7, 1948.

"Take Thirty." TS, CBC-TV, interview by Adrienne Clarkson, November 5, 1968.

"Theatre and the Massey Report: More Than a Pat on the Head." *Saturday Night* 66, No. 49 (1951), pp. 12, 28.

"This Country in the Morning." TS, CBC radio interview on *Riel*, Ottawa, January 17, 1975.

"This Great Experiment." TS, CBC radio, Toronto, 1942.

"Time for Dusting Off the Drama Festival," *Saturday Night* 62, No. 29 (1947), p. 22.

"Toward a Canadian Theatre." *Canadian Review of Music and Art* 4, Nos. 1, 2 (1945) pp. 17-20.

"Why Sabotage the Theatre?" *Canadian Review of Music and Art* 1, No. 4 (1942), pp. 5, 6, 18.

"Words for Music." *Opera Canada* 6, No. 3 (1965), pp. 74-75.

"Words for Music: Confessions of a Librettist," *Theater Arts Monthly* 31, No. 9 (1947), pp. 32-34.

Secondary Sources

ANTHONY, GERALDINE. *John Coulter*. Twayne World Authors Series. Boston: G. K. Hall & Co., 1976.

COHEN, NATHAN. "Interview with John Coulter." CBC radio, Tuesday Night, Toronto, December 3, 1968.

——."Just in Passing." *The Toronto Star*, March 22, 1961.

——."Louis Riel Will Not Die." *The Toronto Star* (November 24, 1966).

——."Riel." *The Toronto Star*, March 29, 1962.

BROWN, WILLIAM. "The Blossoming Thorn." *The Canadian Forum* 27, No. 319 (1947), p. 142.

CLARKE, GEORGE HERBERT. "Churchill." *Queen's Quarterly* 51 (1944): 206.

——."Turf Smoke." *Queen's Quarterly* 52 (1945-46): 493-94.

DEMPSEY, MARION. "Profile: John Coulter." *Performing Arts* 8, No. 1 (1971), pp. 20-21.

MOORE, MAVOR. "Of Oblomovitis." *The Telegram* (Toronto), February 13, 1959.

SINCLAIR, LISTER. "Deirdre of the Sorrows." *Canadian Review of Music and Art* 3, Nos. 11, 12 (1945), p. 42.

SMITH, M. L. "Churchill." *Dalhousie Review* 25, No. 1 (1945), p. 120.

TOVELL, VINCENT. "Riel." *University of Toronto Quarterly* 20 (1951): 272-74.

WHITTAKER, HERBERT. "Mulcahy Evokes a Fascinating Era." *The Globe and Mail*, March 23, 1967.

WOOD, CHRISTOPHER. "A Canadian Opera: Transit Through Fire." *Canadian Review of Music and Art* 1, No. 3 (1942), p. 7.

Two
HERMAN VOADEN
(1903-)

Preface

Like John Coulter, Herman Voaden's contribution to Canadian theatre lies in the two distinct areas of political administration and drama experimentation. Both men are of the same generation; both participated in programs to forward the production of Canadian plays; both used the mass media to make public their ideas for government assistance to the arts; both were leaders in their support of theatre in Canada; both experimented with and provided Canadian drama with new forms.

Herman Voaden and John Coulter are friends. They belong to the Arts and Letters Club in Toronto and they played distinctive roles in the events leading to the founding of the Canada Council. Voaden wrote the Artists' Brief already mentioned in the General Introduction to this book, and Coulter read it to the members of the Turgeon Committee in the House of Commons in Ottawa, 1944. The national arts organizations participating in this "march on Ottawa" formed the Canadian Arts Council (later the Canadian Conference of the Arts) which spearheaded the movement that led to the appointment of the Massey Commission and the founding of the Canada Council. Herman Voaden was the first President of the Canadian Arts Council (1945-48) and the Executive Director of the Canadian Conference of the Arts in 1967-68. He has directed drama and playwriting workshops which were responsible for encouraging many young Canadians toward careers in the theatre. He has also edited a dozen drama collections notable for their Canadian content, which have helped to gain national acceptance for the "play approach" to drama teaching and to train youthful theatre audiences (see Voaden's recent book, Look Both Ways, Macmillan, 1975).

Voaden invented a new theatrical form which he called Symphonic Expressionism, combining music, art, dance, lighting, colour, dialogue and choral speech in a dramatic symphony. Because his personal artistic interests covered equally the arts of music, ballet, painting and drama, and because he saw that all the arts seem to tend toward music, it was natural that he should attempt to combine these four art forms in a unique dramatic unity. According to the reviewers of these productions, presented in the decade of the thirties, Voaden was successful. No doubt the fact that he had seriously studied dance and had attended numerous performances of opera, ballet, and theatre in Europe, accounted for his professional expertise in combining these art forms in a dramatic presentation new to theatre. The antecedents to Symphonic Expressionism were a combination of many artistic movements. Chief among these was that reaction against realism in Germany known as Expressionism. Herman Voaden, in his Introduction to the book, Six Canadian Plays, traces these movements that led up to his new genre. In particular he points to Ernst Toller's play, Masses and Men, and comments on the ballet movements of the characters; the choruses of workers, bankers, jailers; the use of lighting techniques and colour. Gordon Craig and Adolphe Appia influenced Voaden, as did the new techniques of Eugene O'Neill. Poetic, romantic and symbolic innovations in drama as well as new approaches in dance and music — all contributed to the crystallization of Symphonic Expressionism.

Voaden's experimentation had, sadly enough, no followers either in Canada or elsewhere. The reasons he gives in a letter to this editor, dated March 21, 1977 as follows:

> It was not done elsewhere and there were no followers. In the eyes of theatre folk in New York and the big European centres, Toronto was a small and unimportant provincial capital. I was too wrapped up in what I was doing to think of publicizing it elsewhere. I was happy with the reaction here to my experimentation. There were no followers here in Canada

because the creative approach to the productions was so personal and difficult. Only a producer deeply interested in all the arts would think of attempting to produce the plays. "Romeo and Juliet" was a mimed retelling of the story, to the Overture, with the light and colour orchestration added. It was this orchestration that was "symphonic" and not easy to imitate. "Ascend as the Sun" was produced in 1942. The worst years of the war followed; I was involved in arts and political crusading, with editing, teaching, writing libretti, and I produced no more symphonic theatre. So, not being seen, Symphonic Expressionism was forgotten — until the seventies.

In 1974-75 the University of Toronto and Queen's University in Kingston, Ontario, presented an exhibition of Voaden's work in photographs, programs, and reviews.

As noted above, Voaden's urge to create a new dramatic approach began in 1930 just before he went to Yale University for a course in playwriting. Like Gwen Pharis Ringwood, who had won a grant to Fred Koch's regional Playmaker's School at the University of North Carolina in Chapel Hill, Voaden was trained in America. He attended America's foremost drama writing school, the George Pierce Baker Workshop at Yale University, in 1930-31. Eugene O'Neill had earlier studied under Baker at Harvard and had written his first plays there. Under the same Professor Baker, Voaden was encouraged to refine his techniques and to write the realistic play, "Wilderness" (1931), about the Canadian North which Baker presented in a Yale Workshop production.

It was this play that Voaden, the following year, stripped of its realistic trappings and produced as "Rocks" (1932), the first of the new genre, Symphonic Expressionism. Owing much to the paintings of the Group of Seven, it presented the setting of the little fishing village of Port Coldwell, on the northern shore of Lake Superior, which Lauren Harris used for his painting, "Above Lake Superior." Deeply committed to the Group of Seven's beliefs, Voaden was almost obsessed by the Canadian North — its austere, lonely but serene moods. Lowrie Warrener, a young protégé of the Group of Seven, was Voaden's travelling companion. Together they wrote "Symphony," a painter's ballet. While in Port Coldwell, they met a fisherman's *wife who suggested to Voaden the character of the old mother in "Rocks." She is the woman who fears and hates the wilderness while her son is inevitably attracted to it.*

"Rocks" was the first in a series of Symphonic Expressionism plays, a genre which, in Voaden's hands, developed gradually in depth and lyricism. His chief concern was thematic. He attempted in "Rocks" to develop the thesis that the North possesses an elemental strength that uplifts the strong but warps the weak. Theme governs his whole technique in Symphonic Expressionism. In "Rocks" the North is personified in an unseen actor.

The plot involves a young woman schoolteacher who begins her work in the wilderness, where she meets the man who acquaints her with its grandeur. Eventually he is destroyed by the wilderness he so admires as he is lost in a blizzard. The resultant conflict in the woman's mind finally resolves itself in a spiritual transformation caused by the splendour of the wilderness itself.

The characters in Voaden's play are mirrors reflecting the main character, the North. He uses cyclorama lighting and clearly defined stage areas with mood tones through which the characters move as their emotions change. They reveal their true thoughts and emotions in ritualized movement and speech, just as O'Neill's characters in Strange Interlude *reveal their true selves in their asides. The lighting contributes to the symphony.*

The emotional themes developed in the actor's lines are introduced by simple melodies on violin and cello, and by the rhythmic drumbeats of gathering emotional intensity which prepare for the motif of fate. Two groups of dancers provide the rhythmical counterpart of the speeches. As a result, Voaden's play uses all these art forms without subordinating any one to the other. Thus the audience is presented with an artistic exposition of a thesis.

There followed in the next few years several more plays of Symphonic Expressionism: Earth Song *(1932), "Hill-Land" (1934), "Murder Pattern" (1936), "Ascend as the Sun" (1942), and adaptations of plays and a novel into Symphonic Expressionism in "Murder in the Cathedral" (1936) and*

"Maria Chapdelaine" (1938). Voaden also experimented in Symphonic Theatre Dance in "A Dance Chorale" (1936) and an adaptation for dance in "Romeo and Juliet" (1936).

With music so important in Voaden's Symphonic Theatre it is not surprising that "Ascend as the Sun" was followed by the libretti for an opera, "The Prodigal Son," composed by Frederick Jacobi, and a dramatic symphony, "Esther," composed by Godfrey Ridout. His last play, "Emily Carr," about the great West Coast painter and writer, was produced at Queen's University, Kingston, in the summer of 1960, and again at the McPherson Playhouse in Victoria in 1966. He is now working on his theatre biography, but hopes to return to playwriting when he has completed it.

It is worth noting that Voaden anticipated with his Symphonic Expressionism the Symphonic Drama of the great American playwright Paul Green. Green began his experiments in combining the different performing arts in the 1930s and they have continued, sometimes with great success, to the present day. Green works with a huge outdoor stage which allows him to more easily combine music, dance, and panoramic effects in the working out of a genuine play containing plot and characterization.

A reawakening of interest in Voaden's contribution to Canadian theatre should be an enriching experience. In Symphonic Expressionism he has bequeathed to Canada a new artistic synthesis, and to theatre a spiritual transfiguration.

In Toronto in the twenties, thirties and early forties the spiritual forces which have given us a separate identity as a nation and as a people were in full play. In those years I made a series of experiments in which I searched for an expressionist, many-voiced, symphonic theatre that would be, I hoped, uniquely Canadian.

My life-long enthusiasm for the theatre began with comprehensive courses in modern drama at Queen's University, Kingston (1920-23). Even then, while I enjoyed every kind of drama, I was attracted to the revolt against realism—against what Eugene O'Neill called "the banality of surfaces." Poetic, romantic, and symbolic drama, and particularly the post-war German expressionist plays, appealed to me strongly. Gordon Craig and Adolphe Appia opened challenging vistas. Eugene O'Neill was the subject of my M.A. thesis, which I completed in 1926; plays like *The Emperor Jones*, *The Hairy Ape*, *The Great God Brown* and *Strange Interlude* pointed the way to the theatre I should like to make.

Intensive play-going confirmed this interest in innovative theatre. It began with my year of teacher training in Toronto, 1923-24, and continued during two years of teaching in Ottawa and my first English headships in Windsor (1926-27) and Sarnia (1927-28). In these years I saw a wide range of theatre in Toronto and Detroit and made frequent trips to New York. Anna Pavlova, the Duncan Dancers and the Denishawn troupe aroused a keen and life-long interest in dance. I saw and heard Thomas Wilfred play the clavilux—the colour organ. Each new O'Neill play as it appeared was a highlight of New York visits. And always I took keen delight in music—from symphony concerts to the great soloists and the Metropolitan Opera.

Acting strengthened my preference for the new theatre. In a summer play production course at Hart House Theatre in 1926 I played the young gangster in O'Neill's *The Dreamy Kid* and Aglovale in Maeterlinck's *The Death of Tintagiles*. It was a stirring experience to work in Canada's most beautiful theatre, alive with memories of the days of Roy Mitchell. And while teaching in Windsor I acted with the Detroit Repertory Theatre in George Kaiser's expressionist play *From Morn to*

Midnight and played the younger brother in O'Neill's *Beyond the Horizon.*

In Sarnia, as the first director of the city's Drama League, I sought to strengthen the community theatre movement by showing how a small centre could have a vital theatre with the highest artistic standards—a proposal that later became known as "The Sarnia Idea."

The theatre in these smaller centres had been weakened by the collapse of the "road" touring system. Even in many of the well-established little theatres in the larger cities there was indifference to serious and experimental drama.[1]

This was the scene when I came to Toronto to teach and to work in the theatre in September, 1928, after my first thrilling summer of play-going in Europe. The theatre I had helped to launch in Sarnia, and above all what I had seen in Europe that summer, gave me confidence and ideas.

The arena for my efforts was an unusual one in today's terms. There were few professional opportunities for a life in the theatre in Canada in the twenties. Canadian universities taught drama as literature; theatre was an extra-curricular activity. But vocational schools were free from rigid examination requirements. I had been appointed Head of the English Department at the Central High School of Commerce, with a mandate to try to win my students to a love of the arts, particularly books and the theatre. Theatre was an integral part of my teaching by day, and in the evening I directed an adult play production course. I produced Shaw, Barrie, Synge, Yeats, O'Neill. We built a permanent unit setting of curtains, arches, pylons, steps, platforms and screens in the Gordon Craig fashion, and installed a switchboard and lighting equipment with which effects could be achieved that rivalled those possible in Hart House Theatre.

Here I began to work toward my goal. My search for new directions in the theatre had quickened with seeing the Diaghlieff Ballet in London, the Pitoeffs in Paris, Max Reinhardt's *Danton's Tod* in Berlin and *Jedermann* in Salzburg and, during three marvelling weeks at the Bayreuth Festival, watching *The Ring of the Nibelung* unfold, and seeing *Tristan and Isolde, Lohengrin* and *Tannhauser*—many of the productions evoking the sense of space, the mystery and beauty of the Appia designs.

Most important of all, I came back an ardent nationalist. Leave your land when you are young; returning, you will love it deeply. My passionate pride found a focus in the idealism of the Group of Seven painters.

In creative intensity and artistic significance the early years at Hart House Theatre matched the thrust of the Group of Seven. But they lacked the nationalistic fervour which was at the heart of the Group's activity. The only playwright of stature in Roy Mitchell's team was Merrill Denison, and his biographer calls him a mugwump, his mug on one side of the Canadian-U.S.A. border and his wump on the other.[2] The realistic plays he wrote were unique and important in our theatre's story, but they dealt with the *unheroic* north. In the Brooker 1928-29 *Yearbook* Denison's savage attack on nationalism in drama is at odds with the whole mood of the book and its clarion call to a new adventure in a new land.

I loved the north and our wider margins, and found friendship and ideas to be shared with the Group. I was in my mid-twenties. They were older, but keenly interested in what I was trying to do. By this time they were widely recognized and accepted. Their philosophy, their love of their land, were clearly set forth, not only in their own writings, but in *A Canadian Art Movement: The Story of the Group of Seven*,[3] by their close friend, F. B. Housser, and in Bertram Brooker's *Yearbook*. Inspired by these two books, and helped by their authors and several members of the Group, I planned a one-act play competition that would encourage an authentic Canadianism in subject and design by requiring that the plays have an exterior northern setting and suggesting that contestants follow in mood or subject matter the paintings of artists whose work they considered Canadian in character. At this time I wrote the Honourable Vincent Massey proposing a play festival competition and the formation of an organization along the lines of the British Drama League which I had studied in England.

The contest was publicized by the Modern Drama Course offered by the University of Toronto's Department of

University Extension, which I directed in 1929-30. Merrill Denison was one of the judges, along with J. E. H. MacDonald, the poet-painter of the Group, and Professor J. D. Robins. The three prize-winning plays, and three others which I chose, were presented on the Commerce stage, and were published in 1930 as *Six Canadian Plays*[4] — the first of a dozen theatre anthologies which I have edited (see Bibliography).

Those were memorable days. Recalling them, I think of Hamlet's words: "Rightly to be great/Is not to stir without great argument."

The argument is in Housser's account, in Brooker's opening essay in his *Yearbook*, called "When We Awake." Emerson's cry: "Why should we grope among the dusty bones of the past? Why should not we also have an original relation to the universe?" sets the mood for the Introduction to *Six Canadian Plays*, in which I proclaimed, with an apostolic fervour that is strange and intense in its conviction as I reread it, that the great argument could pitch us forward to a vital native theatre.

Six Canadian Plays by its very nature was more Canadian than any collection of plays yet published in Canada. Now I myself had to accept the challenge of the Introduction and seek to create new combinations of the arts which might be universal, "being the reflection of the vision and the beauty of a new people in a new land."

I needed to know more about theatre and playwriting. After two years of teaching at my new school, I obtained a year's leave of absence (without salary), and spent the season of 1930-31 at the Yale School of Drama. I studied all aspects of theatre, with the great George P. Baker, mentor of Eugene O'Neill, my teacher and guide in playwriting.

There I wrote a realistic one-act play, "Wilderness," which was directly inspired by the Group of Seven. It was given a workshop production at Yale. Then I began my first full-length play, *Earth Song* — a play for the symphonic theatre. It was not finished when I returned to Toronto, and I wanted to have something of my own to present with my evening play production group.

One day, in a rare moment, I realized that "Wilderness," which was full of the idealism and belief of the Group of

Seven, was in reality the stuff of my expressionist theatre. I stripped away its realistic detail and presented it on the Commerce stage as "Rocks," the first example of symphonic theatre, on April 22 and 23, 1932.

Augustus Bridle, music and drama critic of *The Toronto Star*, saw that first production. He wrote:

> Nothing quite like it has ever been done in Canada. The story, mainly in two monologues from both ends of the stage, is used as a word-continuity for the use of light and colour.
>
> The set—just a few low bare rocks—looks like some modern paintings. Over the rocks and a cyclorama backdrop, with a few posed pantomimic figures arranged like a frieze, lights and colours change, with incidental music from cello and violin, to the cadences of the voices that tell the story.
>
> The sequence of lights is very beautiful and mystic. Each change of light and modulation of color presents a varying mood in the play which is written in rhythmic prose. The posed figures do slow pantomimes to illustrate various dramatic changes in the story.
>
> The production was highly successful and popular with a large audience, and is likely to develop into something very striking as a new language of drama.

There was so much interest in "Rocks" that I repeated it six months later in four performances on the two weekends beginning September 23. To complete the program I offered seven poems for my new kind of theatre: I called them "theatral" poems—I disliked the word theatrical.

Among the critics who saw this evening of "The Theatre of Many Voices" was Edward W. Wodson, whose column "Music Notes" appeared in *The Telegram*. Commenting on "Rocks," he said, in part:

> "Mr. Voaden's play is deeply tragic—the story of a girl in the north country whose lover is lost in the storm. . . . There are many beautiful lines in the play, but not an accent in them is over-emphasized. On either side of the stage the two women stand, chanting their hopes and fears and history as though they were things outside of their experience. Across the stage are grouped kneeling dancers, who by their gestures emphasize the tragedy that moves inexorably onward. The

viola (played by Mr. Walter Rennie) sings softly a haunting little melodic phrase that has an augmented interval which grips the heart. And distant drum-beats—like the fateful throbs of Beethoven's 5th symphony—mark out the toilsome path of destiny. Behind and around all this is a subtle changefulness of color and lighting—variable as the moods of the human mind, yet broad and restful as a poignant memory long gone to sleep; this lighting robs feeling of its sting many a time. Its effect is beautiful, restful, like a whisper of comfort to an overwrought heart.

One critic, Ernest A. Dale, reviewing the production in *The Canadian Forum*, November, 1932, had doubts about the new language, particularly the restrictions it imposed on the actor. But the review concludes:

We must remember, however, that this is experiment, and that simplicity of theme may be to the director the necessary educative stage in what is meant to become a medium for the expression of what can only imperfectly be rendered by the traditional art of theatre. The method may look forward to the subtle suggestion of underlying thought and emotion at variance with the overt attitude of the characters; and, in any case, a final judgement must await further experience of the method as applied to other themes. Mr. Voaden's work is tentative and extremely ambitious: it has the great merit of not seeming utterly absurd, as departures from tradition so often appear. It is to be hoped that he will continue his pioneer efforts and bring his method to greater perfection. For the present at least, no serious student of the drama should neglect any opportunity of studying his productions."

On the Saturday following the first performances Lawrence Mason, drama and music critic of *The Globe*, wrote a lengthy article, "Symphonic Expressionism" in which he discussed the production and the possible sources of my inspiration— from Greek tragedy to Wagner's music dramas and Pater's thesis that "all art aspires to the condition of music." Finally he made two points:

"1. The soundness and vitality of the inspiration afforded by the Canadian North. Symphonic expressionism, like the painting of the Group of Seven, is far removed from effeminate sentimentality. The harsh title 'Rocks' and the uncompromising virility of the plot, language, and treatment keep the play and the production free from any taint of pretty-pretty aestheticism. The scented muse of Maeterlinck, of Fiona Macleod, of Tagore, finds no place in this vigorous Canadian art-movement.

"2. The great importance of Mr. Voaden's work in helping the Canadian theatre and drama to break away from stultifying borrowed traditions, and to find its own soul by going back to the soil for its subject-matter and inspiration, and by going forward beyond the horizon of realism for its producing methods and theatral art."

The final production of "Rocks" (it had also been performed at the first Central Ontario Regional Festival of the newly formed Dominion Drama Festival at Hart House Theatre, March 25, 1933) was included in the performances, August 9 and 10, 1934, which closed my summer play production course at Queen's University, Kingston. I believe this was the first practical theatre course offered by any university in Canada.

The theatral poems which were presented with "Rocks" were the first of several experiments that paralleled productions of my own plays and were part of my search for a symphonic theatre. In the poems I sought to blend spoken poetry with a visual pattern of ritually moving or sculpturally posed figures in a surround of orchestrated light and colour.

I finished *Earth Song*, my first full-length play for the new theatre, in the summer of 1932, and after the "Rocks"-Theatral Poetry program, returned to Sarnia to direct it for the Little Theatre, which I had helped to found five years earlier. I had secured my second leave of absence, to direct the play and to spend the balance of the school year writing, studying new developments in the teaching of English in England, and theatre-going there, on the continent and in the East. *Earth Song* was presented on December 16 and 17, 1932, on a small stage on a flat-floored public school auditorium.

I described the idea of the play, which came to me while at the Yale Drama School, in an article which I wrote for the *Sarnia Observer:*

I spent many long days rambling over New England hills, walking from morning till dark. These were very happy days. I began to feel that the secret of content and greatness lay in being very much in harmony with nature—in harmony with the movement of the seasons and the cycles of the days. So I wrote the play in five cycles of light and growth—each cycle consisting of four scenes—spring dawn, summer noon, autumn sunset, winter night. Through these cycles my two characters, whom I have called Adam and Eve because they represent the promise of life in a new world, move through experiences which finally lead to the perfection of their own characters and their completion in each other. This final consummation I have called symbolically, their godhood.

The play was a box-office success. Reviewers R. V. Howard in *Saturday Night* and Rica McLean Farquharson in *The Mail and Empire*, were impressed, but had reservations. Lawrence Mason, writing in *The Globe*, seemed most to appreciate the performance. As a critic of music, as well as of drama, Mason, as well as Edward Wodson and Augustus Bridle were in a better position to judge productions which, to repeat Pater's words, aspired "to the condition of music."

Dr. Mason praised the lighting as a "kind of visible orchestration of the text and action," and the music, which was taken from the first and fourth Brahms symphonies, as "so felicitously chosen and timed that the emotional impact of the words and scenes was immensely enhanced. Moreover, largely under the catalytic influence of this overwhelming music, the miracle of the synthesis veritably took place: all the various component parts of the production actually fused and blended in a unified whole . . . "

"Hill-Land," my next full-length play, was begun during my travels in Europe and the East, and completed in time for Play Workshop production on the Commerce stage on December 13 and 14, 1934. The long central fifth scene (Act II, Scene I) was presented at Hart House Theatre in the Dominion Drama Festival Regional Finals on March 27, 1935, and at Queen's University, Kingston, on August 9 and 10 of that year, following the second summer drama course which I gave there.

The Play Workshop, an extension of my evening play

production courses, was patterned on the workshop procedures I had seen at the Yale Drama School. The plays of some twenty-five aspiring dramatists were given weekly laboratory production and examination; the best of these, rewritten, were shown in public productions, along with plays by well-known Canadian writers. The goals of the Workshop were: "To develop a distinctively Canadian art of the theatre; to encourage the writing of Canadian drama."

"Hill-Land" is set in the wooded, rocky, lake country of Haliburton, northeast of Toronto. It is more "real" than *Earth Song;* it tells the story of a pioneer grandmother, her daughter- in-law, her grandson and his young wife, in this hill-land. But like *Earth Song* it is intensely subjective and lyrical. Each of the two acts follows the sequence of spring, summer, autumn and winter.

In "Hill-Land," symbolic, choral or narrative figures are more important than they were in "Rocks" or *Earth Song.* I had seen such figures strikingly used in the youthful Tyrone Guthrie's production of Thornton Wilder's *Pullman Car Hiawatha* at a weekend workshop in Liverpool, and in the Compagnie des Quinze production of André Obey's *Le Viol de Lucrèce* in Paris.

Dance, also, was a more integral part of the production. I had watched dance productions in England, France, Italy and Germany, and had studied dance at the Kurt Jooss School in Essen, Germany; Jooss' ballet, "The Green Table," made a profound impression on me. I realized that actors should be dancers, that dance was the key to opening the door to the symphonic theatre. To quote from an article I wrote for the English periodical, *The Dancing Times,* July, 1933, in the dancer "the rhythms apprehended through the ear and eye are one."

The program note for "Hill-Land" begins with a quotation from Santayana: that the arts have "no higher function" than to renew the "moments of inspiration" which are their source. The symphonic theatre, I said, should seek to re-create these moments by visual picturization, and by using music, dance and choral comment to sustain and lift them to significance.

Dr. Mason judged this production "Mr. Voaden's most

successful effort in his chosen field. . . . his 'message' is an ardent and virile Canadianism which should appeal."

B. K. Sandwell of *Saturday Night* was the dissenting critic. On the flat school auditorium floor he could not see and hear some of the choral figures who were below the stage level, and he was critical of what he heard. He praised the company, but took issue (rightly, I now believe) with some of the claims I made for the symphonic theatre in the program note.

Essentially, he was a traditionalist. For example, Eugene O'Neill was to him one of those "lesser dramatists" who, "deficient in verbal power, have found it necessary to cover up that deficiency by resorting to other and less inspiring mechanisms."

Augustus Bridle in *The Star* summarized and commented on the remarks of the British adjudicator, Malcolm Morley. The work "impressed the London critic as a new Canadian combination of Greek tragedy, music and symbolism. But his comments on the production were rather superficially clever. He failed to analyze so unusual a production on its unconventional merits."

Pearl McCarthy (later well known as an art critic) had high praise. She found "Hill-Land" to be a "gripping work of art. It not only used speech and some stylized acting, music and lighting orchestration, but relied on form and plastic sculptural effects to achieve amazing poignancy. . . . The piece was so original that it scarcely seemed to have a place in what has ordinarily been considered theatre. But it was too vital to be denied a place in art, and it did seem to bespeak a new theatre."

How fortunate I was to have such sensitive and receptive critics! What I was trying to do was something that was understood in the climate of the time.

"Murder Pattern" was first produced at the Play Workshop on January 24 and 25, 1936, and repeated at the Regional Dominion Drama Festival at Hart House Theatre on March 25 of that year. It was an attempt to create a "pattern" in which the story of a famous Haliburton murder, realistically enacted and described, is blended with lyrical comment and the visual and musical elements of my symphonic expressionism. This, I hoped, would make a total statement about the area, which I knew and loved—one that would be more true and memorable than a realistic portrayal of the event. Lawrence Mason commented in his review of the Festival performance that the play uses "the characteristic media of several arts in order to suggest a larger than merely factual significance."

Two critics considered "Murder Pattern" a step forward in the search for a new kind of theatre. Reviewing the Workshop production, Augustus Bridle wrote: "As done by a large well-drilled company it was highly effective; much better focused in drama than 'Hill-Land' and much less self-conscious in lighting effects than 'Rocks.' In fact this production definitely stamps Voaden as having something to say by means of a four-dimension drama that he could not do so well by the ordinary method."

B. K. Sandwell in *Saturday Night*, commenting on the Festival production, wrote that "Murder Pattern" " . . . had a great deal more drama than its predecessors, and showed particular improvement in the poetic quality of the lines given to the various narrators, voices and other personages extraneous to the drama." And he made the shrewd observation that the second contestant in the struggle is "the spirit of the country" and said that this spirit "is rather effectively evoked by the speeches of the symbolic person-ages, the scenery, and the narrative." But he still disapproved of "the method," and called the result "an adorned recitation" rather than an "acted play." How he would evoke "the spirit of the country" with his traditional concept of the play, he did not say. The Group of Seven had done so in painting. Louis Hémon, in my favorite Canadian novel, *Maria Chapdelaine*, had effectively captured the spirit of the Lake St. John region. Why should I not try? Why shouldn't the theatre have the wider range, the freedom?

"Murder Pattern" has many parallels with recent plays about the Donnellys, particularly those of James Reaney. In the thirties I was looking toward the freer forms of theatre we have today.

I should mention briefly other experiments in which, as with the theatral poetry performances, the words or dramatic ideas were not mine. It is not easy to separate them from the productions of my own plays. In each I tried new combinations of the arts. Symphonic techniques were webbed into their very texture; they belonged to the search for a different stage language. And because the musicians, dancers and writers involved were outstanding in their fields, they added interest and excitement to the experimental theatre scene at the time.

Six of these were performed in the two years of the first Play Workshop, 1934-36. There were two poetic plays. *The Toll Gate*,[5] by George Herbert Clarke, was written for the 1934 summer course at Queen's University, and repeated in the opening presentation of the Play Workshop; it is based on Clarke's poem, "Halt and Parley." E. J. Pratt's *The Iron Door (An Ode)*[6] was dramatized by Nathaniel Benson, himself a poet and playwright, and shown at the Workshop performances on February 14 and 15, 1935. Productions of two unusual expressionist plays, "Within" and "The Dragon," by Bertram Brooker, artist and novelist, were mounted in each of the two Workshop years.

Finally there were two experiments in dance, using symphonic theatre techniques: a "Dance Chorale," to Richard Strauss' tone poem, "Death and Transfiguration," danced by Saida Gerrard, pupil of Mary Wigman, and "Romeo and Juliet," a dance-drama, to Tchaikovsky's Overture, first given at the Workshop and repeated at the Promenade Symphony Concert conducted by Reginald Stewart in the University of Toronto Arena on June 25, 1936.

These were followed by my productions (the first in Canada) of T. S. Eliot's *Murder in the Cathedral* at Queen's University at the public performances closing my third summer course, and then at Massey Hall, Toronto, on October 30 and 31, 1936.

"Romeo and Juliet" and *Murder in the Cathedral* reached the biggest audiences of any of my productions. Over 5,000 saw the dance pantomime at the Varsity Arena, and at least an equal number attended the three performances of *Murder in the Cathedral* at Massey Hall. Both were highly praised. Augustus Bridle in the *Toronto Daily Star* wrote that in "Romeo and Juliet" my five-year experiment in symphonic theatre was lifted for twenty minutes "into Reinhardt dimensions." As for *Murder in the Cathedral*, B. K. Sandwell called the Kingston performance "a most noteworthy production of a truly wonderful play."

My next project belongs with these experiments: the adaptation of Louis Hémon's novel *Maria Chapdelaine*, for the symphonic theatre. I was eager to test the composite language with a novel, as I had with poetry, dance, and poetic and expressionist plays. Hémon's classic struck the note of Canadianism in Quebec where our roots as a people are oldest and deepest.

It was to be a full-length play, and I needed time to write it. Again I was given leave of absence, without salary. It was my third leave in seven years; this was how, while a teacher, I was able to write plays and be deeply involved in the theatre. In December, 1936, after the *Murder in the Cathedral* production at Massey Hall, my wife and I left for eight months of play-going and writing in Europe.

The first part of the play, dealing with the tragic love of Maria and François Paradis, was presented at the Workshop; it was repeated at the Regional Drama Festival Finals at Hart House Theatre on March 28, 1938. Nine years later I directed a cast of players that included Lorne Greene and Charmian King in a reading performance of the full-length play.

Reviewing the Hart House production, Nancy Pyper in *Saturday Night* called it "a very moving, very beautiful presentation." "It was marked throughout by harmony—harmony of music, of colour and of voice." Rose Macdonald in *The Telegram* said that I was more successful than usual in differentiating between "characters of the flesh and spirit."

The report in *The Globe* quoted the British adjudicator, Malcolm Morley, as saying that he was "overawed" by the beauty of the production, but that it was too "static." Augustus Bridle in *The Toronto Star* called it "a phase in the development of a big idea."

I took the title for my next play from Whitman's line, "We also ascend, dazzling and tremendous as the sun." *Ascend As the Sun* was the first play of a projected cycle developing the idealistic themes of *Earth Song* and "Hill-Land." It was an ambitious effort, and I found it difficult to find time to complete it. My teaching, headship and editorial responsibilities were heavier each year. The Second World War added additional burdens. No more leaves of absence were possible. The play was finally presented at Hart House Theatre, April 13-16, 1942.

Augustus Bridle wrote in the *Toronto Daily Star*, July 12, 1941: "This is an enormous work, not in length, but in concentrated vitality and plan . . . portraying by all the arts of the theatre the life of a young man from birth, through adolescence, into the realisms of modern life."

Playwright John Coulter also read the play before the presentation. He wrote:

> Voaden proposes a symphony in which orchestral musical instruments are but partners with dialogue, choral speech, ballet, dynamic modulations of colour and light, all chiming together in a stage spectacle on a theory crystallised by Walter Pater in the famous phrase that all the arts tend to the condition of music. . . . His theme is one of imaginative ambitiousness too, for it is nothing less than the ascent of a soul out of the pre-natal night, through the dawn of consciousness in childhood and adolescence, into the broad light of the adult's intellectual day.

I had notable help with both music and dance. The distinguished young composer Godfrey Ridout wrote the music—for choir, trumpets, percussion, harmonium and piano. The dancers, from Boris Volkoff's Ballet, helped me create the choreography; they included Mildred Herman— later world-famous with Balanchine as Melissa Hayden.

But there were question marks in my mind. *Ascend As the Sun* had taken four years to complete. Where would I find time to write the next play of the cycle? More important, *Ascend As the Sun* was conceived and largely written before the war became a frightening and all-engrossing charge on our consciences. By the time it was produced, I knew in my heart that the idealism and ardent, heroic belief of the early plays which it developed with almost embarassing conviction were no longer tenable. We were not, in Whitman's words, a prelude to better players.

Rereading the play, I should like to strip it of its heroic pretensions and leave it, still a score for a symphonic production, an account of a young Canadian's life from birth to manhood—another thrust of the unseen powers toward a more humane world.

I went back to the Yale Drama School the summer of 1942. There I met the distinguished American composer, Frederick Jacobi, and began a close and happy collaboration, writing during the next three years the libretto for an opera, "The Prodigal Son." Here I had to write to order, objectively, with great economy. But I was still experimenting, searching— exploring the relations between the word, and music, and the theatre.

As the Second World War continued and the casualty lists lengthened—the names of many of my own students among them—I was increasingly unhappy and concerned, like many other Canadian artists. This was the second war fought to make a world fit for heroes to live in. What would life in Canada be like after this war? I began to wonder whether I should come down from my lonely and shining tower and join forces with the beleagured fighters who wanted more of the good things of life for everyone.

Thus came the great change in my life's direction. I did not turn my back entirely on writing for the theatre. In addition to "The Prodigal Son," I wrote the libretto for a dramatic symphony, "Esther," for Godfrey Ridout. Also a play about the great Canadian painter and writer, "Emily Carr," (who like me, was strongly influenced by Whitman and the Group of Seven) in which I sought to bring painting and theatre together— continuing my search for a theatre that seeks union with the other arts. It was performed first at Queen's University in the summer of 1960, with Amelia Hall in the title role, and repeated in 1966 at the McPherson Playhouse in Victoria.

But "crusading" in politics and the arts took centre stage, apart from teaching and editing. I joined the CCF party (Co-operative Commonwealth Federation)—now the (New Democratic Party)—in 1943, and contested the Toronto riding of Trinity for the party in three federal elections and a by-election, 1945-54. Also in 1943, I became deeply involved in another cause: the arts for the people. I helped with the preparation of artist briefs to the House of Commons Committee on Reconstruction and Re-Establishment, and was a member of the delegation in the famous "March on Ottawa" on June 21, 1944, when the artists of Canada appeared before the Committee and confronted government for the first time, demanding increased support for the arts and a wider dispersal of cultural opportunity.

On December 5, 1945, the sixteen national arts bodies which had organized the march on Ottawa met at the Arts and Letters Club in Toronto to set up a permanent organization. The Canadian Arts Council (now the Canadian Conference of the Arts) was formed, and I agreed to accept the presidency, which I held for three years. This organization spearheaded the demand for government action which led to the establishment of the Massey Commission and later the formation of the Canada Council and provincial arts councils. I have been active with it since its inception and was its National Director in 1967-68.

The decision to accept the presidency that night was a fateful one. While I continued, as I said, to do some writing and to be interested in the relation of the theatre to the other arts, this decision meant an end to the main thrust of my experiments toward a new composite theatre language—an end to the first intensely creative period of my life.

I have pondered this decision deeply in these last years when there has been a revival of interest in my symphonic theatre. Has it been worthwhile to give the second half of my days trying to help change the character of a nation and the quality of its life?

Is not the artist, finally, more important than the crusader?

I suppose the answer depends on what was created and what was achieved by the crusade. The final judgment will be made by those who read the plays, and perhaps see future productions of them, and by those who study and assess the development of the arts in Canada.

A last word. In truth, teaching had become so demanding that I had no alternative but to make the dramatist play second fiddle, short of a Gaugin-like break from all responsibility. There were no Canada Council grants then; there was no subsidized professional avant-garde theatre. It gives me some satisfaction to know that the crusade I have helped to lead has made it possible for the dreamers and innovators of today's theatre to follow their dreams and continue their innovations, as I would have liked to continue mine.

NOTES

1. See Carroll Aikins, "Amateur Theatre in Canada," reprinted from *The Canadian Forum* in Bertram Brooker's *Yearbook of the Arts in Canada, 1928-1929* (Toronto: The Macmillan Company of Canada Ltd., 1929).
2. Dick MacDonald, *Mugwump Canadian: The Merrill Denison Story* (Montreal: Content Publishing Ltd., 1973).
3. (Toronto: The Macmillan Company of Canada Ltd., 1926.) Reprinted in 1974.
4. Herman Voaden, ed., *Six Canadian Plays* (Toronto: Copp Clark Publishing Company, 1930).
5. George Herbert Clarke, *Halt and Parley and Other Poems* (Toronto: The Macmillan Company of Canada Ltd., 1934). Reprinted in *Look Both Ways: Theatre Experiences*, Herman Voaden, ed.
6. E. J. Pratt, *The Iron Door (An Ode)* (Toronto: The Macmillan Company of Canada Ltd., 1927).

Chronology

1903	Born January 19, in London, Ontario, son of Louisa (Bale) Voaden and Dr. Arthur Voaden, Principal of St. Thomas Collegiate Institute and the Arthur Voaden Vocational School.
1920	Graduated from St. Thomas Collegiate Institute. Entered Queen's University, Kingston, Ontario.
1923-24	Graduated from Queen's University with Honours Degree in English and History. Medalist in English. Teacher training courses at College of Education, Toronto.
1924-26	Taught at Glebe Collegiate Institute, Ottawa. Received M.A., Queen's University.
1926-27	Head of Department of English, Windsor-Walkerville Technical School, Windsor.

1927-28	Head of Department of English, Collegiate Institute and Vocational School, Sarnia. First Director, Sarnia Drama League.
1928	Appointed Director of English, Central High School of Commerce, Toronto.
1928-29	Initiated and played a leading role in arranging a tour of Ontario schools and communities by the Hart House Touring Players in *A Midsummer Night's Dream.*
1929-30	As Director of the Modern Drama Course, Department of University Extension, University of Toronto, was responsible for a tour of *As You Like It* by two casts directed by Dora Mavor Moore and Glen Liston.
1930-31	Studied at the Graduate School of Drama at Yale University; playwriting classes with George Pierce Baker. Wrote "Wilderness," which was produced at the Yale Workshop. Began *Earth Song.*
1931-33	Presented "Rocks"—a non-realistic version of "Wilderness"—as an example of symphonic theatre. Directed *Earth Song,* first full-length symphonic play, for the Sarnia Drama League. Completed "Hill-Land."
1934	Directed the first of three summer play production courses at Queen's University.
1934-35	Launched the Play Workshop in Toronto to encourage the writing and production of Canadian plays and experimentation with new stage techniques. "Hill-Land" produced at the Play Workshop; the central fifth scene presented at Hart House Theatre in the Dominion Drama Festival Regional Finals.
1935	Married Violet Kilpatrick.
1935-36	"Murder Pattern" produced at the Play Workshop and Regional Drama Festival. "Romeo and Juliet," dance-drama to Tchaikovosky's Overture, presented at the Workshop and repeated at a Promenade Symphony Concert in the University of Toronto Arena conducted by Reginald Stewart.
1937	Received Canadian Drama Award.
1938	Scenes from "Maria Chapdelaine" presented at the Workshop and at the Regional Drama Festival.

1942   "Ascend as the Sun" presented at Hart House Theatre, with the Boris Volkoff dancers and music by Godfrey Ridout.

1943   Dance drama based on *The Masque of the Red Death*, by E. A. Poe, presented on the Commerce stage, with music by Godfrey Ridout.

1943-45   Collaborated with American composer Frederick Jacobi in writing the libretto for an opera, "The Prodigal Son," a version of the biblical legend based on four early American prints.

1944   Member of Committee representing fifteen national arts organizations which had prepared briefs for presentation to the Turgeon Committee (the House of Commons Committee on Reconstruction and Re-establishment). Wrote the brief summarizing these submissions. Member of delegation which presented the summary brief to the Turgeon Committee on June 21.

1945   Elected first President of the Canadian Arts Council at formation meeting, December 5, at the Arts and Letters Club attended by representatives of the above national arts organization. President until 1948. Continued as an active member of the Council— now the Canadian Conference of the Arts—since then.

1946   Member of Canada's delegation to the First General Conference of UNESCO, the United Nations Educational Scientific and Cultural Organization, in Paris.

1948   As President of the Canadian Arts Council played a leading role in arranging for Canada's participation in the 1948 Cultural Olympics.

1949-50   Writer member of Committee which prepared and presented brief, summarizing the recommendations of the member organizations of the Canadian Arts Council to the Massey Commission (The Royal Commission on National Development in the Arts, Letters, and Sciences).

1952   Adapted the text for "Esther, a Dramatic Symphony," by Godfrey Ridout, performed at Massey Hall, Toronto, by the Royal Conservatory Symphony Orchestra.

1953	Wrote "Coronation Ode," music by Godfrey Ridout, commissioned by the CBC and presented as part of the Coronation celebrations.
1954	Supervised the production of "The Prodigal Son" for the Forest Hill Concert and Theatre Series, Toronto. Two-piano accompaniment.
1956	Writer member of Committee of the Canadian Arts Council which prepared and submitted brief to the Royal Commission on Broadcasting (the Fowler Commission).
1958	"Emily Carr" written and entered in the play competition sponsored by the Stratford Festival and the Toronto *Globe and Mail*. Judged one of the ten best of the 185 scripts submitted.
1960	First production of "Emily Carr" by the Department of Drama at Queen's University, Kingston, directed by William Angus, starring Amelia Hall.
1964	"Esther" presented at the MacMillan Theatre, Toronto, in the ceremonies opening the Edward Johnson Building.
1965-66	For the Canadian Conference of the Arts prepared two submissions which were presented to the Royal Commission on Bilingualism and Biculturalism on the role of the arts in contributing to Canadian unity and a sense of national identity.
1966	"Emily Carr" presented by the Greater Victoria Centennial Society at McPherson Playhouse as part of the British Columbia Centennial celebrations.
1966-68	Associate Director, then National Director, Canadian Conference of the Arts. Led a research team in writing a two-volume report, "The Arts and Education." Organized the Ste. Adèle Seminar, 1967, which examined Centennial initiatives and future directions for the performing arts in Canada.
1968-70	President, Canadian Guild of Crafts. Gave leadership in the first steps to establish a single multi-media craft organization in Canada.
1970	Elected Fellow of Royal Society of Arts (F.R.S.A.).
1974-75	Appointed member of the Order of Canada (C.M.). Exhibition of photographs, programs, and reviews of experimental productions shown at Hart House

Theatre, the Arts and Letters Club, Toronto, and Queen's University, Kingston.

1977   Engaged in writing his family genealogy and biography. "The Book of the Voadens." Also writing a memoir of his theatre experiences.

Selected Bibliography

Primary Sources

PLAYS

"Ascend as the Sun." MS, 1942.

Earth Song. Toronto: Playwrights Co-op., 1976.

"Emily Carr." MS, 1960.

"Esther." Libretto for dramatic symphony composed by Godfrey Ridout. Text in program, 1952.

"Hill-Land." MS, 1934.

"Maria Chapdelaine," Adaptation, MS, 1938.

"Murder Pattern." *The Canadian Theatre Review,* No. 5 1975, pp. 44-60.

"The Prodigal Son." Libretto for opera composed by Frederick Jacobi. MS, 1952 and 1964.

"Rocks." MS, Play Workshop Production, 1932.

"Wilderness." MS, Yale University Workshop Production, 1931.

PLAYS AND PLAY COLLECTIONS EDITED

A Book of Plays. Toronto: Macmillan Company of Canada Ltd., 1935.

Drama IV. Toronto: Macmillan Company of Canada Ltd., 1965.

Four Good Plays. Toronto: Longman Canada Limited, 1944.

Four Plays of Our Time. Toronto: Macmillan Company of Canada Ltd., 1960.

Human Values in Drama. Toronto: Macmillan Company of Canada Ltd., 1966.

Julius Caesar. Toronto: Macmillan Company of Canada Ltd., 1966.

Look Both Ways: Theatre Experiences. Toronto: Macmillan Company of Canada Ltd., 1975.

Murder in the Cathedral. Toronto: Kingswood House and Faber and Faber, 1959.

Nobody Waved Good-bye and Other Plays. Toronto: Macmillan Company of Canada Ltd., 1966.

Nobody Waved Good-bye. Toronto: Macmillan Company of Canada Ltd., 1971.

On Stage. Toronto: Macmillan Company of Canada Ltd., 1945.

Six Canadian Plays. Toronto: Copp Clark Publishing Company, 1930.

ARTICLES

"The Arts and UNESCO." *University of Toronto Quarterly* 17 (1948): 161-67.

"The Arts in Canada." In *Canada Overseas Reference Book.* London: Todd Reference Books Limited, 1949.

"Canadian Plays and Experimental Stagecraft." *The Globe* (Toronto) April 23, 1932, p.18.

"Creed for a New Theatre," *The Globe*, December 17, 1932.

"Dance of the Theatre: Impressions of the Dance in Four Countries." *The Dancing Times* (London), July, 1933.

"Drama Festival Thoughts." *The Globe*, November 26, 1932, p.7.

"Dramatic Art in Canadian Higher Education." In *The Humanities in Canada.* Ottawa: The Humanities Research Council of Canada, 1947.

"The Future of UNESCO," *Food for Thought*, Vol. 7 (April, 1947), pp. 4-8. Toronto: The Canadian Association for Adult Education.

"Government Owned Theatres." *The Globe*, November 29, 1929, p. 12.

"Producing Methods Defined." *The Globe*, April 16, 1932, p.15.

"Toward a New Theatre." *The Globe*, December 9, 1934.

"What is Wrong with the Canadian Theatre?" *The Globe*, June 22, 1929.

Secondary Sources

BROWN, ERNEST. *"Look Both Ways: Theatre Experiences."* The *Canadian Theatre Review*, No. 14 (1977), pp. 103-104.

DALE, ERNEST A. "Mr Voaden's *Rocks.*" *The Canadian Forum* 13, No. 146 (1932), pp. 75-76.

EVANS, CHAD. "Herman Voaden and the Symphonic Theatre." *The Canadian Theatre Review* , No. 5 (Winter, 1975), pp. 37-43.

HINCHCLIFFE, JUDITH. "Look Both Ways: Theatre Experiences." *Canadian Drama/L'Art dramatique canadien* 2, No. 2 (1976), pp. 234-36.

MASON, LAWRENCE. Symphonic Expressionism." *The Globe* , *April 30, 1932, p. 6.*

Three

ROBERTSON DAVIES

(1913-)

Preface

Robertson Davies has enjoyed a distinguished and multi-faceted career as novelist, essayist, critic, playwright, actor, director, journalist, editor, publisher, wit, humanist, scholar, professor, and academic administrator. Possessed of an urbane, sharp, critical mind and a vast store of learning, this cultured writer has known the company of intellectuals since his childhood. Educated at Queen's University in Canada and at Oxford in England, he followed an acting career for a time with the Old Vic Company in London. All this prepared him well for his future role as distinguished Canadian novelist and dramatist.

Of Scottish, Welsh and Dutch ancestry Davies is primarily a satirist who uses the conventions of satirical romance to develop the perceptions that motivate his art. The philosophical ideas energizing his complex literary and dramatic output seem to be threefold: his concern for the artistic plight of the imagination in the narrow, cultural confines of Canada; his fascination with heredity, particularly Jung's theory of the collective unconscious; his absorption in the world of the spirit and its concomitant relationship to the real. A study of his work over the past thirty years reveals a grappling with these issues at first individually and then collectively as he gradually integrates them in his later work.

To understand the complexities of the Davies canon, one must examine the whole corpus — including the novels and essays — in order to understand the plays. Each sheds light on the other. He approached the novels from drama; yet it is the novels that clarify the meaning behind his works for the theatre. Where the plays sometimes mystify and perplex the audience, the novels enlighten and stabilize Davies' concepts in their philosophical, psychological, political, and social implications. The novel has become his most powerful mode. Here he best develops character in a detached, objective manner.

Although his early plays are often solid dramatic structures, he tends in his later stage works to make characters abstractions of ideas. The plays become more dense so that only the initiated seem able to grasp their true intentions. Davies is a self-conscious artist wrestling with the integration of form and dramatic purpose in his playwriting. As the novels become more profound, the plays seem to become more opaque.

A chronological study of Davies' entire opus is highly rewarding in its revelation of the development of his ideas and style. The early satirical essays to be found in The Diary of Samuel Marchbanks (1947) and The Table Talk of Samuel Marchbanks (1949) reveal his use of a kind of neo-classical wit and invective through the persona of the irascible Marchbanks who lashes out against Canadian mediocrity and provincialism. The characters are merely caricatures. His early interest in heredity is apparent in one of his first plays, King Phoenix (1948) in which Old King Cole manages to live on in his successors just as the phoenix rises out of his own ashes. Davies here proclaims that reason and ability are meaningless without passion and imagination, and that life needs constantly to be rejuvenated by the spirit.

In 1949 Davies wrote six plays: Hope Deferred, a good-natured satire on French Canadian Bishops' narrow-minded views of theatre as a corruption of moral life; Fortune, My Foe, a winner of the Dominion Drama Festival's award, is a satire on Canadian provincialism in art using a puppet master as a symbol ol the position of art in Canada; Overlaid, one of his best one-act plays, is also a satire on Canadian materialism and the failure to invest in the arts; The Voice of the People treats of small town ignorance of the arts; Eros at Breakfast introduces his dramatic use of the psychology of Freud and Jung; At the Gates of the Righteous develops George Bernard Shaw's theme of the respect accorded by society to the successful scoundrel, in a Shavian type of satire.

In the 1950s Davies wrote the Salterton trilogy, entering for the first time the field of the novelist. At the same time he produced six more plays. The satirical romance novels: Tempest-Tost *(1951)*, Leaven of Malice *(1954)*, and A Mixture of Frailities *(1958)* continue the 1940s play themes of the failure of the imagination in Canada and the general cultural poverty of Canadians. Set in the fictional town of Salterton (Kingston, Ontario), these novels reveal Davies' struggle with character development. They show a gradual improvement in characterization from the early caricatures (influenced by the Marchbanks essays) and the stereotypes (influenced by his early plays) to the final fascinating creation of the real Monica Gall in A Mixture of Frailties. It is evident in this last book that Davies is no longer dealing with symbols but with real Canadians struggling to liberate themselves from mediocrity. In drama he depended on the power of the actors to breathe life into his characters (see the Preface to his play, At My Heart's Core). In the novel he could resort only to the printed page and he mastered the techniques of this genre to such an extent that he became a more compelling novelist.

The plays of the fifties include: A Masque of Aesop *(1952)* in which he employs Ben Jonson's masque and uses a theme later used in the novel The Manticore: *self-knowledge produces serenity of spirit;* A Jig for the Gypsy *(1954)* in which he combines romance and politics in a satire on Canadian middle class pretensions; Hunting Stuart *(1955)* in which he celebrates heredity in the recurring human spirit that informs and revitalizes descendants; General Confession *(1959)* in which he develops Jung's analytical psychology through the four major characters each symbolizing one of the four major archetypes of the "collective unconscious" all seeking self-knowledge. It was this last play that led him to the creation of the Deptford trilogy of novels in the 1970s.

In the 1960s Davies produced only two plays: A Masque of Mr. Punch *(1963)* and The Centennial Play *(1967)*. But Davies was gathering his forces for the decade which was to prove the peak of his literary life. Three novels and three plays constitute the work of the first seven years of the 1970s. His now famous Deptford trilogy of novels: Fifth Business *(1970)*, The

Manticore *(1972)*, and World of Wonders *(1975) form the high point of his work as a novelist. They succeed in integrating his ideas on the use of the imagination, on heredity, and on the world of the spirit. His characters are real people: Eisengrim, the magician; Ramsay, the historian; Staunton, the materialist. Yet they also symbolize his preoccupations with the spiritual and magical rather than the real, time rather than history, and the imagination rather than crass materialism.* Fifth Business *offers a psychological examination of motivation and a criticism of Canadian sensibility through its search for the integration of empiricism and mysticism.* The Manticore *continues this theme with the probing of Staunton's Jungian analyst which reveals moments of illumination freed from the limitations of time. The manticore, a legendary animal with the head of a man, the body of a lion, and the tail of a scorpion is Davies' symbol of the noble but confused condition of contemporary man. Staunton's rebirth in the cave reiterates Davies' theme of heredity which strengthens Staunton psychologically.* World of Wonders *continues his preoccupation with magic and the spirit in the realm of the real. Ugly Leisl becomes the transfiguring spirit in the lives of these characters who dwell in a kind of nightmare world of the devil and God, of Flesh and spirit.*

Two of the plays written recently include the television drama, Brothers in the Black Art *(1974) which uses black comedy in its ironic combination of the art of printing, loving, and living; and* Question Time *(1975) which forms a further quest for individual and national self-knowledge in a movement toward psychic integration.*

As a dramatist Robertson Davies has changed gradually over the past thirty years from a straightforward satirist employing realistic characters to a denser, more complex ironist whose characters, while real people, are symbolical. Psychologically the plays move from a simple conception of personality to a testing of the Jungian conception; thematically they continue to gather force in their preoccupation with the Canadian sensibility, the influence of heredity, and the relationship of the world of the spirit to reality. Structurally Davies employs traditional dramatic techniques in settings extending from medieval to contemporary life. Robertson Davies is consistent in his on-going search for self-knowledge and wholeness both for the individual Canadian and for Canada itself.

Dear Sister Geraldine:

Here is the chapter you asked for. I am writing it in the form of a personal letter to you, because I have always had a weakness for nuns, and do my best to oblige them when I can. Let me tell you why: when I was a small boy, taking piano lessons at the Convent in Renfrew, Ontario, I learned one of the great lessons of my life, for which I have always been grateful. It happened thus; I was scuttling through the corridors toward the door, having finished my half hour of instruction in playing Czerny and a piece appropriately named "Convent Bells," when I came upon an elderly nun rebuking a very young nun—I suppose a novice. "But Reverend Mother, I didn't have time," the girl was saying, tearfully. "My dear, then you should have *made* time," said the Superior. I thought about that all the way home, through the winter dusk, and it stuck in my mind; to *make* time—what a splendid idea! I have been doing it ever since. So now I am making time to answer the questions you have sent me. They appear to me to be excellent questions, and to cover all the necessary ground, so here goes.

Why did I begin to write drama?

Because I loved the theatre, and it seemed to me to be the best sort of entertainment that anyone could wish for. I inherited this passion from my parents, who were enthusiastic theatre-goers, and took me and my brothers with them whenever a suitable play visited any of the towns where we lived. Of course there were unsuitable plays; I remember one—a problem-play—called *The Unwanted Child*. I was told sternly that it was not "suitable" and of course I wanted to know why, so I asked a great friend and teacher of mine (her name was Victoria Campbell, and she was our cook-general, a woman of fine character and a natural philosopher) and her reply was, "Don't ask me." But I did ask, and continued to ask, until she produced this gnomic answer: "It was about a girl who Went The Limit." And with that I had to be content.

There were other "unsuitable" plays, and some of these belonged to a category called Mutt and Jeff Shows; they were burlesques, and dealt heavily in indecency. But I knew that they were about comic-strip characters, and so I determined to write a play of my own, based on my favourite comic strip—Our Boarding House, drawn and written by Eugene L. Ahearn. It was not an action strip; it was about people in a boarding house, owned by Major Hoople and his wife, who talked, and talked and talked, in large balloons that almost filled the space in the single panel. My play (featuring Major Hoople) ran to three closely written pages, and gave me immense satisfaction; I did not show it to anyone, because I wrote it when I should have been doing my homework, but I treasured it, and I think it was a lasting influence on me. Our Boarding House was an exposition of character through dialogue, and that seems to me to be in great part, what a play is. And that brings us to your second question:

What is your conception of a good play?
To begin with, it is a play that makes people sorry when it is over; it is a play that seems too short. All kinds of plays come into this category: I remember when, as a schoolboy of fifteen, I went to see Hamlet for the first time; I was very sorry when it ended; I would have been happy to sit in the second balcony of the Royal Alexandra Theatre for another four hours. This was not always my response to great drama. Not long afterward I attended my first performance of The Master-singers of Nuremberg; although I am very fond of music, I had had enough of those tedious burghers long before the end, and even after much time has elapsed, and several more performances have been faithfully endured by me, I feel that in that opera too much is sung and too little is done. Conversation alone is not enough. Not long after Hamlet a company from Stratford-on-Avon came to Canada, playing in a repertoire of Shakespeare, and I saw everything they brought with them. Now there's a playwright for you! Wonderful things are said, but there is plenty of action, too, and good, strong, memorable characters.

Not that I was exclusively devoted to the classics, during my formative years. I saw plays of all kinds, and I formed a particular affection for melodrama, which used to be performed in Canada by Sir John Martin-Harvey, on his many transcontinental tours. *The Only Way, A Cigarette Maker's Romance, The Corsican Brothers* were all wonderful to me; the stories were good, the characters vivid, and they were heavily infused with chivalry, and romance, which appeals to me still, though it is much out of fashion. Later, as I shall tell you, I tried my hand at writing some plays that owed much to these melodramas, because I liked their central idea: they were about a single character under stress, who had a choice of behaving worthily or contemptibly; it was the choice, and his decision, that made these plays vivid. Melodrama has never seemed to me to be an outworn mode of theatre; I see melodrama all around me in daily life, and whenever I pick up a newspaper I find melodramatic plots on every page. Of course they are not in the rhetorical style of the nineteenth century, but the importance of the central character, and his decision as to which of two paths he will take, is the same. Many years after I saw these plays, and was impressed by what seemed to me to be their essential truth to life, I became an enthusiastic student of the plays of Ibsen, and I was delighted to find that Ibsen drew most of his plots from things he read in newspapers. Newspapers and the Bible—this was his reading; a melodramatist (and Ibsen was a very great one) needs no more.

When I first began writing plays I was often accused by critics of imitating Bernard Shaw. Certainly I never did so consciously, but it is difficult for anyone writing plays after Shaw not to be influenced by him in some degree. For two centuries Shakespeare seemed to dominate playwriting in English; Shaw's influence, though not so great, is strong. Not to be drawn toward the limpidity, the elegance and the sprightliness of his dialogue suggests insensitivity in a playwright. But imitation—the conscious desire to write *like* Shaw and produce a reflection of a Shavian play — never occurred to me. So many of my ideas about life are unlike Shaw's, and my conception of human character and the mainsprings of human action are so utterly un-Shavian, that this criticism always surprised me. But I think the critics felt that anyone who made his people speak literately and amusingly must be a Shavian imitator; whereas all I felt was that literacy and lightness of touch are pleasing to play-goers, and it was for these qualities I strove. Which brings us to your third question:

What playwrights influenced your work?

That is very hard to say. Writers of melodrama, like those I have mentioned above, certainly. And also writers whose names I never knew, who wrote the scenarios for the innumerable films I saw, and which impressed me by the rapidity of their storytelling. Writers of some of the plays in which I acted when I was a schoolboy and an undergraduate, and whose dialogue I tested by the practical method of speaking it on the stage, and feeling its impact on an audience. This amateur experience was truly helpful, because in those days amateurs often put on plays of slight quality which had enjoyed a long run in London and New York; it was clear enough to me (though I do not suppose I phrased it in quite this way) that what could be made palatable and unquestionably charming by actors of high technical skill and personal grace was not strong enough in itself to sustain amateur players; on the other hand, plays by masters of drama, or great technicians like Pinero, positively buoyed up an actor of ordinary talents and made him seem better than he was. It is not impossible, but it is difficult, for amateurs to kill a play of fine quality completely, whereas a trivial play may die under their feet, even when they are doing their best. I learned something from playwrights who were not very good technicians, but who were fine writers of prose and whose plays never failed the amateur completely because they had an inherent distinction; I think especially of some plays by John Masefield in this category. Later, when I became a professional actor, this truth became even clearer; fine plays were hard to act because they demanded so much, but they were worth any amount of work because the result was deeply satisfactory; whereas a play of ordinary or meretricious quality asked for great gifts of charm and personality in the actors and could not be performed where these qualities were lacking, or where the actors, however good, were not the right people for that play. I never had the opportunity to act in any plays of strong social or political theme—I was not the right kind of actor for them—but I presume that the same rule holds true for them as well.

Some excellent opportunities came my way to observe the technique of master playwrights. It was once my luck to understudy a leading actor in the role of Dr. Stockmann in Ibsen's *An Enemy of the People*. I watched the play through rehearsal and night after night, with a constantly awakening perception of the extraordinary craft that made it progress inevitably from beginning to end; I observed that it began at its crisis and did not labour toward it from the moment the curtain rose; I also observed that when the curtain fell another play—which was not exposed to the audience—had begun.

Perhaps a greater opportunity, for a person of my temperament, came with a production of *She Stoops to Conquer*; I learned it by heart, and can repeat much of it still. It contains the perfection of a certain sort of comic dialogue. Very rarely does anybody in that play say anything that can be extracted from the play and quoted as a joke, but all of the dialogue is rich in the sort of comedy that is inherent in a dramatic situation; what the characters say is funny, not because of the words, but because of the character who speaks them; it is the comedy that lies in the situation, and in sincerity—or what the characters accept as sincerity—at the moment of speaking. Later I acted in Goldsmith's other play, *The Good Natur'd Man*, which is often dismissed as a bad play but which comes to life surprisingly on the stage. If I had to plump for an "influence" on my work, I think it would have to be Goldsmith. His dialogue is supreme in its field. He is often lumped with Sheridan, but the two are far apart in technique and outlook. Sheridan was a great wit, and page after page of his dialogue is made up of splendidly funny sayings; but Goldsmith is the great writer of dialogue that exposes character; none of his people say anything merely to be funny, but because the speaker himself is funny, and is usually quite unaware of that fact. But one does not write like Goldsmith merely by wishing to do so, and that brings us to your next question:

*Did you meet with any obstacles in the creation of
dialogue, characterization, plot, scenes, etc.? How did you
overcome these?*

Endless obstacles with all of them! In the first place, nobody
wants a play now written in dialogue that sounds superficially
like Goldsmith. Dialogue must sound believable in the mouths
of the characters to whom it is given, and when I began to
write plays seriously I had to try to find a way of creating
something like the Goldsmith effect without writing fake
Goldsmith. My first really successful play, I believe, was a
one-acter called *Overlaid*. It has been performed hundreds of
times and people still seem to like it. It is about an elderly
farmer who spends his Saturday afternoons listening to the
broadcasts from the Metropolitan Opera in New York; it is his
recreation, the food of his spirit, and in his special way he is a
real opera enthusiast. But his daughter keeps house for him
and she is not fond of opera, or indeed of anything except her
reputation for respectability, which she has created with
extraordinary sacrifice of herself and those around her.

The play begins at the crisis of a situation that has been
developing over many years. Pop's life insurance policy is paid
up, and he has come into a little money. What is to be done
with it? To tease his daughter, and to please himself with a
flight of fantasy, he says that he is going to take it to New York,
where he will go to the Opera, eat fancy food, flirt with gay
girls and have a high old time until the money is gone. This
scandalizes his insurance agent and also Ethel, his daughter.
She makes such a fuss about it that the old man asks her what
she would do with the money if she had it, and the sad truth
comes out. What Ethel wants more than anything else is a
large gravestone, to commemorate herself and her family in
the local cemetery. The old man is moved with pity by the
pathos of her desire, and gives her the money. She thinks she
has won the struggle, but it is plain to the audience that Pop is
a man of humane spirit, and that he is a lover of Life and a
conqueror, whereas poor Ethel is wedded to Death and
dissolution.

This is not a story to be written in an imitation of
eighteenth-century dialogue, but Goldsmith's lessons can be

applied to it. Every speech must be true to the nature of the character who speaks it, and there must be no funny dialogue for its own sake. This means that the dialogue cannot be what people call "realistic"; there can be none of the repetition, bumbling, half-explaining and muddle that is involved in everyday speech. So I wrote it in a language that is certainly not that of any farm people I have ever known, but which might be called heightened rural speech.

I sent this play off to a playwriting contest and won. I was much impressed by the comment of the adjudicator, who said; "This little play is fit to stand beside the best of E. P. Conkle." Who, I wondered, was E. P. Conkle? I had never encountered his work. I hunted him up. He wrote plays for Scout and Guide groups, and for Church Entertainments. Clearly the adjudicator, with that simplicity of mind and faith in his own judgment that is given only to critics, though *Overlaid* was a rube play and must therefore have been written by a rube. A friend of mine, who knew of my enthusiasm for Goldsmith, was much amused. "You had better call your next piece He Honks to Conkle," said he.

Instead, I called it *Eros at Breakfast*, sent it to the same contest, with the same adjudicator, and won again; the adjudicator (who saw the plays signed only with pseudonyms) did not detect that *Eros* was from the same hand as *Overlaid*, and he praised its sophistication and smoothness of finish. No Conkle this time.

Eros at Breakfast takes place inside the body of a young man who is in love; the scene is his Solar Plexus. The characters represent aspects of his physical being—his Heart, his Brain, his Liver and his Lower Centres. Acting as a Civil Service, they prepare to deal with the problem of a man in love. The dialogue was suited to an artificial comedy, all the characters spoke in a pointed, literary style, and the play works well on the stage.

Much later I wrote two other plays, to be acted by schoolboys, which were not unlike *Eros* in this respect. They were *A Masque of Aesop*, and *A Masque of Mr. Punch*; in both of them the dialogue is spare; the characters say what they have to say as economically as is congruous with the sort of people they are, and then they shut up. This sort of dialogue is not very hard to write in plays of this kind, for they are frankly artificial, and the brisk, no-nonsense dialogue suits their style. Where it is difficult to be economical is in plays that present the surface of ordinary life, hoping thereby to reveal something important that lies below the surface. In such plays it is hard to avoid padding and unimportant lines which somehow seem to be necessary to get characters on and off the stage.

As for plot, it is always a difficulty, because a play cannot afford the rather slow-moving passages that are perfectly acceptable, and perhaps necessary, in a novel. A play has to go on surprising its audience until the end, and somehow this must be achieved without being merely explosive. Therefore a strong scenario has to be constructed before any writing of dialogue can begin, so that the writer can judge what the comparative importance of his scenes will be, and how much time can be allowed to each of them. Very great playwrights have managed without this sort of construction; Shaw said that he simply invented a group of characters, set them talking in his head and wrote down what they said. Molière seems often to have started a play with nothing more than an idea of a leading character—a citizen turned gentleman, or a man whose hobby is illness—and let the play proceed as it would. But what works for genius is dangerous counsel for others, even if they have a good deal of talent. I could not trust myself to set out on the dark seas of a play without some sort of chart, even if I suspect that I shall arrive at a port other than the one I intended.

Characters do not trouble me. That is to say, I have no difficulty in finding them—because I do not invent them. I meet them in the streets. But once they have been defined and set talking, they trouble me very greatly, because they want to say all sorts of things that do not push the play forward. Sometimes these things are so amusing, to me at any rate, that I cannot bear to throw them away, and I acknowledge that this is a grave fault. Recently a critic was taking me to task because, in the second act of my play *Question Time*, I introduce a character called The Beaver, whom I liked very much. But, said the critic, quoting Dr. Johnson, the Beaver was a naughty superfluity, and should have been removed. Doubtless, if I had been a critic, I might have done so, but I am not a critic; I am a playwright, and when I think of a joke, I cannot hold it in. I do not want my epitaph to be:

> Why did the playwright Davies croak?
> 'Tis said, of holding back a joke;
> The jest did in his pipes expand
> And blew him to the Promised Land.

Playwrights may try to shape their plays carefully, but if they have any real talent it is not likely that they will always be able to do so. When I have finished a play I never think: Is it perfectly shaped? No, I think: There, I hope that will fetch 'em! . . . Now let me see, what did you ask next? Ah, here it is:

How do you proceed in creating a play?

First, there must be an idea, and with me an idea usually means a character. In my play *Hunting Stuart* the leading character is a man in the middle ranks of the Civil Service, whose wife is a strong United Empire Loyalist impressed by what she believes must have been the moral splendour and devotion to principle shown by her ancestors. She is married to a man who, although he is named Benedict Stuart, is known to have European blood and some queer relations, and she is rather ashamed of him. Now, thought I, how interesting it would be if it turned out that he was the one with the splendid ancestry? Suppose he were a descendant of the Royal House of Stuart, descending through the Stolbergs and the Sobieskis? Suppose he took it into his head that he was the rightful occupant of the Throne of Britain? Imagine a minor Canadian Civil Servant harbouring such an inadmissible idea? What would he do? And so the germ of a play grew.

All kinds of problems have to be solved. How does he find out that he has royal blood? How can it be demonstrated on the stage? What would be the attitude of his family and neighbours? What might distinguish a real aristocrat from a U.E.L.? Once he had discovered the truth about himself, could he ever go back to his tedious job?

The play is a comedy, but not a haw-haw-haw farce. Like many comedies, it has a serious idea behind it, which is this: what we are is to a great extent what we believe ourselves to be, and kingship is a condition of mind more than it is a question of the balm, the sceptre and the ball. And just as much as some people yearn for greatness, there are many more who are terrified of it, and in this play it is Stuart's daughter who pleads with him not to wreck her common-place life by suggesting that she is a princess. The play has been well presented on the stage by excellent actors, and it makes its effect. It is difficult for amateurs, because the leading role calls for so many rapid transitions of mood.

The most interesting part of writing a play for me is the composition of the dialogue, because it is in this that the finer shades of character can be touched in. There is danger, however, in being too interested in one's dialogue, because if it is worked over too carefully it may lose spontaneity. The desire of the playwright, it seems to me, is to establish a characteristic rhythm and vocabulary for each character; in *Hunting Stuart* it would not do for Stuart, who is a humble man of gentle character, to talk in the same style as his aggressive and aggrieved wife, or his daughter's fiancé, who is a university graduate student in psychology. The words people choose, and the way they put them together, are the constant study of the playwright. Any imitation of real-life dialogue is likely to become dull if it is continued for long; what he aims at is, rather, an abstraction of the speech of the sort of character he is drawing. This may be achieved by a process of fine-tuning once the broad sweep of the dialogue has been sketched. Choosing the right words is one of the most amusing parts of the playwright's craft. Nor should it be supposed that a play about people who are not highly educated or ready of tongue excuses the writer from this obligation; such people display character in speech as clearly—sometimes more clearly—than the educated, and

they can be extremely eloquent. I have said a good deal here
that bears on your next question:

What inspires a play's conception?

First of all, you must be sure it is a play you have thought of,
and not a novel or a short story. The two things are not
interchangeable. A play must have a fairly simple and direct
line of action, though this does not by any means mean that it
is simple-minded. A novel may deal with a very broad theme
and great numbers of characters. It may, for instance, be about
the life of a whole town or a city. Thornton Wilder hâs given us
a fine play in *Our Town* by means of a special technique,
which owes much to Oriental theatre, but on the whole such
ventures present extreme difficulties for the playwright. Ideas
for novels and ideas for plays are of a different order.

This was brought to my attention in the most forcible and
painful way some years ago when I was asked by a New York
management to make a play from my novel *Leaven of Malice*.
It is about life in a small Canadian university city, as it is seen
from the point of view of the editor of the local newspaper.
The principal character of the novel is the city itself. I
submitted a plan for what I thought might be achieved, and
the New York people wrote back at once to say that it would
not do because they wanted a three-act play, taking place in
the editor's office, and it was to be a love story. I was a
newspaper editor at the time, and I knew that love stories do
not usually develop in editors' offices, and I was sure that I
could not crowd the whole life of a city into such a small
compass. So that plan fell through. Later, the Theatre Guild
asked me to dramatize the same novel; they thought the play
ought to be free in construction, but they wanted the town to
be an American town. I replied that my town wasn't an
American town, and several subtle considerations forbade its
being transformed into one, the characteristics of a cathedral
city and the nature of American small-town newspapers being
two of these. But we reached an agreement of a kind, and I
went to work. I cut about two-thirds of the plot of the book,
and produced a play which was certainly free in form and

was even more free when the director, the late Sir Tyrone Guthrie, had finished tinkering with it. But then the Theatre Guild had a new objection: the play contained no star part. I replied that the town was the star of the piece, and all the parts were of roughly equal value. But, said the Guild, New York likes stars, and one part must be fattened up to suit the personality of a star.

What was I to do? What would you do, Sister Geraldine, in my position? I wanted the play to appear on Broadway, and I did not want to appear as a pompous writer who could not accommodate himself to the necessities of Broadway production because of rigid artistic principle. So I did the best I could, and the play was a flop. It had been messed with too much, and the idea was not, in the first place a theatrically viable one.

It was not total loss, however. In 1975 the Shaw Festival at Niagara-on-the-Lake produced the play again. The first-night audience seemed to like it very much, but the much-read New York critic, Clive Barnes of the *Times*, wrote of it in terms of such scorn and loathing, such inflamed and engorged contempt, as have never greeted a play of mine before. This was a New York response. But Canada behaved quite differently. The play continued throughout the season, doing what is called "eighty-per-cent-biz"—meaning that the audiences averaged eighty percent of capacity throughout the run. Audiences laughed heartily, and wrote me letters to tell me about it. Which means, if it means anything, that Canadian taste is not New York taste, and that a play about Canada may appeal to Canadians without necessarily transferring success-fully across the Border. But I still do not think the play a good play. Perhaps I may be allowed to say that it was, and remains, a good novel, and might make a good film.

Not all plots are good plots for plays, nor are good plays necessarily transferable to the screen. The methods of storytelling and character revelation in plays, and films, and novels, are all different in ways that may be obvious or subtle. I have never, except in this one instance, tried to make a play from an idea that came to me as material for a novel. And that leads us to your next question:

What do you normally write about? . . . the family? . . .
underprivileged groups? . . . the fringes of society? . . .
politics? . . . history?

I write about a single, dominating character, whose problem shapes the play, and who is surrounded by people who in some way throw light on him and his predicament. My first long play to have any success was *Fortune, My Foe*, and it is about a young university teacher who has two problems; he is in love with a girl who does not love him, and he cannot make up his mind to go to the United States, where he could get a better job and more money. Essentially it is the same problem: the girl doesn't love him, and his country doesn't love him either—both quite like him, but they can get along perfectly well without him. Everybody in the play throws light on his trouble in one way or another. The old professor, who is disgusted with Canada, shows him what may lie in the future for him. The keeper of the speakeasy shows him that fortune favours the bold rather than the reasonable. The Czech puppet master shows him that the quality of life is more important than financial reward. The social workers show him that the tendency of life in new and prosperous countries is toward what is catchy and easy rather than what is demonstrably good. The newspaper editor shows him that success is often bought by compromise. But the character of Don Quixote, who appears in the puppet show (and whom analysts love to describe as the "dominant symbol" in the play), shows him that some people must do irrational and indefensible things for the sake of ideals, or mankind may as well close up the shop. The play is essentially about Nicholas Hayward, the man who has to decide whether he will stay in Canada or go elsewhere.

A family may take this central position, as it does in *Hunting Stuart*, though here again it is the problem of Benedict Stuart that dominates the play.

Underprivileged groups and the fringes of society do not occur to me as material for plays because I do not know enough about them to reach far into their psychology, yet I am too much aware of the pain and wretchedness of their situation to risk falsifying it. I think that politics is a dismal and dangerous theme for drama. Do you know of any play of first-rate quality about politics? When we examine what appear to be political plays—*Julius Caesar* for example—we quickly discover that they are about interesting people, and not about principles. I have written one play about history; it is a one-acter called *Hope Deferred*, and it tells of Count Frontenac's struggle with the clergy, who did not want him to present Molière's *Tartuffe* in Quebec because of its anti-clerical bias. It is a true story, and a bitter one, and it is still relevant to some Canadian attitudes toward theatre.

Now, what next? Ah, yes, here we are:

What style seems best for you?

Comedy, in the broadest sense of the term. But I take it to include a great measure of romance, of pathos, of the rueful awareness that life is short in time and that what we can understand of it is only a trifle of the whole; the extraordinary variety of life inclines it toward the comic rather than the tragic. Tragedies are usually about people with a limited sense of reality who live in closely contained worlds of their own making; they may be great figures because of the vigour of their passions, but they have no power to see themselves objectively. Shakespeare usually gives us some sense of a world other than the tragic world in his tragedies; Hamlet encounters the Gravediggers, who give a wholesome sense of another world to the complexities of the court; at the hour of her death, Cleopatra talks with the Asp Seller, a countryman whose simplicity brings a breath of country air into the death chamber. French dramatic theorists reproached Shakespeare for what seemed to them his want of full tragic seriousness. But Shakespeare was too large in nature to be utterly possessed by the idea that anyone's death, whatever the circumstances, was more than a trifle in the sweep of human destiny. We would not want to be without tragedy, but the greater part of life is lived in the mode of comedy, using the word in its widest sense. Because I do not believe that birth is the beginning, or death the ending, of our lives, I am not inclined toward the tragic point of view. But for the same reason I am greatly inclined toward an attitude which expresses itself in some of my plays—the sense of life as mystery, insoluble by any means available to us, and certainly not to be solved or terminated by the favourite tragedy device of suicide.

This sense of life as a mystery has made trouble for me with some of my plays. One, which has been seldom performed, and which has been sharply criticized when it has achieved production, is *King Phoenix*, which is about the indomitable spirit of man. Another, which has never been performed, is *General Confession*, in which I try to explore some of the elements that shape the life of every man. I think the form of it confuses some readers, because it seems on the surface to be a romantic costume play, written in language which is not that of everyday, and demanding performances of a type not immediately available in most theatres.

It is about Casanova, the great lover and adventurer. It has long fascinated me that this romantic figure ended his life as Librarian to that Graf Waldstein for whom Beethoven wrote one of his finest piano sonatas. There, in a somewhat remote castle library, sat the old enchanter, writing those *Memoirs* which give us one of the liveliest pictures of eighteenth-century life that we possess. What did he think and feel at that time? As he drew near to death, did he not draw some conclusions about the strange life that had been his? Did he not, at least for his own satisfaction, make some defence of all those ambiguous adventures in which he had been involved? It is such a defence that he offers in the play.

Casanova had known many extraordinary people. One was Cagliostro, the reputed magician and rascal who caused such a stir in European courts—certainly an evil figure. Another was Voltaire, the apparent epitome of reason and intellect, but rather a slippery person in some of his relationships. And of course there were those scores of women, some of whom Casanova seduced, and some of whom seduced him, and to whom he devoted so much of his energy and undoubted charm. In the play I bring them on the stage. Cagliostro represents all the ill luck that had come Casanova's way; Voltaire represents the ingenuity and occasional callousness with which he braved his way out of hundreds of tight corners; and a third, called the Unknown Beloved, speaks for all the women in his life. With these three he acts out, in recollection, some of his most famous adventures, from his comparatively innocent and likable youth, through his tough and opportunist middle age, into his years of declining power. In the end these figures of his fantasy demand that he provide a justification for what his life has been, and he gives one: at all times, he has tried to shape his life into a work of art, and, for good or evil, that is what he has done. He makes his general confession, and it is that he has done the best that lay within him with the opportunities that came his way. He is not a good man, but he insists that he cannot be called an evil one because he has left no portion of his destiny unlived; he has drained his cup to the bottom, and at the end of life he is at peace.

This is not an ordinary theme, and it does not seem to appeal to acting companies, but I hope that at some time I shall see the play satisfactorily performed. It calls for actors of special quality and a sympathetic director. If I may permit myself a small vanity, it is my belief that the play is somewhat ahead of its time.

The theme of the portion of life that is unlived, for whatever reason, has long appealed to me. Another of my plays, *At My Heart's Core*, explores this subject. Its setting is the Canadian backwoods, and the time is 1837, when Canada was making one of its early revolts against the stifling, second-hand traditions of the Europe that gave it birth. Three women living in pioneer conditions, are brought face to face with what their lives might have been if fate had been kinder—or if they themselves had been a little more courageous. One might have been a writer of substantial achievement; that is Susanna Moodie. Another might have been a natural scientist of wide renown; that is her sister, Catharine Parr Traill. The third might have had an adventurous love and a high place in society; that is Mrs. Frances Stewart. They are brought to a realization of what might have been by a gentleman settler whom they have, in various ways, offended, and who revenges himself on them by making them discontented; he seems to be no more than a silver-tongued stranger, but there is a suggestion that he may also be the Father of Discontent, the Devil himself. Only Mrs. Stewart, because of qualities in her nature that her neighbours lack, survives the temptation without regret. I have seen this play acted several times, and occasionally it has been performed by people who appeared to see no more in it than yet another play about pioneer life. But it is about the qualities of life that a new country demands of its pioneers, and the gifts a new country does not want— or does not know it wants. There is a reminder in it that in this respect the pioneer days are not yet completed, because Canada is not yet a country that asks for and uses all the possibilities of its people.

This last aspect of Canadian life I attempted to explore in *Question Time*, in which a Canadian Prime Minister, lost in the Arctic, is confronted with a question that politicians do not seem to ask themselves very often. It is this: can a man be a leader of his people in the truest and most effective sense if he has devoted his best energies to the external life of statesmanship, and has permitted the feelings and obligations of a fully realized human being to wither away? Critics were divided about this play; a few liked it, but others thought it a failure because, I think, they did not understand what it was saying. They thought it was about politics, and about the fate of Canada, and the nature of the Canadian people. Of course it was about all of these things, but it was principally about what a man must do to make himself a completed human being, and the pathetic gaps and holes that appear in his life when he has failed to do so.

It is this theme of the unlived portion of my characters' lives that chiefly concerns me as a playwright, and I do not feel that I have in any sense come to the end of it. If I have anything of my own to say to theatre-goers, this is the area in which it lies.

What else did you ask me?

What characters do you like ... dislike ... and why?
It would be untrue to say that I dislike any of my characters. Even such apparently unsympathetic ones as Lilian, the bewildered wife in *Hunting Stuart*, are not portrayed with dislike; after all, considering what her life has been, and the

chances she has had to understand life, she is not a bad person. Her daughter, who is terrified by the idea that greatness might be demanded of her, is not ridiculous—only limited in outlook. Cagliostro, in *General Confession*, is certainly a villain, and so is Mr. Cantwell, in *At My Heart's Core*, but they have a dimension of splendour, of unrepentant enjoyment of their evil, which I find attractive.

Even my hypocrites, in *A Jig for the Gypsy*, have a point of view of their own; in spite of their religiosity they mistrust the Other World of the Gypsy and Conjuror, but they are sturdy in defending their own opinion.

Indeed, I do not write about people I despise. Even Shorty, the bumptious little barber in *The Voice of the People*, is a charming, self-important little fellow, not in the least contemptible. The people I despise in life are the self-regarding, close-fisted, nay-saying men and women who see nothing in the world except chances for personal advantage. I put them in novels, but not in plays.

Why? Because I regard it as one of my jobs to provide actors with juicy, actable roles, in which they can display their art to advantage. A musician who writes what are called "dull inner parts," where whole sections of the orchestra are confined to a tedious deedle-deedle-deedle while the violins and horns have all the fun, is not usually a favourite with instrumentalists. I want actors to like me, because if they do, they will give their best work to my plays; I can only expect that if I give them something interesting to do. The theatre is a cooperative art; that is one of its great satisfactions. The playwright is important, but he is not the whole show, and as he learns his craft he discovers that actors can do as much with a look or a gesture as he can do with half a page of dialogue. I have been an actor, and I like actors, and I want to give them something that is worth their effort and worthy of their sometimes extraordinary skills.

Now let us go on to . . .

What are your future plans in drama?
That depends on other people. I am not one of the young new generation of playwrights in Canada, and my plays, as

comedies, are not really in the fashion of the present moment. But from time to time I am asked for a new play, and I am usually happy to do what I can to provide one. At this moment, Sister Geraldine, I ought not to be writing to you (pleasant though that is) but should be working on a new play that I have been asked to provide for a particular occasion. It is a challenge because it is to have music and dancing, and that appeals to me greatly. I have always had a feeling that a truly satisfactory play ought to be one in which people sing and dance as well as speak. Some people call that Total Theatre, but I just think of it as Real Theatre. It sets the playwright free to do all kinds of things that are not dictated by the necessities and realities of life; it makes anything possible that he feels is desirable. The theatre began, after all, as a temple; it was a place where people expected to experience the full range of human emotion; sometimes the outcome was joyous, and sometimes it was the revelation of what was godlike in man, which provoked feelings of the highest solemnity. Unfortunately, for several hundred years we have associated temples only with what is *good*, and we have narrowed our ideas of what is good to a meagre range of emotions. But the true theatre, the great theatre, is a temple not of goodness, but of *wholeness*, of the complete scope of human action and aspiration. I try to create a theatre of wholeness. I may not get as near it as I could wish, but that is my aim.

Chronology

1913	Born August 28, in Thamesville, Ontario, son of the Honourable William Rupert Davies, a Senator, and Florence Sheppard (McKay) Davies.
1919-38	Educated at Renfrew and Kingston Schools; Upper Canada College, Toronto; Queen's University, Kingston; Balliol College, Oxford (B.Litt. 1938).
1938-40	Experience as an actor in the English provinces.

	Joined Old Vic Company, London, to act and teach in its Drama School and to do literary work for the Director.
1940	Returned to Canada as Literary Editor of *Saturday Night*. Married Brenda Mathews February 2, 1940 (former Stage Director of the Old Vic).
1942-62	Editor of *Peterborough Examiner*.
1949	Won Barry Jackson award for *Fortune, My Foe*, in the Dominion Drama Festival, and the Louis Jouvet Prize for directing *The Taming of the Shrew*.
1953-71	Governor of the Stratford Shakespearean Festival.
1955	Awarded Stephen Leacock Medal for Humour for *Leaven of Malice*.
	Hunting Stuart performed at the Crest Theatre, Toronto.
1957	Awarded Honorary LL.D. by the University of Alberta.
1959	Awarded Honorary D.Litt. at McMaster University, Hamilton.
1960	"Love and Libel" produced on Broadway, Martin Beck Theatre, December 7.
1960-61	Visiting Professor, Trinity College, University of Toronto.
1961	Awarded Lorne Pierce Medal from the Royal Society of Canada for his contribution to Canadian Literature.
1962	Awarded Honorary LL.D. from Queen's University, Kingston.
1963-77	Appointed first Master of Massey College, University of Toronto (a college for post-graduate work). Helped to establish the Drama Centre for Graduate work.
1967	"The Centennial Play" performed in Lindsay, Ontario. Awarded Honorary D.C.L. from Bishop's University, Lennoxville, Quebec. "The Centennial Play" performed in Ottawa. Made a Fellow of the Royal Society of Canada.
1971	Awarded Honorary D. Litt. from the University of Windsor.
1972	Awarded Honorary LL.D. from the University of Manitoba. Made Companion of the Order of Canada.

1973   Received the Governor General's Award for Fiction (*The Manticore*). Awarded Honorary D.Litt. from York University, Toronto, and from Mount Allison University, New Brunswick.

1974   Awarded Honorary D.Litt. from Memorial University, St. John's Newfoundland, from the University of Western Ontario, from McGill University, Montreal, and from Trent University, Peterborough, Ontario. "Brothers in the Black Art" performed on CBC-TV, Toronto.

1975   Awarded Honorary D.U.C. from the University of Calgary. *Question Time* performed by the Toronto Arts Productions, the St. Lawrence Centre.

1977   Wrote the play *Pontiac and the Green Man*, which was produced at the MacMillan Theatre as part of the University of Toronto's sesquicentennial celebrations.

Selected Bibliography

Primary Sources

PLAYS

At the Gates of the Righteous. In *Eros at Breakfast and Other Plays*. Toronto: Clarke, Irwin & Company Ltd., 1949. In *Four Favourite Plays*. Toronto: Clarke, Irwin & Company Ltd., 1968.

At My Heart's Core and Overlaid. Toronto: Clarke Irwin & Company Ltd., 1966.

"Brothers in the Black Art." TS, CBC-TV, Toronto, February 14, 1974.

"The Centennial Play." MS, Ottawa, 1967.

Eros at Breakfast and Other Plays. Toronto: Clarke, Irwin & Company Ltd., 1949. In *Four Favourite Plays*. Toronto: Clarke, Irwin & Company Ltd., 1968.

Fortune, My Foe. Toronto: Clarke, Irwin & Company Ltd., 1949. In *Four Favourite Plays*. Toronto: Clarke, Irwin & Company Ltd., 1968.

Four Favourite Plays. Toronto: Clarke, Irwin & Company Ltd., 1968.

General Confession. In *Hunting Stuart and Other Plays.* Toronto: New Press, 1972.

Hope Deferred. In *Eros at Breakfast and Other Plays.* Toronto: Clarke, Irwin & Company Ltd., 1949.

Hunting Stuart and Other Plays. Toronto: New Press, 1972.

A Jig for the Gypsy. Toronto: Clarke, Irwin & Company Ltd., 1954.

King Phoenix. In *Hunting Stuart and Other Plays.* Toronto: New Press, 1972.

"Love and Libel" ("Leaven of Malice"). MS, Hart House Theatre, Toronto, 1973.

"Leaven of Malice." MS, Hart House Theatre, Toronto, 1973.

A Masque of Aesop. Toronto: Clarke, Irwin & Company Ltd., 1952.

A Masque of Mr. Punch. Toronto: Oxford University Press, 1963.

Overlaid. In *Encounter*, edited by Eugene Benson. Toronto: Methuen Publications, 1973. Also in *Ten Canadian Short Plays*, edited by John Stevens. New York: Dell Publishing Company, 1975.

"Pontiac and the Green Man." MS, Massey College, Toronto, 1977.

Question Time. Toronto: Macmillan Company of Canada Ltd., 1975.

The Voice of the People. In *Eros at Breakfast and Other Plays.* Toronto: Clarke, Irwin & Company Ltd., 1949. In *Four Favourite Plays.* Toronto: Clarke, Irwin & Company Ltd., 1968. Also in *Cues and Entrances*, compiled by Henry Beissel. Toronto: Gage Publishing Ltd., 1977.

HISTORY OF DRAMA AND CRITICISM

Renown at Stratford (with Sir Tyrone Guthrie). Toronto: Clarke, Irwin & Company Ltd., 1953.

The Revels History of Drama in English, Vol. VI 1750-1880 (with Others). United Kingdom: Methuen Publications, 1975.

Shakespeare for Young Players. Toronto: Clarke, Irwin & Company Ltd., 1942.

Shakespeare's Boy Actors. London: J.M. Dent & Sons Ltd., 1939, and New York: Russell and Russell, 1964.

Thrice the Brinded Cat Hath Mew'd (with Sir Tyrone Guthrie). Toronto: Clarke, Irwin & Company Ltd., 1955.

Twice Have the Trumpets Sounded (with Sir Tyrone Guthrie). Toronto: Clarke, Irwin & Company Ltd., 1954.

Upstage and Down (with Daniel McGarity). Toronto: Macmillan Company of Canada Ltd., 1968.

A Voice from the Attic. Toronto: McClelland and Stewart Ltd., 1960.

ARTICLES

"The Genius of Dr. Guthrie." *Theater Arts Monthly* 40, No.3 (1956), pp. 28-29, 90.

"Notes on the New Theatre." *Stratford Festival Souvenir Program*, 1957.

"Stratford: 2nd Year An Air of Certainty." *Saturday Night* 69 (July 17, 1954), pp. 7-9.

"The Theatre." In *The Arts As Communication*, edited by D. C. Williams, pp. 17-31. Toronto: University of Toronto Press, 1962.

"The Theatre. A Dialogue on the State of the Theatre in Canada." In *Royal Commission Studies: A Selection of Essays Prepared for the Royal Commission on National Development in the Arts, Letters and Sciences* (1949-1951), pp. 369-92. Ottawa: The King's Printer, 1951.

FICTION

The Diary of Samuel Marchbanks. Toronto: Clarke, Irwin & Company Ltd., 1947 and 1966.

Fifth Business. Toronto: Macmillan Company of Canada Ltd., 1970. New American Library, 1971. Penguin Books, 1977.

Leaven of Malice. Toronto: Clarke, Irwin & Company Ltd., 1954 and 1964.

The Manticore. Toronto: Macmillan Company of Canada Ltd., 1972 . Penguin Books, 1976.

A Mixture of Frailties. Toronto: Macmillan Company of Canada Ltd., 1958 and 1968.

Samuel Marchbanks' Almanack. Toronto: McClelland and Stewart Ltd., 1967. New Canadian Library edition, 1968, introduction by Gordon Roper.

The Table Talk of Samuel Marchbanks. Toronto: Clarke, Irwin & Company Ltd., 1949 and 1967.

Tempest-tost. Toronto: Clarke, Irwin & Company Ltd., 1951 and 1965.

World of Wonders. Toronto: Macmillan Company of Canada Ltd., 1975. Penguin Books, 1977.

Secondary Sources

BARCLAY, PATRICIA. "Noble and Confused" *(The Manticore)*. *Canadian Literature*, No. 56 (1973), pp. 113-14.

BISSELL, CLAUDE "World of the Master." *Canadian Forum* 55, No. 657 (1975-76). pp. 30-31.

BJERRING, NANCY E. "Deep in the Old Man's Puzzle." *Canadian Literature*, No. 62 (1974), pp. 49-60.

BUITENHUIS, ELSPETH. *Robertson Davies*. Canadian Writers and Their Works Series. Toronto: Forum House, 1972.

COHEN, NATHAN. "Theatre Today; English Canada." *Tamarack Review*, No. 13 (1959), pp. 24-37.

DAHLIE, HALLVARD. "Self-Conscious Canadians." *Canadian Literature*. No. 62 (1974), pp. 6-16.

HALL, W. F. "The Real and the Marvelous," *(Fifth Business)*. *Canadian Literature*, No. 49 (Summer, 1971), pp. 80-81.

Journal of Canadian Studies, February, 1977. Entire issue is devoted to critical essays on the work of Robertson Davies.

LISTER, ROTA. "*Question Time*, A play by Robertson Davies." *Canadian Drama/L'Art dramatique canadien* 2, No. 1 (1976), 118-19.

McPHERSON, HUGO. "The Mask of Satire: Character and Symbolic Pattern in Robertson Davies' Fiction." *Canadian Literature No. 4 (1960), pp. 18-30.*

MOORE, MAVOR. *Four Canadian Playwrights*. Toronto: Holt, Rinehart, and Winston of Canada Ltd., 1973.

MORLEY, PATRICIA. *Robertson Davies*. Profiles in Canadian Drama Series. Toronto: Gage Publishing Ltd., 1977.

————."Comedy Company of the Psyche." *Canadian Drama/L'Art dramatique canadien* 2, No. 1 (1976), pp. 9-19.

NEW, WILLIAM H. "Lives of Ghosts and Lovers" *(Hunting Stuart and Other Plays)*. *Canadian Literature*, No. 59 (1974), pp. 104-106.

NOONAN, JAMES. "*Hunting Stuart* and Other Plays." *Queen's Quarterly* 80 (1973): 466-68.

SOLLY, WILLIAM. "Nothing Sacred. Humour in Canadian Drama in English." *Canadian Literature*, No. 11 (1962), pp. 14-27.

STEINBERG, M. W. "Don Quixote and the Puppets: Theme and Structure in Robertson Davies' Drama." *Canadian Literature*, No. 7 (1961), pp. 45-53.

Four

GWEN PHARIS
RINGWOOD

(1910-)

Preface

Western Canada's theatre owes much to the pioneering work of Gwen Pharis Ringwood. In the early thirties when theatre was relatively unknown in Alberta, Ringwood assisted Elizabeth Sterling Haynes in the first rural community drama movement on the prairies, under the auspices of the University of Alberta. Through a 1937 Rockefeller Foundation Fellowship, Gwen Pharis was brought to the famous Fred Koch's Playmaker's School for regional drama at the University of North Carolina, Chapel Hill. There she learned her craft from such distinguished playwrights as Paul Green who won the Pulitzer Prize for his play, In Abraham's Bosom. *She was taught perfection in form, tightness in style, sensitivity for regional nuances, and the wide range of effects in the folk play. Under the tutelage of master craftsmen, she wrote five one-act plays and had them produced at Chapel Hill. Judging from the royalties she has consistently been receiving since 1939 for one of these plays, it would not be incorrect to estimate that this play,* Still Stands the House, *has probably been performed more often than any single Canadian play in the U.S. and Canada.*

Ringwood's dramatic output during the past forty years includes twenty-four stage plays, three musicals, ten children's plays, and twenty-eight radio plays, all produced in Alberta and British Columbia. Since 1953 she has lived in the Cariboo at Williams Lake where she successfully brought the community together in a united effort to produce stage plays. In 1971 the people of Williams Lake built and dedicated the Gwen Pharis Ringwood Civic Theatre as a tribute to her involvement and total commitment to community activities.

The nuances of Canada's West, whether it be voice, tone, atmosphere, character, or values, is caught and reproduced in Ringwood's plays. One can hear and see the hardy farm people of the prairies; the French Canadian gold miners of Goldfields, Saskatchewan; the Ukrainian Immigrants of Edmonton, Alberta; the Chilcotin Indians of the Cariboo; the gold miners of Billy Barker's northern B.C. gold rush; the cowboys and Indians of the Calgary Stampede. Regional drama is her forte, not only because of her education in the folk play at Chapel Hill, but also because her sense of humour, gentleness of manner and her warm response to people, as well as her comic instinct for play, which make her uniquely able in this form of drama. The critic must accept this fact and use it as his starting point if he is fully to appreciate her contribution.

Conflict and paradox are at the root of the Ringwood experience of life and character. In Still Stands the House she creates conflict between two prairie women who confront each other in a struggle over the land — one eager to relinquish it in favor of an easier town life, the other bitterly obsessed by it and ready to sacrifice all in order to retain ownership of the house and land. A passionate play, it reveals Ringwood's talent for creating emotional conflicts. Her play, Pasque Flower (1938), and its extension into the three-act play for her Master's thesis, "Dark Harvest" (1939), also explores conflict, this time one man's interior conflict between his love for his land and his love for his wife.

A deep sensitivity for the problems of immigrants is revealed in a number of her plays: the Scandinavians in "Chris Axelson, Blacksmith" (1938), the Ukrainians in The Drowning of Wasyl Nemitchuk (1946), the Greek immigrants in "The Deep Has Many Voices" (1971), the Italians in her prize-winning children's play, "The Magic Carpets of Antonio Angelini" (1976). With Indians, Gwen Ringwood seems to have special rapport, having worked briefly on the Blackfoot Indian Reservation in Montana, and more recently at the Cariboo Indian School in northern B.C. Her sensitive response to native people and their problems is dramatically reflected in the plays Maya or Lament for Harmonica (1959), and in "Jana" or "The Stranger" (1971).

A wry sense of humour and an instant reaction to the comic in life impelled her to create colourful western characters out of fact and fantasy. Hatfield, The Rainmaker (1943); Widger in Widger's Way (1952); John Ware (Nigger John) who is a real person and great Albertan figuring in "Stampede" (1945), recalling the last days of the great ranching era of Alberta; the pioneers of Edson, Alberta, in "Look Behind You Neighbor" (1961); the archetypal figure of Billy Barker in "The Road Runs North" (1968) —all these folk heroes are made memorable in her plays.

If her plays lack the dark pessimism and sharp social criticism that mark many contemporary works, it may be that Ringwood is unable to cope artistically with the tragedies she has personally known and the social problems of which she is so well aware. It could not have been ignorance or innocence of Canada's very real problems, for these are apparent in her unpublished verse and letters, but rather an artistic temperament that found its only outlet in comedy and farce, which lent her scope for distancing and subtle comment. As well, the folk play offered her a medium for rich re-creation and a means for a kind of gentle social criticism that provides an effective nudge for the audience.

Her contemporary plays, however, do mark a change in her style as she moves gradually away from folk drama toward satire and uncompromising social criticism in her short satiric sketches on national problems in "Encounters" (1971), the prejudices of narrow-minded Canadians in "A Remembrance of Miracles" (1975), and the pragmatism and greed of the family in her latest play, "The Lodge" (1976). Yet these plays (with the possible exception of "The Lodge") seem pallid in comparison with her regional drama.

Gwen Pharis Ringwood's work comprises a substantial body of plays on Canada's West. She not only pioneered the drama movement in Alberta and British Columbia but she brought to bear on this genre a professional skill and a talent for experimentation as she re-created the colourful past and gently probed the weaknesses in the social structure. She used a variety of techniques including: fantasy, realism, comedy, farce, classical tragedy, multi-media presentation, musical, *myth, parody of melodrama, poetic dialogue, in a body of work that essentially celebrates and enlarges the possibilities of regional drama. The quantity and quality of her work attest to her single-minded and total dedication to the art of playmaking as an expression of deeply felt life.*

The theatre has always seemed to me the most exciting of the arts because it combines poetry, flowing motion, dance, song, the music of speech. There on the stage people move to and away from one another in anger or passion or despair. Again people crawling on all fours meet nose to nose in ludicrous, undignified surprise. The theatre can provide all the colour and rushing and larger-than-life representation of that thinking animal who came late to the planet. And often the theatre has enlivened the mind, restored the soul. While I've written in other forms — short stories, verse, two novels — my ambition is to write a new and better play.

At eight years old my conception of a good play was *The Bells*, at eleven *Macbeth*. *Macbeth* holds up very well! Now I'd add *The Frogs*, *Antigone*, *Medea*, *Hamlet*, *Tartuffe*, *The Cherry Orchard*, *The Skin of Our Teeth*, *Waiting for Godot*. Those are good plays. They hold one's attention.

And I think of the young Marlowe's excitement as he penned his great "purple passages." And of how Chekhov cherished his gentle, charming, foolish or pretentious people so that his plays express some poetry of ordinary lives lived out waiting for something more. In rich and earthy language John Synge depicted the lives of men and women who work hard to wrench their living from land or sea. These people always remind me of the men and women I knew as I grew up on the prairies of Alberta.

And in my time Samuel Beckett has distilled in a stark poetic form the fears and the nightmare, the sense of isolation, despair, futility that sometimes overwhelms each one of us. Nowhere has the confusion of shabby, brave little people caught between mud and stars been so well expressed.

Our Town set up echoes in my mind and blood. The bare stage, the use of a narrator, the country and small-town people all have made an impact on playwrights of this century. I think it was 1940, too, when I read Saroyan's first one-act "My Heart's in the Highlands." His non-sequitur comedy, teetering on the edge of farce, struck a chord of recognition and delight and set me free as a writer to sometimes take off and dance with my own shadow.

Paul Green's plays, particularly *In Abraham's Bosom* and his *The Lost Colony*, have meant much to me. His plays transcend the folk-play genre to become universal in the way that Synge's plays are universal. In writing regional plays I've always hoped to avoid the mere expression of regional idiosyncrasies.

Among Canadian plays I think of three: Elsie Gowan's *The Last Caveman* because of its clear statement of an important theme; Bob Gard's *Johnny Chinook*, imaginative and lyrical; Lister Sinclair's *The World of the Wonderful Dark* with its drums and masks and swelling sound. And I must not forget George Ryga's *The Ecstasy of Rita Joe* because it plumbs the dark springs of human agony.

In the years of my growing up there were not many productions of plays, but I read plays and think perhaps I was much influenced by reading. I loved language. I truly wanted to use a language nearer to poetry and away from ordinary "dried out cat-gut" speech. Often this desire has carried me into the "purple passages" realm where thin air billows about.

The feel of words and sounds in the mouth, the rhythms of great speeches, the swell of blank verse all seem important to me. Consequently I'm always "prosing down" the first draft of a play, trying to keep the language human and sound, while still moving towards a place where words can take off. That "heightening of language" Aristotle talked about is not an easy thing to do.

My playwriting goes back a long time. *Still Stands the House* was written and produced in 1939. I suppose I could date myself B.CBC (Before CBC) when we had no radio plays, few amateur little theatres, no university theatre departments, and because of the depression the touring companies had stopped coming West. Sometimes *Aunt Millie's Secret* or *Aaron Slick* or *You Never Can Tell* were done and the proceeds bought a new church organ or school uniforms. Then in the late twenties Elizabeth Sterling Haynes started a new kind of play production. Before Elizabeth was through, Western Canada had a loosely knit federation of amateur theatre groups under Dominion Drama Festival sponsorship;

it had also the *Banff School of Fine Arts*; and everywhere in little theatres, high schools, universities, people were learning the techniques of acting and directing and were staging productions of great plays, old and new. Elizabeth Haynes had founded and was nurturing the Prairie Theatre. I was her student, later her assistant and her friend. Without Elizabeth and my admiration and devotion for her, I would probably have written in other forms. She encouraged my playwriting and gave me insights into the requirements of the stage.

At the time of my first playwriting, young writers were nearly always admonished to write about what they knew. This is good sense but I would add that young writers must also gamble on writing what they feel, sense, magically glimpse. The young writer should not forget that anything, any thought which comes knocking at his brain more than once may be worth exploring. And he should save old notebooks—those explorations may propel a writer into further work in later years.

In 1936 Sheila Marriott, director of Radio Station CKUA for the University of Alberta commissioned Elsie Gowan and me to write a series of radio plays "New Lamps for Old," about people who had changed the course of history. We each wrote ten scripts varying in length from one half-hour to an hour. (At CKUA, time was an elastic thing stretching between great fanfares of music, with no advertisements to confine or disfigure the reaches of the imagination.) Elsie and I searched through history from Socrates to Nansen. I think of those radio plays with affectionate dismay. I destroyed the manuscripts eventually because the long speeches embarrassed me, but I still recall the zeal and excitement with which I hurriedly researched the lives of Socrates and Galileo, Beethoven and Henry the Navigator, Florence Nightingale and Oliver Cromwell (a hard man to write about is Cromwell) and Nansen of the North. With passion, purple passages galore, and Dick Macdonald's fine sound effects our radio plays were sent out live. The final play was about a brave man risking his life to dismantle a laser ray that was set to destroy the earth. The play was accepted but I was told that it was a fantastic and unbelievable idea.

Elsie and I were paid five dollars a play. Writing isn't an easy way to make a living! Perhaps young women writers are better advised to marry liberated young men. Marriage is more secure than a Canada Council Grant and a lot more fun.

In 1937 I went to the University of North Carolina on a Rockefeller fellowship. There in the Department of Drama, as Carolina Playmakers we wrote, directed, acted in and talked about one another's plays. Our plays seemed important. We felt we were breaking new ground. My first one-acts (long lost and a good thing) were termed "trite," "contrived," and "Hollywoodish"—this the unbearable blow! I went back to the Graduate Women's residence downcast, a sad Canadian, tearful and alone in a strange land where people talked funny.

My first production at Chapel Hill came in the spring of 1939 after I'd written a play about the prairies. *Still Stands the House* remains the work of mine that most people know. My reputation as a writer rises and falls with that House. Several comedies followed in production. Chapel Hill was a good atmosphere for writers in those days and I think it still is, thanks to the great Paul Green, dear Sam Selden and the creative climate they manage to induce.

I tried with the Playmakers several times to write politico-social plays. The depression was heavy on the land; the dust bowls spread from Texas to Saskatchewan; long lines of unemployed men waited at soup kitchens from Vancouver to New Orleans. In New York, Clifford Odets was writing about the need for social change; his plays were produced by the Group Theatre, that great acting ensemble.

I managed just one social-problem play—"One Man's House" produced in 1940. In this play a labour leader, Jan Lodeska, loses his job because he leads a strike for better working conditions in his plant. At the end he is rejected by management, by the workers he fought for, and by his own family, when he goes out to speak for continued strike action.

The actor who took the role of Jan was a young socialist from New York. Later the McCarthy investigations caused him to lose a teaching job and to become a non-person for some seven years. Lots of us might have been termed "fellow travellers" in those depression years. We saw oranges and wheat ploughed under while people starved. I became a kind of mild fence-sitting socialist. I did not write many plays of protest—a few short sketches in the sixties and early seventies.

At Chapel Hill I wrote my first long play, *Dark Harvest*. Garth Hansen's wheat field was a symbol in somewhat the way the cherry orchard was to the Ranevsky family. And Hansen's tragedy was that he lost faith in his dream when his wife rejected the dream. The play was given a good production at the University of Manitoba in 1945 and was later movingly done with Bud Knapp as Garth Hansen on CBC Wednesday Night radio.

My children and their friends find it hard to understand that most of us were naively blind to the threat Hitler represented right up to 1939. We truly thought that World War I had ended war. This, despite the march into Czechoslovakia, despite the publication of *Mein Kampf*, despite the whispered stories of genocide and pogrom filtering out of the Third Reich. We shrugged these stories off as "communist propaganda." The declaration of war, the reality of World War II, left us shaken and stunned and many of us were too confused to write about our immediate concerns.

I had returned to Canada in 1939, married, and gone in 1940 with my husband, Barney, to the north shore of Lake Athabasca. For two years the war was a distant cloud, brooding, inert. In the north we were hardly aware of it, no battles, no threat to us. I wrote *Marie Jenvrin* and bore our first son, joyous events.

But in 1941 my brothers, husband, cousins, and friends went off to war, and I who had been a pacifist was forced out of an ivory tower to confront rocket bombs falling on the just and the unjust alike; a shaky alliance with the U.S.S.R., now fighting for its life; Hitler's Third Reich bent on living space and power; the fact of twentieth-century genocide. And before the end there was the destruction of Nagasaki and Hiroshima, the violent advent of the atomic age.

This was more than my brain or heart could encompass or

surround, more than I could write about. In some verses I tried to express what seemed inexpressible, admiration for the stand at Leningrad, my feeling about Canada, my country, my hatred and fear of war. But mostly I lived from day to day, in Edmonton, with our two children, waiting for my husband to come home.

Robert Gard was collecting Alberta folklore and history under a Rockefeller Grant to the province. His interest in my work culminated in a commission to write some Alberta plays —*The Jack and the Joker* (about Bob Edwards and the Calgary *Eye Opener* ;) *Hatfield, The Rainmaker* based on a true Medicine Hat contract with Hatfield for rain; and *Stampede*, a full-length play about the early ranching era and the first Calgary Stampede with John Ware as a principal character.

My husband returned from overseas in time to see the University of Alberta and the Banff School productions of *Stampede*, directed by Sydney Risk and including Ted Fallowes, Vincent Tovell and Gordon Peacock in the cast. Obscure cowboy songs from Lomox's book *Cowboy Songs* were used throughout the play, many now well known through The Weavers and other singing groups.

Of the three plays, I like *The Rainmaker* best. It employs a large cast, seems to me to express the time and the people of the prairies, and the earth and the elements somehow inform the shape and action of the play. Also, the language naturally took a poetic turn without seeming forced or artificial. *The Rainmaker* received the finest productions I have seen of any of my plays—one by Sydney Risk in Banff and one, directed by Tom Kerr with the Kamloops High School appearing in Victoria.

When the war was over, and the cold war with the U.S.S.R. was just beginning, we lived for two years in Lamont. There I came to know some Ukrainian Canadians of both the first and the second generations. They are a people of temperament, dark and brooding and silent at times, volatile and effervescent at other times. My little one-act comedy, *The Drowning of Wasyl Nemitchuk*, employed for comedy

Ukrainian Easter eggs wrought by hand, a henpecked husband, and oil wells drilled on the rich wheat farm of Wasyl.

In writing *Wasyl Nemitchuk* (its first title was *A Fine Colored Easter Egg*) I experienced a heightened awareness of shapes in space — the sculptural and dance aspects — and also of the concomitant variation in sound when strange juxtapositions are used. I'd always appreciated multi-level sets but in this play, as I wrote, I visualized relationships in space, and seemed to hear or imagine the pitch, tone, vibration of sound of the spoken lines. This increased awareness of space and sound makes writing more exciting and interesting.

A play for radio I enjoyed writing was "The Wall" asked for by an Edmonton station for a United Nations Day. We knew a young musician, Bruce Haack, and I had always wanted to try a music drama where the music was integral to the script, so "The Wall" was a collaboration with Bruce on a comedy about racial intolerance. Our eldest child, eleven, played the little black boy in the play. Bruce played the piano and organ version of his own music. The music and words seemed to belong together. It was a good production. Later the play was revived in Winnipeg but Bruce had gone to the United States; his music had been written on old envelopes and had been lost. The play was not the same.

In 1950 at Robert (Imbert) Orchard's suggestion I began the long play *Widger's Way*. I wanted to employ full-bodied acting, colour, farce and satire, a "classical comedy" in a Western setting. I think I liked writing *Widger* best of all my plays.

I remember some of its scenes with fondness. The miserly fearful old Widger, generous at one moment and appalled and regretful of his own generosity the next, giving with one hand and taking back with the other, critical, nagging, querulous, longing for some richer life but afraid of his own best impulses — Widger somehow seemed to me an interesting and very Canadian character. The play is a bit lumpy. Its theme doesn't always come through clearly. But the theme was what Widger said when the police had arrested him and he was deep in trouble: "Now the giant closes his fist on Widger and since it were so, I'd wish myself a bigger fistful."

Then, despite his fear of "unnatural nature" he escapes into the dreadful dark to try to save his daughter. He's a little bigger fistful at the end of the play. Much that is in *Widger* is still important to me.

In 1952 we moved to British Columbia. I gave up playwriting for awhile, wrote short stories and a novel. And I didn't write at all for several years.

One year I was to adjudicate one-act play finals. The plays came. I read them all calmly until I came to the last one, *The Chairs*, by Ionesco. The sweat ran down my brow. I was up against the unknown! Strange how the years change one. . . . *The Chairs* seems reasonably straightforward now. But then it set me on a journey in which I found out about Sartre, Brecht, Beckett, Genet. These European plays left me shaken, bewildered, somewhat aghast. I admired *Waiting for Godot* but the rest of the plays I hated, then wondered at, and finally embraced. Anti Theatre. The Theatre of the Absurd. The theatre of cruelty. Some of these plays will last, as have the plays of Strindberg and Pirandello before them. Some will disappear. But they have brought back mystery, enigma, paradox, the sense of things rather than the appearance of things, to the stage.

I tried an anti-theatre play. In those years I was a prey to fear, doubt, disillusion. Clichés sat on my shoulder like vultures pouncing on my written pages. I had sensed that words could be as futile as nutty putty thrown against a wall. Our younger children were rebelling against baby sitters and bedtime. Our older children were rebelling against everything. I started "The Carpenter Ants" but it never got finished. Just not enough despair, I guess. Some of it was later used in "The Deep Has Many Voices."

In the sixties I collaborated with musicians on two community anniversary shows—one for Edson, Alberta, celebrating its fiftieth anniversary was "Look Behind You, Neighbor" with composer Chet Lambertson, about the laying of steel of the Grand Trunk Pacific Railway and the impact of World War I on a small Western town. The other, "The Road Runs North," was a Centennial production in Williams Lake about Billy Barker and the Cariboo Gold Rush.

The late Art Rosoman composed the music for the Cariboo show. Both were big, splashy productions with large casts, good costumes, simple multi-level sets, and both were highly popular with their audiences. Plays with music and songs and comedy do seem to be a sure way to the heart of an average play-goer.

In the sixties, too, I tried in several forms, novel, stories, three one-act plays, to write about the Indian people, whom I have long known and whose temperament and anger and joy seem the stuff of drama. The plays were not to be social documents but plays about the tragedy of wasted and misunderstood people.

The first play, *Lament for Harmonica*, was to be full length but reduced itself to a shorter form. It has been produced several times but I have never seen it. The "Stranger" employed the legend of Jason and Medea in a Chilcotin Indian setting and was done here with an Indian cast. Earlier with Indian school children I had written and produced *The Sleeping Beauty*, transforming the old fairy tale to a Western and Indian setting, and the English dialogue in the play was written with a sense of the rhythms and tones in our local Indian languages. The timbre and resonance of Indian voices is a joy to hear. Some of the choruses in both of these Indian plays were spoken as a writer dreams of hearing his or her words spoken, rich in full tone and breath and in belief.

In "The Deep Has Many Voices" (1969) again I tried for poetry and to move away from naturalism. I suppose all of us have our favourite plays and this play, only produced here, directed by me, with amateur actors and an outdoor setting, remains one of my plays I care about. In it there seems a fusion of some of the shock and despair of the sixties with some middle-aged optimism I carry with me.

Then I wrote a book. Then I stopped writing for a while. Nearly five years. I wrote "The Lodge" in 1974. It received its first production at the West Vancouver Little Theatre in October, 1976.

Some plays were commissioned, suggested, asked for, and that always was a pleasing thing because it made you feel needed as a writer. *Widger* was at Bob Orchard's suggestion and derived from an old Plautus play which got lost early in the Alberta oil, dinosaurs, politics and love. But whether the plays were commissioned or suggested, or whether they came out of my own decision to write them, the process is very similar. Many yellow pages of notes about how one might treat the subject, names of possible characters, descriptions of places or people or actions written at random at first. Some small returning thought must be explored, perhaps for gain, perhaps to be thrown away. Scraps of mandalas, notes put aside or scrambled up until a few names emerge with faces, or a glimmer of the ending is glimpsed. Characters move forward briefly but for some reason some slip back into some limbo where might-have-been characters wander, lacking the energy of Pirandello's six characters to demand a hearing. Other characters seem to move about a little; their names elicit shapes, fat or thin or tall, straight or crooked. Suddenly there you are beginning a play with a vague idea of the ending but no sure path to get there.

For me the first draft is an attempt to move forward, sometimes fearfully, sometimes with tremulous excitement, to move forward and get somewhere.

A well-articulated plot is something I often pray for, but occasionally when I've outlined one I have found I never wrote that play or story. The pursuit of a fitful light seems my way of going about the initial stage of creating.

In "The Deep Has Many Voices" I welded together many musings and notes and bits of dialogue. In one "story" I'd explored the mind of a middle-aged woman whose despair stemmed from the nightmare of the concentration camps and disposal termini, the atomic destruction, the cold-blooded disregard for life, that had been a part of our once-vaunted "civilized" twentieth century. The woman is half mad with the attempt to surround the times she lives in, to find some way to be of use. "Miriam stands at the window looking at the village and in the hall her empty travelling bags are packed for nowhere."

A second piece used in "The Deep" is an ironic story about the death of Einstein, the genius of our time, simply stating how little ordinary people understood of his mind or his work. And Gandhi, too, walked across those pages. At another time I'd written notes too about a young high school graduate writing a valedictory with rage and contempt for the education she had received. Feeling that these were variations on a theme, I started the first of many attempts to write a play on that theme—how to make a life. Finally Melissa, the young graduate, was sent on a simple pilgrimage through her village, eliciting from various people at various levels of consciousness or understanding some answers to her question. She saw young men training for war, she experienced a little of various forms of religious and drug experience, rock music, as well as seeing people past middle age or old, some broken, some aware. And finally Melissa "puts away childish things" and with her young lover sets off on a kind of search to change the world . . . the search perhaps is all.

Writing a play is difficult. Certainly it is for me. I never have "tossed anything off." I still sometimes burrow among books from Aristotle to Allardyce Nicoll to John Howard Lawson and the Paris Review *Writers at Work* hunting for the recipe "how to write a play." And I go to the theatre searching for that experience when a play unfolds as a unified, flowing whole, enveloping me with stage realities, suspending my disbelief for its own purposes, sometimes illuminating the high adventure of being alive.

A tremendous amount of energy must be generated early in a play to carry forward the action throughout an evening. A number of times I've thought I was writing a long play only to find I was compelled to reduce it to the shorter form. The one-act play can make a strong statement without extraneous adornment. The full-length play can easily become diffuse and its action can seem elongated and perhaps unbelievable unless great forces have been set to work.

A difficulty is to fully dramatize the story, to show what happens, not to talk about it. I shy away from violence and from stripping my people down to the core of being. And often if I reread a scene in past plays I realize that I have diluted and diminished its energy by *telling* what happened when I could have *shown* it on stage.

Hardest of all seems to be a blending of theme and story. To decide "this is what I want to say and this is how I will say it" sounds like a writer's first job, but it is one I find very difficult. As I said above, I am probably writing towards the glimpsed ending of a conflict, trying to find out what the emerging characters stand for and against. The first draft is pure exploration, hoping to discover through the conflicts of the newly known people what lies at the back of my mind to want to write about these conflicts and these people.

I think Ginsberg said "How do I know what I think until I see what I say?" Kazantzakis too, wrote that his great novels and poems were written to find out what he thought about his world. I take comfort in them. I hope a theme will emerge even if it is as simple as the celebration of love or living or man's capacity to endure. When I can discipline myself to write, to sit at the typewriter and to return the next day to sit again, I am always glad after I get started trying to capture something in words. It is like setting off on a journey in which one tries to let the unconscious or subconscious mind take the lead at first; this part of the mind flits ahead, flashing a torch down unknown but possible paths. After awhile the characters begin to take on form and the story or plot emerges.

The first version then is to explore and get to some ending, the second is to make the story logical, to further enrich and understand your characters, to find the spine of the action and get rid of extraneous material, to believe harder in the people and the conflict, to go deeper under the whole piece of work, keeping open to change and inspiration and the opportunity to follow up vague premonitions and to explore new ground. I know it is very important to keep this second stage from "jelling" too soon, to keep one's sense of the flow of the play fluid and free and alive.

The third time through calls on you to give your play everything you have left in the way of belief, enrichment, polish, ruthless pruning and cutting—everything you have discovered about the play should be considered now. This before anyone else sees the script would be the best way, if you can wait before trying it out on someone sympathetic and informed.

Where I live has always influenced the settings of my plays and stories. I seem to need a long time to soak up the atmosphere of a place and all my work has been set in Western Canada except for a few expressionistic short stories. I normally write about country or small-town life, family groups or large groups of people at some holiday or ritual function. Usually there are some underprivileged or "unassimilated" people in the cast. My people are sometimes working people or farmers, often middle class. In comedy I employ characters who preen themselves in some way—vain, shallow, affected, snobbish or hail fellow well met, hypocritical or ambitious. My sense of political intrigue is poor. My sense of history is poor. I seem to do best with a country or small-town outdoor background, lovable people caught unawares. I love the colour of fairs and birthdays, movement, music and bright dateless costumes and I love nice people taking themselves very seriously about the small details of living.

The style comes with the idea, I think. Perhaps a writer just keeps exploring the same material in different ways and when he's written a lot, his own voice is clear enough that a reader can recognize his style.

Most of the plays I've written would fall into a kind of "heightened realism" category with touches of symbolism. Sometimes I've enjoyed doing short satiric sketches with political or social implications—coffeehouse sketches—and this makes me feel that I'd like to experiment further with the very short play such as Jacinto Benevente or Lope de Vega wrote in Spanish.

The Rainmaker (the original title), *Widger*, "The Stranger," and "The Deep Has Many Voices" are my favourite plays of all I have written. But there are scenes and moments in others that I loved writing. "The Lodge," "A Remembrance of Miracles," "The Magic Carpets," are the new plays and so, of course, I like them best right now.

There were and are obstacles to the creation of a play all the time. The rule that the creative process requires going through the work at least three times—maybe many more—helps to overcome some obstacles. Sometimes you can truthfully say "I can't do anymore—for good or ill this must now stand on its own." Unfortunately one always has a few plays, stories, that last unpublished novel, that you grudgingly realize should be worked at once again.

The Rainmaker, "The Stranger," *Still Stands The House*, *Widger's Way*, *Dark Harvest*, and perhaps *Marie Jenvrin* are plays I know I now cannot help by revision. They are too far in the past. But many others I feel would be improved if I could cherish them once again as "unfinished work." Unfortunately there is so much to do.

I do not feel quite easy in myself if I'm not testing experience and observation by trying to shape it to some acceptable form that makes the material understandable or illuminates the experience in some way.

I dislike Claude Dinsmore in *Marie Jenvrin* because I don't believe in him very much and I dislike Michael in the same play because he spanks Marie and I'm embarrassed to think how unliberated I was in 1941. Allan in *Lament for Harmonica* doesn't seem true and I have trouble believing in Lisa and David in *Dark Harvest* all the time. And of course there are other unrealized, unreal characters in my plays. Usually actors have liked the characters I created. Black Jake in *Widger* is a hard role to make plausible. Perhaps Jason in "The Stranger" should be more deeply explored. But mostly I've approved of my characters. It's theme and plot that are hard to manage.

I like Widger, Jana, and the old woman in "The Stranger," Miranda and Joe in *The Rainmaker*, the little old ladies who talk about Einstein and Gandhi in "The Deep Has Many Voices." In fact I like most of the people in "The Deep" because when I think of them I have a sense of their vitality and three-dimensional reality. I like Wasyl Nemitchuk running away from oil drills and his wife Olga and pretending to be drowned. And I like Billy Barker and Flynn and Rosa and the Widow Manders in "The Road Runs North." These people I've mentioned seem real to me. There's a line in "The Deep has Many Voices"—"And Macbeth's as real as Diefenbaker." W. O. Mitchell's *Jake and the Kid* are real and Sarah Binks and the Mad Hatter and Louis Riel and Antigone are real, as are Claudius and Rosencrantz and Hamlet—the printed page won't hold them.

We who have helped to shape Canadian theatre since the

twenties have seen many of the things we hoped for come about—the establishment of professional theatres in the main cities of Canada, the employment of Canadian actors by those theatres, the children's plays and the tours to high schools throughout the country, the Canadian content on CBC radio. We have theatres now devoted largely to the production of Canadian plays. I enjoy the small City Stage in Vancouver with its lunch-hour productions, the informal atmosphere of arts clubs, galleries, summer outdoor productions. Vigorous theatrical companies have been formed to experiment with the improvised action, the instant plays, the masque, the mime, the protest play. So I think we are well on the way to a good theatrical future.

Somehow our audiences are not always happy with the plays they see, and I hope ways will be found to enlist the interest of wider, more heterogeneous audiences who will feel affection for their theatre, some responsibility for its survival.

I think we need to cherish our artists in the theatre more than we do, to give young actors a long period to mature, not to expect from them "sudden success" but rather to be prepared to support them while they learn how to use their talent. We seem intolerant of small failures on the part of our artists and to be looking for brilliant performances every time.

If the theatre is a civilizing agent in man's progress, then the medium of television should serve the theatre more than it does now. Great plays from Sophocles to Beckett are occasionally done for a mass audience, but why could they not be a regular occurrence? Why can we not see one another's productions—the Théâtre du Nouveau Monde one week, Winnipeg or Calgary productions the next week and something from British Columbia or the Maritimes in continuing sequence? Why cannot the careers of our playwrights be followed by seeing their works as a body over a period of some months? And these without the interruption of advertisements and blaring claptrap! The CBC can do more for us than it is now doing.

I hope playwrights of the future will be encouraged to work closely with acting groups, creative directors, in interesting and warm surroundings to bring their plays to production.

Too many plays have to be put together in a rush in cold, barn-like rehearsal rooms or crowded basement corners, with everyone concerned wearing fur hats and mittens. Playwrights can be helped by commissions to write for stage, radio and television, by invitations to join players' companies, by competitions, by their friends' insistence on their continued efforts, by sympathetic and helpful comments and criticisms from critics and audiences.

In Athens in a period of fifty years a lot of fine plays were written. The Irish Theatre produced notable plays at the Abbey during its most productive twenty years. Who knows? The next twenty years may see a burst of energy such as we have not had before, and a Canadian theatre will emerge, comprised of plays of significance for our time, and times to come. There is a trembling in the air. And somewhere young playwrights are aware of where the wind might take them.

Chronology

1910	Born in Anatone, Washington State, August 13, daughter of Leslie and Mary (Bowersock) Pharis.
1913	Moved with family to Magrath, southern Alberta. Attended elementary and high school (1914-26).
1926-28	Moved with family to Valier, Montana and attended the University of Montana.
1929	Obtained position as bookkeeper for Browning Mercantile on the Blackfoot Indian Reservation. Returned with family to Alberta and attended the University of Alberta, graduating in 1934, with a B.A.
1932-37	Secretary to Elizabeth Sterling Haynes, Director of Drama, University of Alberta, Department of Extension. Then became Registrar of newly established Banff School of Fine Arts where her play, "The Dragons of Kent," was produced. Wrote radio plays for CFCN radio, and CKUA, which produced her ten plays, "New Lamps for Old."

1937-39	Awarded a Rockefeller Foundation Fellowship to the University of North Carolina, Chapel Hill, Carolina Playmakers School, where she wrote and had produced the plays: "Chris Axelson, Blacksmith," *Still Stands the House*, *Pasque Flower*, "Dark Harvest," and "One Man's House." Awarded the Roland Holt Cup for outstanding work in drama. Graduated with an M.A. in Drama.
1939-40	Director of Dramatics for the Department of Extension, University of Alberta. Married Dr. John Brian Ringwood, M.D., in Edmonton, September 16, 1939. Moved to Goldfields, northern Saskatchewan, a frontier mining town where Dr. Ringwood was the company doctor.
1941	First child, Stephen, born April 22. Awarded the Governor-General's medal for outstanding service in the development of Canadian drama.
1942	Second child, Susan, born November 19. Wrote and had produced the play, *The Courting of Marie Jenvrin*, at the Banff School of Fine Arts. Judged Best One Act Play of 1942 by Carolina Playbook, University of North Carolina, Chapel Hill.
1942-46	Returned to Alberta when her husband enlisted in Canadian Army Medical Corps, Second World War. Awarded a Playwriting Fellowship and Grant under the Alberta Folklore and Local History Project to write three plays: "The Jack and the Joker," *Hatfield, The Rainmaker*, and "Stampede," all produced at the Banff School of Fine Arts. Wrote radio plays: "The Fight Against the Invisible" and "Niobe House," produced on CBC radio.
1946	Husband returned from the war. Moved to Lamont, Alberta. Third child, Carole, born December 15.
1948-53	Moved to Edmonton where Dr. Ringwood set up practice. Wrote *A Fine Colored Easter Egg* or *The Drowning of Wasyl Nemitchuk*, produced in Banff and on CBC radio. Fourth child, Patrick, born January 13, 1949. Wrote *Widger's Way* or *The Face in the Mirror*, produced at the University of Alberta. Wrote radio plays, "Right on Our Doorstep," "Health Scripts for Children," and "Frontier to Farmland,"

	for CBC radio, 1952. Wrote the political musical, "The Wall," and the play, "The Bells of England," for CBC radio.
1953	Moved with her husband and family to Williams Lake, B.C. Revived the Players Club and initiated her Coffeehouses, evenings of short plays. Wrote the novel, "Younger Brother."
1959	Wrote the play, *Maya* or *Lament for Harmonica*, and won first prize for it at the Ottawa Little Theatre Competition. Adapted "Heidi" for CBC radio, Toronto.
1961-66	Wrote the lyrics for the musical, "Look Behind You Neighbor," for Edson, Alberta's fiftieth Anniversary. Volunteered to teach dramatics and creative writing at Saint Joseph Mission for Indians in the Cariboo. For them she adapted the play, *The Sleeping Beauty*, published their legends in the two-volume work, *My Heart Is Glad*, adapted the fable, "The Lion and the Mouse," and "The Three Wishes."
1967-75	Awarded a Certificate of Merit for her outstanding contributions to the British Columbia Centennial Celebrations and the Canadian Confederation Centennial Celebrations. Wrote the play, "The Deep Has Many Voices" or "The Edge of the Forest," for the opening in 1971 of the Gwen Pharis Ringwood Theatre at Williams Lake—a tribute to her by the local community. Wrote the lyrics for the musical, "The Road Runs North," for the Williams Lake Centennial. Wrote the novel, "Pascal." Gave courses in Modern Drama, Playwriting and Acting at Cariboo College, Williams Lake (1967-75). Wrote the play, "Jana" or "The Stranger," for the opening of Centennial Park and the Gwen Pharis Ringwood Theatre, 1971, Williams Lake. Wrote a series of short plays, "Encounters," for her Coffeehouses which have since become a community theatrical institution. Gave writing workshops and adjudicated numerous play festivals throughout British Columbia and Alberta. Awarded in 1973 the Eric Hambert trophy from the British Columbia Drama Association for her continuing commitment to theatre. Wrote an adaptation of "The Golden Goose."

1975   Made Honorary President of the B.C. Drama Association for Amateur Theatre. Wrote the play, "The Lodge," winning second place for it in the New Play Centre Women's Playwriting Competition.

1976   Won first prize for her children's play, "The Magic Carpets of Antonio Angelini," from the Ontario Multicultural Theatre Association 1976 National Playwriting Competition. Play produced at Winnipeg. *Widger's Way* revived for the Kawartha Festival. "The Lodge" produced by the West Vancouver Little Theatre at the West Vancouver Recreational Centre.

Selected Bibliography

All manuscripts and typescripts are in Gwen Pharis Ringwood's possession at her home near Williams Lake, B.C.

Primary Sources

PLAYS

"The Bells of England." TS, CBC radio, Edmonton, May 7, 1953.

"Chris Axelson." MS, Chapel Hill, North Carolina, May 26, 1938.

"Christmas, 1943." MS, Edmonton, University Women's Club, 1943.

The Courting of Marie Jenvrin. In *Canada on Stage*, Edited by Stanley Richards. Toronto: Clarke, Irwin & Company Ltd., 1960.

"Dark Harvest." In *The Canadian Theatre Review*, No. 5 (1975), pp. 70-128.

"The Days May Be Long." MS, Edmonton, 1940.

"The Deep Has Many Voices." MS, Williams Lake, 1971.

The Drowning of Wasyl Nemitchuk or *A Fine Colored Easter Egg.* Toronto: Gage Educational Publishers Ltd., 1946.

"Encounters." MS, Williams Lake, 1970.

"The Fight Against the Invisible." TS, CBC radio, Edmonton, 1945.

"Florence Nightingale." TS, CKUA radio, Edmonton, 1936.

"Frontier to Farmland." TS, CBC radio, Edmonton, January 30, 1952.

Hatfield, The Rainmaker. Vancouver: New Play Centre, 1946.

The Jack and the Joker, Edmonton: University of Alberta Extension Department, 1943.

Lament for Harmonica or *Maya*. In *Ten Canadian Short Plays*. New York: Dell International Inc., 1975.

"The Lodge." MS, Williams Lake, 1976.

"New Lamps for Old." TS, CKUA radio, Edmonton, University of Alberta, 1936. (Ten plays, typescript not preserved.)

"Niobe House." TS, CBC radio, Edmonton, 1945.

"One Man's House." MS, Chapel Hill: University of North Carolina, April 20, 1938.

Pasque Flower. In *The Carolina Playbook*, Edited by Fred H. Koch. Chapel Hill: University of North Carolina Press, 12, No. 1, (1939), p. 7-20.

"Red Flag at Evening." MS, Edmonton: University of Alberta Extension Department, 1940.

"Remembrance of Miracles." MS, Williams Lake, 1975.

"Saturday Night." MS, Edmonton: University of Alberta Extension Department, 1940.

"Stampede." MS, Edmonton: Alberta Folklore and Local History Project, 1945.

"So Gracious the Time." MS, Williams Lake, 1954.

Still Stands the House. New York: Samuel French Inc., 1939. Also in *Encounter: Canadian Drama in Four Media*, edited by Eugene Benson. Toronto: Methuen Publications, 1973.

"The Stranger" or "Jana." MS, Williams Lake, 1971.

Widger's Way or *The Face in the Mirror*. Toronto: Playwrights Co-op, 1976.

"Younger Brother." TS, CBC radio, Edmonton, Prairie Playhouse, August, September, 1960.

MUSICALS

"Look Behind You Neighbor." MS, Edson, Fiftieth Anniversary, 1961. (Composer: Chet Lambertson.)

"The Road Runs North." MS, Williams Lake, Centennial Celebration, 1968. (Composer, Art Rosoman.)

"The Wall." TS, CBC radio, Edmonton, 1953. (Composer, Bruce Haak.)

CHILDREN'S PLAYS

"Books Alive." TS, CBC Radio, Edmonton. Right On Our Doorstep, December 7, 1951.

"The Dragons of Kent." MS, Edmonton, Banff School of Fine Arts, 1935.

"The Golden Goose." Adaptation. MS, Williams Lake, Cariboo Indian School, 1973.

"Health Highway Series." TS, CBC radio, Vancouver, 1952.

"Heidi." Adaptation. TS, CBC radio, Toronto, 1959.

"The Lion and the Mouse." Adaptation. MS, Williams Lake, Cariboo Indian School, 1964.

"The Magic Carpets of Antonio Angelini." MS, Winnipeg, Ontario Multicultural Theatre Association, 1976. (National prize-winning play.)

The Sleeping Beauty. Adaptation. In *My Heart Is Glad*, edited by Gwen Ringwood. Williams Lake: local publisher, 1965.

"The Three Wishes." Adaptation. MS, Williams Lake, 1965.

"The Voyages of Captain Cook." TS, CBC radio, 1936.

Secondary Sources

ANTHONY, GERALDINE. *Gwen Pharis Ringwood*. Twayne World Authors Series. Boston: G. K. Hall Co., forthcoming.

"Attention Alberta Writers." *Alberta Folklore Quarterly* 1, No. 1 (1945), pp. 27-28.

BRODERSON, GEORGE L. "Gwen Pharis—Canadian Dramatist," *Manitoba Arts Review* 4 (1944), pp. 3-20.

JONES, EMRYS. "Courting of Marie Jenvrin." *The Winnipeg Tribune*, 1941.

ORCHARD, IMBERT. "Widger's Way." *The Edmonton Journal*, March 11, 1952.

TAIT, MICHAEL. "Playwrights in a Vacuum," *Canadian Literature*, No. 16 (1963), pp. 5-18.

TOVELL, VINCENT. "Dark Harvest." *University of Toronto Quarterly* 16 (1947): 266-67.

URSELL, GEOFFREY BARRY. "A Triple Mirror." Microfilm No. 722, Master's thesis, University of Manitoba.

WAGNER, ANTON. "Gwen Pharis Ringwood Rediscovered." *The Canadian Theatre Review*, No. 5 (1975), pp. 63-128.

Five
TOM GRAINGER
(1921-   )

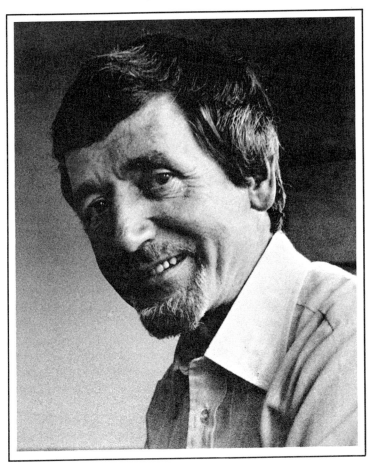

Preface

Tom Grainger, a resident of Vancouver and a naturalized Canadian citizen, is an interesting example of the self-educated man whose innate talent for drama resulted in a playwriting career that has gained considerable momentum since his first national prize-winning play, Daft Dream Adyin', in 1964.

Unlike Voaden, Davies, Reaney, and Ringwood, he did not enjoy the benefits of a secondary and college education. Born in Lancashire, England, in 1921, he began work at 14 years of age as a scavenger in a cotton-spinning mill at $2.25 a week. "There followed over the years a succession of ill-paid, dead-end jobs."[1] Finally in 1956 he emigrated to Canada and four years later had his first short story published in Vancouver. This encouraged him to a dedicated writing career.

He has since written a number of fine stage plays of social protest rising from the social conditions of his own and others' backgrounds. These were then adapted for television and radio since the Vancouver theatres at that time were not, for the most part, producing plays by Canadians. Six of his plays were awarded prizes in national competitions and Grainger was given four Canada Council grants. Obviously his talents have been intelligently assessed by judges of drama. Don Mowatt of CBC radio drama, Vancouver, who early appreciated Grainger's exceptional talents has selected several of his radio plays for production.

In 1965 Grainger was awarded a fellowship in drama at the Yale University School of Drama where Herman Voaden had studied. Grainger learned to refine his craft under the celebrated American critic, John Gassner. Grainger had already adopted a conventional style of realism and Gassner's training helped him to tighten that style. As a result Grainger's plays are conventionally structured, observing the three unities of action, time and place, although their ramifications can extend back in time. In his full-length plays he goes back in time without the help of flashbacks. A character sleeps and dreams; he moves back and forth without any break in the flow of the action. When he uses a narrator, he tries to weave in and out of time without enormous gaps.

Grainger's plays are not Canadian or British or American per se, but seem to be universal in character. For example, in the play, "In Arizona the Air Is Clean," the setting could be anywhere. The noted American actor, Cameron Mitchell, said of the old man in this play: "This is the best role of its kind I've read since Willy Loman in Death of a Salesman." Grainger's play, "The Kill," is set in a Canadian meat-packing plant but it is so universal that it could take place in any large city anywhere. It offers a powerful theme, but there are no local or national references. As a result of the universal aspect of Grainger's plays he is beginning to be recognized in the United States and Germany, and to have them produced in Great Britain.

Grainger gives the audience a chance to think, not guess, so that the choice is theirs. His strong points are character and theme rather than plot. He says: "I try to give my characters a complete life with hints of their past so that they become solid figures without forcing them." The contradictions in characters intrigue him. He observes the foibles in mankind with compassion. His prize-winning play, The Injured, contains murder and incest but the play is really about the reasons for these aberrations. Social injustice is his concern. He examines the plight of the person of blameless life who makes one mistake and is punished by a legal system that takes no account of his past but only of that one mistake. The injured characters are isolated in such a society.

A wry sense of humour is exhibited in his play, The Helper. Christopher Dafoe, writing of its production in 1972 by the New Play Centre in Vancouver, for a review in The Vancouver Sun, August 25, 1972, has this to say of it:

> Grainger's play, The Helper, about an innocent idealist and a temporarily destitute opportunist, works very well in production. The script is tight and makes its points in an amusing and forceful way. . . . While its form is conventional there is nothing stale about what it says. Grainger gives us an aged printer who has given the best years of his life to the mighty struggle against capitalism. For years he has been grinding out fake banknotes, apparently to undermine the monetary systems of the great capitalist nations. He is an enthusiast for whom the fire of the old cause has never dwindled. He is joined . . . by a tramp who . . . exploits the situation to his own advantage.

This combination of concern for the victims of our social system and a balanced sense of humour at man's foibles gives decided richness to Grainger's plays. Of this same play, James Barber writing for The Vancouver Province, August 25, 1972, says:

> Grainger is a simple, direct wordsmith who uses very ordinary images and the limited language of very ordinary people to paint very clever pictures. . . . His simplicities are unforgettable and complicated . . . capable of being appreciated on a number of levels, separately or simultaneously. The basic politics of revolutions, the dynamics of personal relationships, the naïveté of romantics, and the inevitable exploitation of any system for personal gain and comfort. . . . They are all there.

Grainger's play, "The Great Grunbaum," is another example of his creative probing of inconsistencies in character. It contrasts the ways used by different people to control situations that tend to get out of hand. In his reunion of two former circus performers with one of their previous associates the audience is confronted with a situation that may be controlled through fear and violence, or through trust and love. Both the characters in the play and the audience are given the opportunity to make their own value judgments.

The writing of dialogue comes easily to Grainger. He says of it:

> Dialogue is remembering. First I invent a character and then dialogue follows naturally. Somehow from somewhere comes a

plot to hang a theme on. Perhaps a few words about the speech patterns of the characters in The Injured will help in the reading of the play. The play is set in the birthplace of the Industrial Revolution, that so-called 'bloodless revolution,' which, with its handmaiden, the Enclosures Act, forced hundreds of thousands of homeless men, women and children into the coal mines and factories of the new industrial towns. The dialect they had used for centuries, with its biblical rhythms and near-Elizabethan turns of phrase, was, like the countryside, eroded as the generations lived and died under the shadows of the factories and the slag heaps. But the accent remained, with its broad vowels and hard consonants, that accent which almost always kept the 'northerner' in his place. . . . Of course there is no town of Loston in Lancashire . . . Loston is the lost town. . . . [2]

The great dramatists who have influenced Grainger's work have been, for the most part, self-educated writers like himself. From such playwrights as O'Casey and Gorky, and poet-playwrights such as Dylan Thomas, he has perfected his art form and he continues to develop his style. Grainger is a British Canadian dramatist worth watching.

NOTES
1. Unless otherwise noted, all quotations are taken from the editor's interview with Tom Grainger, Vancouver, April 9, 1974.
2. In a letter to this editor from Tom Grainger, Vancouver, April 17, 1974.

Twelve Canadian Dramatists (original working title of *Stage Voices*). The title lies there waiting for the comic cosmic jolt that will make it a reality. Who are the other eleven? Whoever they are, I'll be outnumbered, left staring at a pile of second-class blank paper as they discuss the finer points of dramaturgy and the past, present, and future of Canadian Theatre, subjects of which I know little, so will leave to those who are safely aboard the Great Canadian Arts Band Wagon and Gravy Train, and doing very nicely indeed.

That word "Canadian" bothers me as a prefix to the arts. The leading question tends more and more to be not "Is it good?" but "Is it recognizably 'Canadian'?" If I had to choose between the fig leaf and the maple leaf as a formative influence, the fig leaf would be a front runner all the way. If there is one quality that can lift the saddened heart, that quality is innocence. As the educators and media manipulators make inroads on our young, this quality is becoming as hard to find as clean air in a quiet place. The decay and near-disappearance of blushing is a symptom of a grave spiritual sickness. If to bring back the blush we must also call back the fig leaf, then let us lay in a goodly stock before those crafty boyos in the futures markets get wind of our need.

"It is true," a great man once said, "that I also have to defecate, but for quite different reasons." It may be that I also have to write, but, to judge by the very few writers I have met, for quite different reasons. I think of myself as a dramatist only in moments of desperation, but if I am to be considered by others as a dramatist I must be considered as a late-starting outsider in a race for which I have not been entered. All other things being more or less equal, it is the writer's point of view that gives him the edge, so it is my point of view that must first be made known. As one of the last of the walking wounded in a wheeled society, the problems of the well off—and in my view anyone who has money over after paying for food, shelter and clothing is *rich*—are of no interest to me. Drug addiction, alcoholism, overeating and the side effects of so-called permissiveness touch me hardly at all. A founder-member of Belt Tighteners Anonymous, I would be more at home in the Third World and if there was a fourth I would head straight for it. My income tax return is the high point of the fiscal year. It's the only thing that ever coaxed a tear out of a computer.

My viewpoint is an awkward one. To be down here continually looking up puts a strain on my neck muscles as well as making me an easy mark for nystagmus of the spirit. As the years lurch on, misanthropy insists more and more on a fair hearing and there is a danger of my being flattened by that modern equivalent of the Black Death, General Paralysis of the Indifferent. From the heart-on-sleeve, black-against-white, here-I-am-knock-me-down openness of my first play, *Daft Dream Adyin'*, I have twisted and turned and back-tracked to arrive at the take-it-or-leave-it stand of *The Injured*. In my current work in progress I am searching for a code that will be cracked only by someone who has travelled the same dim paths as I have.

The influences behind *Daft Dream Adyin'* are as obvious as the play's message. Echoes of the early O'Casey, *Strife* and *Love on the Dole*, are loud and clear. A later, fairly long one-act version turned one of the central characters, with a brief nod of thanks to Tennessee Williams, into a narrator-protagonist.

The play is set in the industrial north of England before, during and after the General Strike of 1926. An innocent group of characters—and by innocence here I mean the opposite of sophistication—wanders through this play. Songs are used, including an adaptation of Edwin Waugh's lovely lyric, "Come, Mary, link thi arm i' mine And lilt away wi' me." May the shade of this almost forgotten poet forgive me for it. A real-life character is used, the great miners' leader, A. J. Cook. The tramp, a recurring character of mine, is here the champion clog dancer, Rochdale Jack. An attempt is made through the narrator, Steve Bradshaw, to counterpoint the miseries of poverty with a touch of poetry as he moves from now to the then when his dream was betrayed.

STEVE: *(On ramp)* The canal is not Venice, but the strange light of an evening in early summer will touch it now and then with smooth, nervous fingers. Fingers that know they should be somewhere else. Somewhere

where their presence would add to beauty, like a tiara on the head of a lovely woman. We would sometimes look at this light with a jaundiced eye, as though expecting it to be taken away by a man in uniform. At other times we would swallow it neat through both eyes and come back for a second look, daring it to go back where it belonged, on the sunny side of the class system. The canal is not Venice. No palaces line the banks. But in the strange light of an early summer evening the extravagant façades of the factories have an exotic, Eastern look, so that one half expects to hear the muezzin's call from the chimney tops. And sometimes far away a song is heard . . .

It is later used to introduce A. J. Cook.

STEVE: There is sometimes a heartbreak of longing as the light fades in early summer in Loston. Oh, Mary, Mary Doonan. I dreamed of seeing you in a fine dress, wearing shoes that glittered, with your hair craftily fashioned to set off the great glow of your eyes . . . But it was not to be. Men whose women had scores of dresses would see to that. In their stately homes and great offices they were laying their plans. The guns and truncheons were ready to hand out to the paid patriots. Food was being piled up as though for a long siege. But there was fear in the hurried plans. Fear of a little man in a badly made suit. They knew the price of most of the workers' leaders and were willing to pay it with cash and promises, but they were afraid of the man who had no price. They were afraid of little A. J. Cook. *(He disappears as a spot is focused on the rostrum. A. J. Cook raises both arms as he demands silence.)*

A. J. COOK: And I tell the bosses this right now. There's one part of the British Empire where you won't frighten the natives with the military or a gunboat. There's one part of the British Empire where the natives will one day put the fear of Christ in you. And that part of the Empire is right here, in these coalfields. I say to the bosses, "Go on, lock the workers out. They're your gates." But *we'll* open them, and from then on they'll be *our* coalfields and *our* factories. If you want a test of strength we'll give you a test of strength!

Humour is tried for—that special brand of "I'm all right in meself like. It only hurts when I breathe." Lancashire humour—which is contrasted with the Irish extravagance of Paddy Doonan. Paddy sits in his wheelchair after months of trying, with no success at all, to get compensation after a roof fall.

> MRS. BRADSHAW: How *is* your back, Mr. Doonan?
> PADDY: No change at all, missis. The main nerves and muscles are still paralysed and half the rest are constantly fretting and fuming.
> ROCHDALE JACK: And never a penny compensation! If there were any justice you'd be set up for life after a crippling accident like that.
> STEVE: (*Without looking up.*) Didn't John Fairclough, the country's leading nerve specialist, come down from London? And did he or did he not confirm the compensation doctor's deft diagnosis that you were only coddin'?
> PADDY: Is *Sir* John Fairclough for the working man? . . . He's only to turn thumbs down on ten more claims for Workmen's Compensation and they'll make him a lord.

Another character, black-listed Joe Shovelton, tries to temper the daft dreaming of the others with his realistic outlook.

> JOE SHOVELTON: While A. J.'s ranting and raving in there the bosses are all calmly eating their good dinners. They'll let him carry on for a while longer, then one o' these fine days they'll flatten him between dessert and bloody coffee.
> PADDY: I can remember the time when you were making speeches. You were neck and neck with A. J. then.

JOE SHOVELTON: Happen I've learned my lesson. If speeches and meetings brought Socialism we'd have had it long since. *(Rises.)* But I want you to know something, Paddy. If A. J. Cook were to come out o' yon Institute this minute with a rifle and a few rounds of ammunition and declare an open season for boss-killing I'd be the first to grab the gun.

Although this play was published, long after it was written, in *Best Short Plays: 1969*, edited by Stanley Richards, it has not been produced, so must be considered a failure. Yet, prejudiced as I am, I think there are good characters and good dialogue in it. The plot, often a weak point in my plays, may be a bit shaky.

My next play, a fairly long one-acter, written the same year, has a completely different setting, but has the same kind of innocence as one of the themes. "The Action Tonight" is set in a city loft which overlooks a freeway. George Graham, who has turned his back on society, lives there with Golden Echo Lovejoy, whom he had some time ago rescued from the chaos of a major smash-up on the freeway below. Goldy's mind has been wiped clean. He remembers nothing of his life before the accident. He is a man who is absolutely innocent, whereas George is a sophisticate who has turned to innocence in desperation. As well as giving Goldy his name George has given him a job. He sits in his rocking chair and watches over the freeway. As long as he watches over it there will be no more accidents. They live on handouts. Their tranquil existence is disturbed by Dolores, who tells them that the action will be here tonight. She talks of Binky, drug pusher and pimp, who is also, unbeknownst to her, a police informer. Binky enters, leaves some marijuana for the police to find, then goes off to give them the nod. The police enter, Goldy is killed, George is hauled off and Dolores is left alone on stage as the sounds of a major highway smash-up are heard. It is sometimes difficult to trace influences after many years of indiscriminate reading, but the influence here is probably that of Saroyan.

The character of Binky still seems to me to be well drawn and the two policemen are solid in their scene, but if I were to attempt a play like this now I would add a few more touches to George and Dolores and perhaps to Goldy as well. And of course a few ounces of marijuana would not be enough to trigger the final scene today. "The Action Tonight" was written in 1963, before marijuana received its dubious social accolade and before the present preoccupation by otherwise seemingly intelligent people with things astrological. It was also, I think, before the "drop-out" was recognised as part of the social fabric and before characters such as Binky became more common in Canadian cities. It has been misinterpreted both as a plea for the relaxation of the laws relating to "soft" drugs and as a demand for the harsher implementation of them. What I actually set out to write was a condemnation of the automobile. Very few people, it seemed to me, had at this time any second thoughts at all about this destroyer of cities. I have never owned an automobile and it is unlikely that I ever will. The private ownership and constant use of an automobile in a town or city where there is some form of alternative transport is, to my mind, a crime as reprehensible as those of land, currency and futures speculation, forms of grand larceny much favoured by three-car families. That this message did not come across except as an apparent side issue is the play's gravest fault.

"The Action Tonight" was a competition prizewinner. It was published in *Prism*, then under the editorship of Earle Birney, and was produced non-professionally in Ottawa. Several years later a radio version was produced by the CBC. Its partial success encouraged me to write two more one-act plays within the next year or so. In these, "The Kill" and, "In Arizona the Air Is Clean," innocence is again the starting point, but it is now the innocence which is the opposite of guilt. These two plays are more successful. I really don't mind that my first two plays have been more or less ignored, but that "The Kill" should have received the same or worse treatment bothers me a little. "Arizona" was produced locally by CBC-TV in Montreal and a radio version has been broadcast, also by the CBC, but "The Kill," apart from being awarded a competition prize, has done nothing but gather dust and a little praise.

The main theme of "The Kill," that of responsibility for

almost unthinkable atrocities, is not new. What I considered at the time of writing to be new was the setting, the locker room of a meat-packing plant, and the choice of characters for such a theme. They are pig butchers, labourers and a janitor. The action is simple and inevitable. A casual labourer is killed "according to the laws for killing pigs" after it has been proved that he was an SS man. The obsessed Feldtman is contrasted with the kindly self-taught scholar and fellow pig butcher, Molnar. The brash young Dave gives a little light relief and the old wobbly janitor, Joe, ties it together with his memories of the judicial murder of Joe Hill. Blood is ever-present, visual and talked about. Feldtman has moved from the slaughterhouse of Auschwitz to a slaughterhouse in the Canadian West, but here he wields the knife.

> FELDTMAN: But they made a mistake. On their own kind they put numbers. For every special butcher a number. Some day I will meet a man who has a scar, or a little butterfly, in a certain place. Until then I cut only the throats of pigs.

Certain that the casual labourer, Lindtner, is his man, Feldtman baits him.

> FELDTMAN: You have lived in Argentina? A very interesting country, with many slaughterhouses . . . Why did you leave?
>
> LINDTNER: There was nothing to stay there for. (*After a moment*) There is too much politics there. It is even dangerous. Guerillas everywhere, taking the law into their own hands. Here it is different. Here there is freedom, yet there is also law and order. This is a much better country.
>
> FELDTMAN: This is a nothing country. A get-rich-quick country. A few guerillas could work wonders.
>
> LINDTNER: (*Smiles*) Your sympathies are with the Communists then?
>
> FELDTMAN: It is not a question of sympathy,

Lindtner. It is a question of trust. Marx I trust. Lenin I trust. Mao Tse Tung I trust. Even Stalin I trust. You I don't trust.

As Feldtman continues his baiting against Molnar's protests and Lindtner's seeming calm, it becomes apparent that there is to be an initiation, a ritual, before Lindtner can take his place with the other two men on the kill. The right sleeve of Lindtner's shirt must be cut off.

> FELDTMAN: What is it, Lindtner, that you hope to do tonight? We can take the sleeve off tomorrow, but not now. I offer ten dollars for the privilege. You need money, yet you refuse the ten dollars. What is it you hope to do tonight?
> LINDTNER: *(With an almost successful attempt at lightness)* Tonight? I hope to eat supper, then go to bed so that I will be fresh for work tomorrow. That is what I hope to do tonight. I will come early tomorrow, so that you will have plenty of time for the ritual of the sleeve.
> FELDTMAN: No. *(Rises)* The ritual of the sleeve takes place now.

The ritual takes place after Lindtner has been knocked senseless. The proof of SS membership is made visible, Lindtner is killed and his body trundled off to the pulveriser in the janitor's trolley. I cant help feeling that the very important theme was fairly well handled and that what it may lack in freshness is partly made up for by its insistence that inhuman orders must be disobeyed.

"In Arizona the Air Is Clean" is almost a one-character play. The Old Man, a leftover from the thirties and early forties, is a part a good actor could really get his teeth into. His son, Gershon, now called Harry, is a shadowy figure, not really there, except in the mind of the dying old man. Innocence, sophistication and responsibility are again the themes.

> OLD MAN: I learned one thing, though. You cant get away from people like you. People like you are like

pigeons. You drop your dirt on every town and city in the whole world.

HARRY: I didn't come all this way to go through that again. I'm not responsible. Not the way you think I am.

OLD MAN: Not responsible. *(Approaches Harry)* Look at you. That suit. How much was the suit? Three hundred dollars? You've got a fine suit made out of blood, Mr. Braindirtier.

And later . . .

OLD MAN: You know why you live so good? Why you have so many things you gave up counting them? Why you're so rich you throw food away every day? You're so rich because elsewhere people are starving to death, that's why.

HARRY: *(Goes to Old Man, puts arm around his shoulder)* You're living in the past, poppa. It's not like that now.

OLD MAN: *(Breaks away)* No? He's got a magic three-hundred-dollar suit. From inside it everything looks good.

Later still the Old Man insists on the innocence of the Rosenbergs, and I must point out here that the play was written in 1965, before pens more important than mine began hinting that there had been a miscarriage of justice. He speaks of Mrs. Rosenberg:

OLD MAN: She was a good woman. Nice. A woman you could talk to. A woman who would listen, like your momma. So what did they do? They shaved her head and put her in the electric chair. *(Moves from door and points)* This one, this Mrs. Rosenberg, she's rich. She'll live to be a hundred. Only she's bad. Mean. She never had a good thought in her whole life. They let her live, though. They killed the good one instead.

HARRY: She had a fair trial. She was found guilty.

OLD MAN: Sure, she was found guilty. They were all found guilty. It's easy to find a person guilty when you make a lie shine so much it looks nicer than the truth. They were innocent. They were good people. You know who the guilty ones are? Every last person in the mind-twisting business, that's who. Every last person taking home a fat pay cheque for using his talents to dress up a lie so that it looks good is guilty.

HARRY: It's not like that. There are a lot of dedicated, honest people in communications. They're not in it just for the money. They love the truth too.

OLD MAN: They kept it a secret then. They didn't communicate it to us.

I look upon "Arizona" as one of my better plays. A good actor could make it a moving experience.

In my next play, *The Helper*, my old friend the tramp takes over. Here he is Nimrod Twentyman, an ex-miner who has for ten years been pounding the inhospitable pavements of London. On his way one night to cadge a cup of tea and a lie down in the warm from the lads in the shipping department of the *Daily Mirror* he falls down some steps in a vacant lot and discovers the hideout of Tiggy, master printer and counterfeiter extraordinary; member of The International League of Anarchist Artisans And Intellectuals, London Central Branch; the most innocent revolutionist who ever plotted the downfall of capitalism. For twenty-six years he has been printing the best money in the world, having taken over from Ginger, who did the roubles job. (The "roubles job" is a running joke in the play referring to counterfeit money used in the chaos following the Bolshevik Revolution in Russia, causing even good "Tsarist money" to lose all value.) The idea being, of course, to flood the capitalist world with money so that "it will be useless except in the lavatory, and even there it would only make a second-class wiper." "It's taking a long time, isn't it?" queries Nimrod. "Wouldn't you be better off making bombs?"

As the play opens Tiggy is setting up for a run of pesos on the old hand press, two contacts being on their way to pick them up, along with a load of "cruzyroos." After Nimrod's unexpected entrance Tiggy's wife, Tess, is called in from the kitchen. When it becomes evident that Nimrod is not from the other side and has indeed stumbled upon the hideout by accident, Tiggy swears him in as a member of the League and hires him as his helper, in the forlorn hope that this will stop the two men who are on their way from killing him. Tess having gone back to the kitchen, Tiggy and Nimrod start the run. They are interrupted as they are setting up again by The Nobbler and The Blinder, who have come to collect the pesos and cruzeiros. As the operation has long since, unbeknownst to Tiggy, been taken over by the The Syndicate, The Nobbler and The Blinder know that Nimrod cannot possibly be a member, in good standing, of the League; the only surviving member being Tiggy, who "would never make money just to make money, if you know what I mean," so has been kept in ignorance of the true state of affairs.

By bluffing Tiggy into going into the kitchen to make tea for them, The Nobbler and The Blinder are enabled to make sure that Nimrod is alone in the world, would not be missed and that no one could know that he is in the neighbourhood. Having proved to him that he could not possibly be a member of the League by virtue of the sad fact that there no longer is one, they cart him off to close his mouth forever. Nimrod, however, has put the big adjustable wrench Tiggy had been using to set up the press in one of the capacious pockets of his carry-all of an old raincoat. A few blows with this "original blunt instrument" and the disposal of the bodies in a nearby body of water brings Nimrod back to the hideout where Tiggy, tea ready and on the table, is wondering where everybody's gone to. Nimrod tells him that the two men have had to leave in a hurry. Tiggy questions him about orders for next month's work.

> NIMROD: *(Leans on the press)* *(Casually)* Didn't I tell you? *(After a moment)* I could have sworn I'd told you. *(Looks around the room)* You've got all the comforts of home here, all right. They told me to tell you that the pound is slipping again. They said to give it another push.
>
> TIGGY: Fivers, eh? Did they say fivers?
>
> NIMROD: Yes, Tiggy. *(Moves handle slowly forward and back)* Fivers.

TIGGY: *(Puts sheet on press, takes it off as Nimrod moves handle forward and back)* What else besides fivers?

NIMROD: Nothing else. They said this push should do it.

As the play ends with the two of them almost dancing as they print, and shouting "Up the rebels! Up the bloody rebels!" it is evident that God will soon help yet another who is going to help himself.

I had now written five plays, each tackling sizable themes and each differing to a greater or a lesser degree stylistically. The early stages of my apprenticeship should have been over. Some encouragement had come my way, some recognition in the form of prize monies and awards; one play had been published and another was being favourably considered. Yet what little confidence I had started out with was being whittled away as time passed and no offers of production came. I entered on a period of false starts and sudden sterilities, when my pen was either costive or diarrhoeal. This period was brought to an end when I threw my pen away.

Three years later "The Helper" and "Arizona" won first and third prizes in a competition for a total of $1,000, but I still wasn't having any. Two years after that "The Helper" was given a professional production in Vancouver. The reviews were extremely favourable, but my adoptive birthplace was still Missouri. Soon after this, radio versions of "The Action Tonight" and "Arizona" were produced by the CBC and I sold an original radio play, "The Good Life." The crazy notion that *perhaps* I could become a real dramatist took hold of me again and I tackled *The Injured*.

With this play I entered a darker place. The plot is melodramatic. Murder, incest, rape, the hanging of an innocent man—all have a place in it. The major themes of shame and guilt, and the effect on the lives of poor, simple folk of laws and moral standards imposed from above by people to whom such laws and standards did not normally apply are themes of some consequence. But when, as in present-day England, it is not uncommon to find older people whose lives have been twisted beyond repair by the harsh implementation of these laws and standards, laws and standards *which no longer apply to anybody*, these themes become almost tragic in the classic sense.

For the first time a female character dominates one of my plays. Sarah Slater may be almost fully realized, a major role for a good actress. The character of her husband, Jud, may rank as one of the most sympathetic portraits of a child-rapist-murderer ever put on stage, but is believable for all that. Of the subsidiary characters Rochdale Jack is lifted almost bodily from "Daft Dream Adyin'" and becomes Harry Platt, the hanged man. Jud's father, Matt, and Sarah's mother, Tess, are solid characters when one considers the brevity of their scene. Young Sarah has only to look and sound attractively pathetic for her scene to work. Miss Rogers, the young schoolteacher, was not intended to be a complex, well-rounded character. She is a type, an interloper from "that other England."

The sexual morality of the working class in the industrial north of England forty years ago, when the turning point in the lives of Sarah and Jud was reached, may not be easy for some Canadians to understand. The most shameful thing that could happen to a family in those then closely knit communities, where almost everybody knew almost everybody else's business, was for a daughter to get "into trouble," to become pregnant without a marriage license and, because of some special circumstance, to have no foreseeable chance of getting one.

The more efficient mechanical methods of birth control were beyond the reach of most working-class pockets. Unemployment had been chronic since the twenties. Wages were at such a low level that several wage packets were needed to keep a household out of debt. Mothers would refer to their brood as "scholars" and "workers." "We're not doing so badly. We've got three workers and only two scholars." A "scholar" being a child still at school and so a dead loss. Although their fathers may have been unemployed for many years there was plenty of work in the factories for the very young, who did a six-day forty-eight-hour week with no fringe benefits for just over two dollars a week. It is against this background that the lives of Sarah and Jud must be placed.

I remember, when I was but thirteen or so, being questioned about my relationship, if any, with a certain plump dark-haired girl of about my own age who lived a few doors away. Being a late starter in this as in everything else except hard labour, I had at that time never heard of sex, so was let off with a warning. The topic of this girl in trouble dominated all talk in our neighbourhood for a while. Then one day the girl disappeared, as did her stepbrother, who was roughly the same age. Sent away, each to a different "home" or institution. Some time later they were released and were married. It may be that the child died in its infancy. I don't remember seeing it or hearing of it. Then about two years ago a small item in a local newspaper caught my eye. It had been picked up from an English news agency. A woman in her fifties had just been released from a mental institution. She had been sent there in her very early teens with a child in her belly and had been there ever since. From this and from my memories of the stepbrother and stepsister came *The Injured*.

This play starts with a strong scene in the graveyard of a northern industrial town. Sarah speaks to Jud, who is on his knees at a graveside.

> SARAH: *Pray*, our Jud.
>
> JUD: *(Raises his head, lets arm hang limp)* Gentle Jesus, meek and mild, look upon this little child.
>
> SARAH: A child, Jud Slater. Suffer to come unto Me, little children. *Suffer*, Jud. *(Abruptly)* Whose child then?
>
> JUD: Mine, Sarah. Mine and thine.
>
> SARAH: *I* bore her. When I was but fourteen I bore her. *I* gave her suck. Her were all lovely. Her were that nice I used to kiss her all over every time I changed her. I bore that child with every hand and tongue against me.
>
> JUD: Not mine, Sarah. Not mine.
>
> SARAH: Especially thine, Jud. You hope we'd both go under. Be honest. Didn't you hope we'd both go under, then you'd be shut of us?
>
> JUD: I'm bound to admit that I did, Sarah. I were too young to be trapped like that. Then I saw the babby. Her were a bonny babby.
>
> SARAH: *Pray*.

This scene is soon broken off and is picked up again for the opening of the second act and again to open the third act. This trick has doubtless been used before, but I can't remember where. It certainly comes in handy here. The second scene, as well as introducing the new lodger, Miss Rogers, brings in a stylistic device which is used again and again . . .

> JUD: *(Braces himself, approaches, stands over her)* This is my house.
> SARAH: *(Rises, faces him. There is a change in the relationship. Each knows what the other is going to say)* Ours, Jud. Ours.
> JUD: It was my dad's. Now it's mine.
> SARAH: Your dad's been gone a long time, Jud.
> JUD: *(Retreats left)* Ay.
> SARAH: *(Follows him)* You know what he died of, don't you, Jud?
> JUD: *(Retreats further)* Ay.
> SARAH: *(Follows him)* Say it then. Say what he died of.
> JUD: *(Stands still, blank eyes avoiding hers)* Shame, Sarah. My dad died of shame.
> SARAH: *(Sharply)* What did my mam die of then?
> JUD: Grief. Grief killed your mother, Sarah.
> SARAH: Who caused it then? Say who caused it.
> JUD: *(Hopelessly)* Let me be. It's work tomorrow. Let me be.
> SARAH: *(Relents)* Who do you love then? *(Silence)* Say who you love then. *(Silence)* Say who you love.
> JUD: *(Turns head away from her)* You, Sarah. Only you.
> SARAH: Go on.
> JUD: *(By rote)* You're that bonny, our Sarah. *(Slowly moves backward left away from her)* I mun have you. *(Turns suddenly and escapes quickly)*

Although I have said that it was not my intention to make Miss Rogers a well-rounded character, she brings a needed

breath of goodness and kindness to the play. She is not there
just as an Aunt Sally to be knocked down. Her involvement
with Jud is a natural result of that innocent goodness,
however short-lived it may be, which often follows a sheltered
upbringing. The contrast between Miss Rogers and Sarah is
great. The north is like a foreign country to Miss Rogers. "But
what are foreign countries for if not to visit?" she asks her
diary. She is having a "working holiday" in a strange place.
Sarah's almost all-consuming bitterness sometimes falls away
and we see what she might have been. Her love for her dead
child, her family loyalty, her sense of duty, her strict personal
code of honour are pieces of a whole that was not allowed to
be. Just as Jud's generator, Flossie, is his substitute friend and
the shed is his escape, so the scrapbook of photographs and
newspaper clippings is Sarah's dead child. An attempt to get
the audience's sympathy for her is made in the second act . . .

> SARAH: *(. . . stands near lectern with the book still
> cradled in her arms. She rocks it gently as she speaks)*
> Hush then . . . Wilta not hush? *(Holds book in both hands
> away from her)* Was there ever such a bonny babby?
> *(Clasps book to her breast)* They'll not take thee away
> from me. *(Cradles book)* They'll not. . . They'll not.
> *(Gently rocks book)* Hush then.

And an attempt is made to attain a sad, lonely grandeur for
her near the end of the play . . .

> SARAH: *(Holds open book in both hands in front of her)*
> I bore this child with every hand and tongue against me.
> I bore this child in a place of green walls and uniforms. I
> were but fourteen, but I swore I'd keep my child. I were
> but fourteen and they had no mercy. It weren't for the
> want of asking. I went down on my knees in this very
> room. "Don't let them take me away, my mam. Don't let
> them take me away." But they came with their uniforms
> and their motor cars. *(Cradles book in her arms)* I've
> ne'er asked for mercy since. *(Gently rocks book)* Hush

then. Not even when they brought her home that night all wet and cold. They came with their uniforms and their motor cars then, too. They stood there waiting for me to break down, but I wouldn't give them that satisfaction. "Put her on the kitchen table," I said. "I'll wash her and put her a clean nightie on." "She'll have to go to the mortuary," they said. "She'll be washed there." "I'll wash her," I said. "I washed her when she came into this hell hole and I'll wash her now." Her were blue and that cold. It were all I could do to get the nightie on her. *(Rocks book in cradled arms)* Then they took her away and I ne'er saw her again.

The great Irish working-class novelist turned playwright, James Hanley, is the main influence behind *The Injured*. He has said, "The more insignificant a person is in this whirlpool of industrialized and civilized society, the more important he is to me." It may be, without my consciously seeking it, or even for a long time being aware of it, that this is becoming my standpoint also. I hope so, as it seems to be a good standpoint for a self-educated writer to take.

What then, are the threads that connect my plays? They vary in style and setting, but are for the most part conventional in form. The unities, by and large, are observed. The themes are usually important ones and my point of view colours them in varying degrees. Strong definition of character is always tried for and sometimes attained. A *leitmotif* is often used, sometimes in its true sense as a piece of music or a song, but it is more often verbal, a line or lines which are used in differing circumstances to heighten a scene or scenes. Detachment is sometimes tried for, but rarely achieved. My sympathies are always with the underdog.

As to how one becomes a writer, I don't know. I came to it, in common, I suppose, with most self-educated writers, through reading. One can become a doctor or a lawyer or an engineer by taking the required courses and passing the examinations. All the "creative writing" courses in the world cannot make a true writer. These courses, seized upon so avidly, perhaps as a form of therapy, by lapsed housewives and reformed schoolteachers and social workers, are part and parcel of the false assumption, so popular in North America, that education and culture are synonymous. They are not synonymous and it might do Canadian Theatre some good to be divorced from colleges and universities. At the very least a trial separation should be arranged.

I became a writer because it was the only avenue of expression open to me. I became a dramatist, if I really am one, because I almost always start a work with characters and theme, rather than with a plot. My characters are, for the most part, imagined characters. As they take shape, become fleshed out, they move within my mind's restrictive setting as in the confines of a stage. Also, as a beginning writer, a play seemed easier to tackle than a novel. That this is not so is a lesson I have learned the hard way. I was at one time sure that to be a writer must be a wondrous thing. It is an art that can be practiced into old age, an art that can keep the mind young. Now I am not so sure. A pile of blank paper on a desk can turn both mind and body sour, put a black edge around sun, moon and stars. A drama critic once wrote, after attending a public reading of one of my plays that had been rotting in my drawer for years, that I must have the patience of Job. I may have had some small part of Job's patience. I have never had his faith, so expect neither comforters nor rewards.

There must be a reason, or reasons, for my plays to have been ignored at a time when dramatists are being encouraged more than ever before. The main reason may be that the themes are bigger than the plays, that I have aimed too high. My reach may have exceeded my grasp by an ell or two. Well than, vivas to those who have aimed high and failed. And a black curse on those who uphold the status quo by writing to sell and for no other reason that I can see.

Chronology

1921	Born in Leigh, Lancashire, England, fourth child of Albert and Esther (Fenney) Grainger.
1925-35	Attended St. Joseph's Elementary School, Leigh.
1935	Began working life as scavenger in cotton-spinning mill.
1940-46	Served in Royal Air Force.
1946-56	Succession of ill-paid, dead-end jobs. Found a haven of sorts in a well-known publisher's basement warehouse. Read almost his entire list, which was very big, very catholic.
1956	Emigrated to Canada. More dead-end jobs, but the pay was better.
1957	Married Ann Pulver, January 9.
1960	"Not For Zenocrate Alone" published in *Prism*.
1964	*Daft Dream Adyin'*, winner of National Playwriting Seminar, London, Ontario. "The Action Tonight," winner of Canadian Playwriting Competition, Ottawa Little Theatre. Radio script, "Wouldn't It Frost You," broadcast by BBC London.
1965	"The Action Tonight" published in *Prism*. "The Kill" wins second prize, Canadian Playwriting Competition. "The Action Tonight" produced, Ottawa Little Theatre. Awarded fellowship, School of Drama, Yale University. Studied playwriting under John Gassner.
1966-70	Lived and worked in New York.
1970	Returned to Vancouver. *The Helper* awarded first prize in Playhouse Theatre Company's Centennial Playwriting Competition. "In Arizona the Air Is Clean" awarded third prize, same competition.
1970	"In Arizona the Air Is Clean" produced by CBC-TV, Montreal. Daughter, Helen Rachel, born June 9.
1972	*The Helper* produced by the New Play Centre, Vancouver.
1973	Several plays produced by CBC radio, Vancouver.
1974	"The Great Grunbaum" produced by the New Play Centre, Vancouver. *The Injured* wins first annual Lee Award.

1975   *The Injured* produced at the Studio Theatre, Edmonton. "Down There" produced at the Octagon Theatre, Bolton, England.

1976   "In Agony" produced at Metro Theatre, Vancouver. "Roundabout" produced by the New Play Centre, Vancouver.

1977   Wrote "The Exile." Full length play, "The Sounding," in progress.

Selected Bibliography

Primary Sources

"The Agreement."* TS, Vancouver, New Play Centre, 1973.

"The Action Tonight."* *Prism* (Winter, 1965).

Daft Dream Adyin'. In *Best Short Plays, 1969*, edited by Stanley Richards. New York: Chilton Book Co. Also New York and Toronto: Avon Books, 1970.

"Down There." TS, Vancouver, New Play Centre, 1975.

"The Exile." MS, Vancouver, 1977.

"The Great Grunbaum." TS, Vancouver, New Play Centre, 1974.

The Helper. * In *West Coast Plays*, edited by Connie Brissenden. Toronto: Fineglow Plays, and Vancouver: New Play Centre, 1975.

The Injured. * Toronto, Playwrights Co-op, 1976.

"The Kill."* Vancouver, New Play Centre, 1965.

"In Agony." Adaptation of Miroslav Krleza's *U Agoni ju*. MS, Vancouver, 1976.

"In Arizona the Air Is Clean."* Vancouver, New Play Centre, 1970.

"The Man From Wulfshausen."* Vancouver, New Play Centre, 1974.

"Not for Zenocrate Alone." *Prism*, (Fall, 1960).

"Roundabout "* Vancouver, New Play Centre, 1976.

"Slane."* Vancouver, New Play Centre, 1975.

"The Sounding." MS, Vancouver, 1977.

"Wouldn't It Frost You?" TS, BBC radio, London, England, 1964.

*Typescript reproduction is available from the New Play Centre, P.O. Box 8614, Vancouver, B.C. V7X 1A3, $3.00 postpaid.

Secondary Sources

ALLEN, BOB. "Krleza's Script Better Than the Production." *Province* (Vancouver), June 21, 1976.

———."Playwrights Get Their Chance." *Province* (Vancouver), April 26, 1974.

———."'Roundabout' Fascinating Despite Flaws." *Province* (Vancouver), September 13, 1976.

BALL, ALAN EGERTON. "Arrogant Eloquence in a Cut Rate Trade." *Georgia Straight*, September 16, 1976.

BARBER, JAMES. *"The Helper* Is Vital Theatre." *Province* (Vancouver), August 25, 1972.

CARSON, CATHERINE. "It All Began With A News Item." *The Edmonton Journal*, January 4, 1975.

———."Prize-winning Playwright Doesn't Like to Write." *The Edmonton Journal*, January 11, 1975.

CRIGHTON, TOM. "'Roundabout': Some Great Lines But Too Many False Bottoms." *Georgia Straight*, September 16, 1976.

DAFOE, CHRISTOPHER. "Du Maurier Festival: Play's the Thing." *Sun* (Vancouver), April 18, 1974.

———.*"The Helper* Finds Work After Long, Idle Period." *Sun* (Vancouver), August 25, 1972.

———."This Theatre-goer's Labour Rewarded." *Sun* (Vancouver), April 27th, 1974.

DEMERS, EDGAR. "Le Rideau se lève. . . ." *Le Droit* (Ottawa), May 2l, 1965.

EVANS-SMITH, EILEEN."Prize-winning Plays Well Worth Attending." *The Citizen* (Ottawa), May 21, 1965.

DUCIAUME, MARCEL. "Une Contribution importante à la dramaturgy canadienne." *Le Franco Albertain*, January 15, 1975.

"Grainger Grabs Two Play Prizes." *Sun* (Vancouver), December 19, 1970.

HEALD, JOSEPH. "New Plays at Vancouver East Cultural Centre." Toronto *Motion* (July/August, 1974).

JONES, BERYL. "Tom Adds the Timely Touch." *Manchester Evening News* (England), September 8, 1975.

MULLALY, EDWARD. "West Coast Playwrights." *The Fiddlehead*, No. 106 (1975), pp. 38-40.

RICHARDS, JACK. "Prophet Or Not, Grainger Finds Profit in Writing." *Sun* (Vancouver), July 17, 1964.

SALDMAN, LARRY. "The Injured." Edmonton *Poundmaker*, January 21, 1975.

SHIELDS, ROY. "Canadian Workers Lucky-Playwright." *Province* (Vancouver), September 22, 1976. (Later printed elsewhere in Canada via Southam News Service.)

SHORTER, ERIC. "A Gripping Tribute to the Miner." *Daily Telegraph* (London, England), September 10, 1975.

"Studio Theatre World Premiere . . . *The Injured.*" *Edmonton Gateway* (University of Alberta), January 16, 1975.

"Three One-act Plays Have Première at OLT." *Journal* (Ottawa), May 21, 1965.

THORNBER, ROBIN. "Down There at the Octagon." *The Guardian* (London, England), September 10, 1975.

W., N. "Bolten Down There." *The Stage* (London, England), September 25, 1975.

WOOLNER, DAVE. "Powerful Drama But a Worn Theme." *The Edmonton Journal*, January 10, 1975.

WYMAN, MAX. "Metro's 'In Agony' Exposes a Major Yugoslav Playwright." *Sun* (Vancouver), June 21, 1976.

———. "Pain and Pleasure." *Sun* (Vancouver), September 10, 1976.

———. "This Vivid Gallery of Grotesques Does Their Author Proud." *Sun* (Vancouver), September 11, 1976.

Six

JAMES REANEY
(1926-   )

Preface

James Reaney is a major Canadian poet turned playwright who has introduced a new kind of theatre into Canada. His complex symbolic and poetic regional drama defies categorizing. Folk play is not comprehensive enough and poetic drama is too narrow a term. As Herman Voaden had to introduce the new term Symphonic Expressionism to describe his contribution to Canadian theatre, so James Reaney will have to provide the critics with a term to denote that fine mixture of symbol, metaphor, chant, poetic incantation, choral speaking, improvisation, miming, and child play which combined in one perfect union is the Reaney play.

The recipient of two Governor-General's awards for books of outstanding poetry (1949, 1958), and well on the way to a solid career as a major Canadian poet, Reaney turned suddenly to drama in 1960 and his third Governor-General's award was for The Killdeer and Other Plays *(1962). He had found his true métier. Today his position as dramatist overshadows that of poet, or like Yeats, whom he admires, Reaney has become the poet/playwright par excellence.*

Reaney was one of the first in that new stream of Canadian playwrights who opted to write solely for the stage when the 1960s provided them with small theatres across Canada dedicated to the production of Canadian drama. He was one of the fortunate inheritors of that long struggle waged by the older stream of radio dramatists, such as John Coulter, who pleaded for theatres to produce, and Canadians to write, an indigenous Canadian drama. The Shakespearean theatre at Stratford, Ontario, was only a bicycle ride from his home.

Here the young James Reaney first experienced highly professional theatre.

It is only natural that Reaney, the poet, should bring to his conception of a play all those poetic gifts that eventually made his plays an oral and visual artistic experience. They are dependent on the music of the spoken word, the imaginative and spiritual response to atmosphere, mood, tone, theme. Such plays as Listen to the Wind and Colours in the Dark are rare and memorable experiences.

Reaney uses many small children as well as adults in his plays and he requires a workshop for his actors before the production in order to engage the entire cast in the play impulse, which comes naturally to children but is foreign to adults. Reaney depends on the concept that we are all "children of an older growth" and his audiences have fully responded to this expectation.

During the summers of 1973-75 he conducted three such workshops in Halifax as preparation for the Toronto productions of The Donnelly Trilogy. From these workshops Reaney himself learned what needed pruning or further interpretation for future audiences. He is convinced that his type of play is not meant for long-term production but rather for the circuit, touring from one city to another. With the NDWT Theatre Company, Reaney took the cast of The Donnelly Trilogy across Canada from Halifax to the West in 1976, playing to numerous audiences, who were highly receptive to his work in all the major cities and many small towns.

An assessment of Reaney's plays was made by his son, James Stewart Reaney, in his book about his father's drama James Reaney. He says that all his father's plays really ". . . compose one big play that Reaney keeps writing." His characters, whose names bespeak their essence, belong to either the forces of light or the forces of darkness. They live in a small country town of Perth County, Ontario, similar to Reaney's birthplace. The focus of his drama is the family: the Almedas, McTavishes, Caresfoots, Dells, Donegans, Donnellys, Fays, Farls, Henrys, Kingbirds, Lorimers, Taylors, Thompsons — these people his plays. The adults and children of these families must confront good and evil, and it is the conflict arising from these two forces which provides the tension. Or rather it is the conflict within the minds and hearts of those who straddle the fence, unable to make a decision between the two forces, as James Stewart Reaney has so well perceived in his criticism of the plays. Their agonies of doubt and fear in the confrontation are central to the Reaney drama.

The fact that their conflicts are caused by petty concerns shocks the audience into a realization that Reaney is indeed dealing with the realities of life cloaked under the guise of fantasy, folk drama, regionalism and romanticism. The audience is shaken out of its reverie as it is forced to consider the deeper issues of actual day-to-day living.

The theme of childhood and growth to maturity within the family is a constant with this playwright: the symbolic quest as the children search for truth and end in reconciliation with the adult world. The innocent child is the hope of the future. Hope is a staple of the Reaney play. Although The Donnelly Trilogy, a true story of a nineteenth century feud between two Ontario families, ends in wholesale murder by the Whiteboys, there is a powerful dramatic climax at the end when the audience realizes that, despite the attempt to destroy them, the Donnellys will continue to people the earth.

Reaney's theatre is essentially "play." He is artistically aware that the play impulse is really at the heart of the adult response to life. Throughout his plays one single theme echos and re-echoes in a kind of subtle reverbation—the child's movement from innocence to maturity as symbolic of hope for a fallen world. Now in his early fifties, Reaney has succeeded in developing his theatre into a new kind of genre, rich in its implications for the future. It is this kind of original, experimental work which will give Canada a name and a place in the history of world drama.

Why did I begin to write drama? I don't think that I can give this a very true answer since it could be anything from a neurotic compulsion to bore my community, to a healthy desire to do something that my town could focus on, to things hidden deep in childhood like toys, cardboard cut-out theatres in popcorn boxes and Christmas stockings and so on. I wrote my first play for my high school; they had a tradition of producing plays. A teacher of mine wrote a play which the school produced; the acting of plays (despite the movies and the radio) was still something everyone was involved in. So if you want impetus, then I suggest in the end you have to find out what Southwestern Ontario was like in the first half of the century.

Good plays, which I deeply envy, are the beautiful structures of our heritage—*Pericles* with its wonderful leaping back and forth in reality; years erased by just a word from the bearded old storyteller; *Punch and Judy* with its demonic amoral sudden killings; those Greek plays constructed like jewel weed pods—sooner or later the magic and horrible button will be touched (Polyneices will choose the gate his brother Eteocles is defending) and the tears and blood and screams will pop out. Good plays dance with the audience: make each person use parts of his soul he hasn't been using for some time and make him use various parts of his soul in succession during the evening.

I've been influenced by many playwrights but we'll have to expand the definition of playwright because Walt Disney (or Ub Iwerks) is the artist who most dominated the dramatic side of my imaginative development. I wish there were a proper book that went into the ins and outs of the Disney canon; one scene change I'm rather fond of is the moment when the dwarfs finally go to sleep—last shot of Sneezy's nose with Bluebottle snoring too; shot of moonlit exterior of cottage and then—we're at the Queen's Castle for the transformation sequence. That sort of cheek-by-jowl switch always struck me as being what drama was all about.

What playwrights? Well all the ones involved with any play I've ever seen. Let's take a representative sample though. Start with Thornton Wilder, *Our Town*—revolutionary because after all the modern craze for spectacle and opsis derived from movies, here's a play that does it all with words. The No Set principle. *Skin of Our Teeth*, beautifully produced by Peter Dearing some years ago at the Grand Theatre here in London, Ontario, interested me with its putting everything in; at the end of the evening the cycle behind all the shifting scenes actually appeared—clouds (magic-latern projection) and visions of godlike figures *in a circle*. On the superb proscenium stage of this Ambrose Small theatre as one looked around at an enthralled audience—you felt this is the globe of life, this is the ultimate theatre.

The first years at Stratford Festival showed me the playwright in a more influential way than ever before; I can remember realizing that Cocteau is right when he says that theatrical metaphor is like lace; when the big reading image of Richard III came up—bluebottle, spider in a bottle, or whatever—it just whizzed by in a second, hardly noticed. On the page I used to linger over it. In the Alec Guiness-Tyrone Guthrie production, what one was thrilled by was the larger design around all the scores of metaphors—a malignant shape in the centre of a circle eventually and suddenly banished after bending the circle for a long time in whatever way it pleased.

The bare Stratford stage, of course, designed to create an emphasis on speech and actor that helped one think of new techniques; the fluidity of a bare stage in which this author emphatically does not need to worry about a box set being changed every ten minutes—that impressed. Also here's a writer who was allowed to (and *could*) use rhythm and as many words as he could get in a mouth. The general feeling I've met in our community is that this is all right for the past, but now—why, there are close-ups instead. Alas, one is not a filmmaker although that may be what people say the results of the above thinking may be; when one works with words it is a relief to be asked to use them. In a verismo play the set and the lighting quite frequently are doing what the words used to be able to do, and I object to my soul being squeezed through a fuse box. So Shakespeare, I salute. Naturally, although you can't, one dreams of going back to that world.

Imagine being able to write for a living; there's this busy town by a river and it's got several silo-like buildings where people have got used to going to see plays written in verse. The audience loves to hear people talk and talk well in rhythm with lots of imagery. Not only that, but this audience has staying power; a whole afternoon, not just the thin shank of the evening before the baby sitter has to go home and the buses start going slower. Furthermore, they have quick ears and the actors can go quite fast if they like. What a world in which a verbal invention such as blank verse is a profitable and sought after as now a technological device such as 3-D or Technicolor and is a magnet for audiences. As I see Peele's *Old Wives' Tale*, or the cliff scene in *Lear* or Ariel and Caliban, I envy them their world where they could get away with it; today, there'd be Jack Shenk in New York and Sam Goldwyn in Hollywood asking what it all means.

Admittedly there were evidently some things you couldn't get away with even in such a culturally healthy spot as seventeenth-century London; *Coriolanus* and *Troilus and Cressida* are supposed to have met audience resistance. Some years back I can remember seeing them at Stratford and having a good work-out feeling in my ears; the slightly more difficult texture in both plays (probably because not so much done on this side of the Atlantic) abrades the mind very pleasantly. I like very much the idea that *Twelfth Night* is all built up around the clown with his drum; in thinking about all the plays together you sometimes see the company who must have played them, each actor with some twenty magnificent roles attached to him and of these giant figures, Eternal Actors—the clown with his drum and the beardless page (Moth, Ophelia, Miranda)—are part of one's mental equipment for life.

I can't stress enough the division there used to be in Canada between reading the Shakespeare canon and seeing it. In childhood I don't think it really matters if the only production you can get to of *A Winter's Tale* is the local Normal School; but later on it does. Time after time I used to suffer the anguish of seeing a *Merchant* (summer stock, Royal Alexandra, 1944) or a *Macbeth* (same place with, yes, Redgrave and Flora Robson) which never caught up to Shakespeare; in some ways the grotesque student and staff productions at small provincial colleges are better because their alienation effects, unconsciously, are so complete. I can remember a *Hamlet* at the Agricultural College Auditorium in Manitoba which, despite only two or three good actors, nevertheless got the play in a way the Stratford Festival never has. However it happens, quite often primitive productions force the audience to work out richness in the way that a "properly" designed and "competently" acted version miserably does not.

There is director fault here, of course; quite often one suspects that the subliminal shape of the great plays has not been made out; we are coasting on personality, production values, free association with actors freely admitting they can make up Shakespearese at will. (I'm still in shock from one of the actors in Wolfit's company here in 1947 confessing that when he fluffed he simply raved on in pentameters.) Slowly you get tourist drama: huge costumes, glittering thises and thats—I'm thinking of the Stratford *Cymbeline* wherein the two Tarzan sons have this moment where they speak chorally—and as a texture moment it was phtt! Whereas the Eagle epiphany of Jove, or whatever, had silver in it that took many hours of beating; no time for speech, but all the money in the world for metal. This may explain why I fell asleep in a Richard Burton *Henry V* years ago but stayed bolt upright during a Gielgud *Winter's Tale*. And so the great monuments of our culture are best performed by marionettes; yes, at Brescia College here in the sixties Sister Corona Sharpe with hand puppets did a *Twelfth Night* that swept you right into the magic—and all because the puppet convention simplifies so ruthlessly that you have to get in there and create yourself; partly it was the nun actors too; the cross-casting involved in having a Sister Angelica play Sir Toby Belch can be very charming, particularly if the sister in question can read poetry. I felt I was back at the Globe. Read Arnott's *Plays Without People* for the full gen on this concept; it's a hard idea to sell—what, rag marionettes almost unarticulated are far more moving in Oedipus than live actors balletically whirling? Yes. And I scorn the audience that in puppet plays wants them to be smooth and have five manipulators round one puppet ballerina—why not get a real ballerina?

In the repertoire of this time moments from *Epicoene* (Pamela Terry, Toronto, 1958) and the whole worlds of *Volpone* and *Alchemist* keep saying things to me; *Volpone* (Hirsch, Winnipeg, 1956) had some remarkable Venetian beggars, one of whom had pulled every other tooth, so devoted was she to the director's interpretation, and Victor Cowie's Ignaro—people as animals, the Aesop effect, a whole way of seeing our city lives. The morbid authors of *Duchess* and *Revenger's Tragedy*, of course, are favourites because of the horror; they seem to be made out of insights from *Hamlet*. But any play with a false hand, or someone attacking their shadow (Roland Hewgill, Stratford, 1972), or beating in his mistress' skull or saying "Tis but Annabella's heart" (holding same in palm of hand) gets my money. Also favourites in this period are *Comus* and *Samson Agonistes*. The latter (Marion Woodman, student production, Middlesex College, 1964) is very theatrical and should be done at Stratford; what one loves is the way it moves, slowly but majestically, and with spellbinding words *all* the way. Having supervised several public readings of *Paradise Lost* and felt the power of his words slowly but surely break down the old idea that your attention span should only last three hours (it can last twelve hours quite easily if you just flex a few mental tendons), I hope somebody does a play version, just as Blake's *Jerusalem* and *Beowulf* (also directed or assisted at readings here) have a dramatic shape which some director-author should try someday.

When reading *Prometheus Bound* in 1952 and just on the verge of really going at all the classical repertory, the first interesting thing that struck me was the so-called static quality. Henry James gives one the cue here: if it *means* something just sitting in a chair can be far more gripping than any number of "exciting gallops" in Westerns. It's odd, but I've never yet heard anyone say that they thought that

Prometheus Bound was slow; and it is to despise the audiences that want stimulation and "speed" that the Greek drama teaches one.

Vaguely behind what I've been saying so far (Thornton Wilder at the Grand, remember?) there has been the concept of theatre as a wheel of life. When I learned from critics both ancient and local that tragedies were constructed around turning points and recognitions, I realized that watching a tragedy was like seeing this wheel slowly make an unusual but usual turn—rather like cat's cradles that gradually turn inside out. The more delicated and finessed the turn, the better. In *Oedipus at Colonus* that is just—will the brothers get the old man or won't they. He "dies." They don't. Will Ajax be able to resist Odysseus' cunning, big heavy boy against a whip-mind? No. In Aeschylus' *Supplices* one is close to the Zen idea of if it's boring try it for an hour and you'll find out it's no longer boring.

I'm fascinated by plays that are so slow, there's no point in calling them slow. After seeing failures at chorus acting in productions of Eliot, it was fun to see Guthrie bring off the chorus in *Oedipus* — ballet and motion added, and the infinite possibilities behind really doing the intricate imagery in the Antigone choruses using Carl Orf techniques are part of daydreams. How wonderful it is to have twenty or so good voices really building up a vision; how can Neil Simon resist? Plays like the *Alkestis* or the *Ion* seem so fresh and witty still; you not only have a small boy scurrying across a temple yard somewhat afraid of birds dropping on him, but also a god, and the effect is of low mimetic strangely bulged out with myth, like teacups that are also turning into grails. In the Eliot doubles of these plays I remember being very taken with the picture of Mrs. Caughan saying to Denholm Elliott, "What would you like to know?" implying that if he can ask a good question, he'll get a good answer. In *The Cocktail Party* it is the libation scene that attracts me; Trinity College gave me this, but in Manitoba the libation scene was mysteriously cut.

While we are at modern adaptations I might as well mention the birthday cake in *Family Reunion* (Bob Gill, Hart House) and the language surrounding it; curiously, this language reappears in Agatha Christie's *Witness for the Prosecution*. It's as in the Ivy Compton-Burnett novels—as if you heard old language talking to itself, quite uninterested in sounding like human beings.

Old Comedy is a rich mine of ideas that look new if you steal them straightforwardly enough; I like direct address by the author to the audience (parabasis), the ghost of the marriage ceremony at the end, food thrown to the audience, rather like the Christmas Concert where Santa Claus appears at the end with food. I once saw a wonderfully funny *Ecclesiazusae* at Edmonton (Alberta, Gordon Peacock) in a Niessen Hut on the same bill as Maeterlinck slow mime and a radio play about an Alberta tall character turned into a folk play: "You'll get pancakes for supper if you get home past all those wolves, Bill."

Winter against Summer seems to me the ultimate in what life is always about; the exuberant grotesquerie seems to be held interestingly together with what one suspects is not such a simple device. Since I've done a marionette version of Plautus' *Manaechmi* I've always liked New Comedy's smooth formulae; we're back to the basic theatre family of actors again with the locket or birthmark as the catch that will make them turn inside out and back again. I wish more Satyr plays had survived because the one that has helps explain the New York porno plays (Viveca Lindfors taking some man's pants off!)—I note that one brochure for a glossy college text on Western Drama goes through the greats from Aeschylus to Calderon to O'Neill to a play called *Toilet*. Good. We've reached the end of the tradition and now we can start over again with plays about gods who are fighting demons and satyrs with no ambiguity about it, as in Christ the Centaur and the Dragon (favourite mediaeval carving in Irish church somewhere).

What other plays have I seen? Well, a production of *Secunda Pastorum* where a real lamb at the end gave the Virgin Mary quite a battle; Frances Hyland in *She Stoops to Conquer* (where has Richard Easton gone to?) at the Old Crest Theatre—dazzling. Doug Rain standing on his head on a chair. Pamela Terry's *Waiting for Godot*—a Toronto first and the startling sound of something new—the making of nothing into something, dullness and repetition becoming magnetic.

Now one should really talk about opera—Wagner, Mozart and films. Not only has the musician got words going for him, he's got music and in Wagner this means that the kind of chorus I've been praising for its richness and density can now be carried on with motifs that slip into the viewer's psyche with somewhat more ease than even words do. The same effect in films comes about through the addition to the verbal scenario (mythos of the almost too bewildering subliminal visual wash of effects and symbols and power dives of a camera-eye. It is interesting to me how *much* through working at-a-play-the-way-children-would-play-it-as-if-it-were-a-big-game you can steal some of the power that musical and visual forms do have.

Why not make films, or at least have a try at them? Just at the moment I can see in plays a really wonderful chance that doesn't occur, I think, with films. With a play you've eventually produced a script which stays put, never changes and is a constant ideal—to be slaughtered, finally produced properly, perhaps become a vehicle that is played over a whole continent in ways one never dreamed of. But the ideal production never occurs; it's still there, mysteriously present and not present in your finished script. With the film, the mechanical process freezes your script or your metaphors into a form that remains *so* for ever. Performance simply involves getting a good print and threading it through the projector. With the drama script there's always a great deal more adventure to what will happen to it this year, and as I make contact with young directors and actors I realize that in ten years time there may come along somebody for whom a certain slant of style in character or in mythos really, really clicks.

To talk about the influence of films (Frye calls them spectacular masques, and they are glittering, expensive, photographed *shows*) would be endless; Jean Simmons in Lean's *Great Expectations*; the opening stage sequence in *Tale of Two Cities* (Ronald Coleman); the spatial flashback in *Tets* (not Bergman, but he wrote the script for it); all the stringers and bars and nets through which things are seen in *Lola Montez*; the kids' hands in *Odd Man Out*; the chalking up of the address in *Picture of Dorian Gray*; the first big close-up of Vivien Leigh in *Gone with the Wind*; the plot of the *Seven Samurai*, very much like the very satisfying plot of Bunyan's *Holy War*, the siege of Mansoul sort of thing; the flowerpot in *The Lady Vanishes* (unknown person's hand shoves it onto Margaret Lockwood's head); the end of that movie where the old lady plays the piano, but what she plays is the secret message that had to be got through; Cukor's *David Copperfield* with its big sea image when you first meet Emily; Garbo at the end of *Christina* just looking at you; the coach scene in *Uncle Silas* (Jean Simmons again) and the same lady in *The Clouded Yellow* where that demonic uncle is after her with a meat hook on top of the warehouse.

One could go on quoting film moments that have become part of one's life forever; they get at your dream life in a way no other artform save music quite does; and of the cinemas I've known—the Majestic in Stratford, also the Classic (*Gulliver's Travels*, and *Mr. Bug Goes to Town* which latter I unfortunately missed though I drank in the stills); all the Odeons, the Victoria in London, Ontario, and the Shea's Hippodrome in Toronto (what was that place at Charles and Yonge street called that showed the Danish animated version of "The Tinderbox?")—all great temples where, in their prime, in religious darkness, one drank in silver visions that engraved themselves more deeply when they were not in colour. To close—I always feel that the cannons at the end of *Mother Courage* are never loud enough and that one Broadway production I'd like very much to have seen would have been the adaptation some lady made of Major John Richardson's *Wacousta*. About 1845?—I'd like to have gone with him and that big Newfoundland dog he had; also when it toured, I'd rather like to have seen what the play looked like at the Covent Garden Theatre here in London, Ontario, where Major Richardson's cousins would have had a chance to go. This is the possible beginning of a native theatre right here where I live now.

I like symbolism, so when a green light comes down on a

Glass Menagerie I'm suitably thrilled; all those Tennessee Williams titles get to me, although I tend to drop out after the *Milk Train* one, but a picture of a streetcar in New Orleans named Desire can still send shivers up and down my back. I'm not a fan of verismo drama; the more inner melodrama—symbolic distortion of so-called reality—the better. I like the way things happen in Grimm's Fairy Tales—and when this happens in drama, so much the better. For example, there's a magic top in Chekov's *Three Sisters*—great, or the blue light? In Peele's *Old Wives' Tale*. Incidentally, what a let-down Arnold Bennett's *Old Wives' Tale* is when you've read the great original (nay, seen it in a David Blostein production at Huron College). Can you imagine Elizabethans sitting through a reading of all that description of furniture?

One obstacle in the creation of plays today is the mixed-up state of the world; the society one writes about tends to be one seen at an early age. People keep saying mindlessly. "But we don't live like that any more." So that one is almost embarrassed to write about Stratford, Ontario, circa 1929; it seems archaic. Not quite archaic enough, perhaps. But not an in-period nor an in-place. You are continually facing a barrage of nostalgia-accusations from boobs who don't seem to have read Proust and never walked *Du côté du chez*—a gas station, let alone a house in a landscape with a century of plowing behind its surroundings.

Let's go over the miserable plays and list obstacles: *Sun and Moon*—abortionists have become very popular; farmers on the side of fertility don't go down well; people don't believe a community could be that naive. Actors with Souwesto [southwestern Ontario] accents and feel are extremely rare; in a Montreal production of *Night Blooming Cereus* the one singer from Brantford (and he alone) knew the world I was trying to get at. *Killdeer:* accusations of melodrama—why is she rolling on the floor? The opening up of reality intended by the progressively madder and madder plot twists alienate audiences. *One Man Masque:* what do you mean that after the world of life there is a world of death? I was taught that you went straight to—you know where, or I wasn't taught anything about what happens to me after death; I dissolve back into Nature, don't I? *Easter Egg:* the return of Kenneth to sanity has to be done by some genius of an actor or by some rank amateur; the part has no in-between possibilities. *Listen to the Wind:* but it's a melodrama, isn't it? No, it's a child's view of a melodrama; the melodrama becomes a symbol of the world he lives in. Oh? Say that again? *Ignoramus:* kids wouldn't be interested in education. *Apple Butter*: but Paul Smith's kids who are with me are orphans, don't you know, and now you've given them traumas. Too violent. *Donnellys; Sticks and Stones:* too gimmicky—too many sticks and, stones; too rich; I could only stand one act and then left.

In the Donnelly plays there has been a big problem with the creation of a language for the actors that isn't Irish dialect and isn't the way we talk now; I've been told that Mrs. Donnelly should say begorra more. All these examples show problems I couldn't begin to say I've solved. Perhaps the biggest problem is me; why did I start doing all this? Plays demand co-operation from a community of the most eager and energetic sort; not until I started going down to the Listeners' Workshops at Halifax nor till these got started here at home did I feel this necessary community; but the demands on sticking power are enormous. One of the things that amuses me is the lack of money for a tradition like this; but the way money pours forth in its dollops for some quite dreadful adaptation at a so-called professional theatre in which the amount of listening to words has gone down to the level of a harlot's curse! Let me close this section by saying that most of the obstacles have not been overcome; but there has been an interesting shift in audience participation lately—an acceptance of longer plays, for example.

I think you must love something or somebody very much if you are to create a play. This as in embryology grows into something, usually a design which expands unconsciously into words in a script, gestures by actors, orders of movement that repeat themselves in meaningful ways. You can take a play from the commission—write me a play that uses colours and slides—or you can take a play from something that comes deeply from the past inside oneself. The shaping can involve knowing what actors are going to be in it; you write for them. I think the main idea here is that you hear the heartbeat and you try to give it head, guts, and limbs.

Take *Sticks and Stones*: there is a big slice of local history. There is a notorious family whose deeds and characters practically glow in the dark. You are told one version of their fate when you're a child: they were horrible, their shanty had no doors because squatters have no doors, don't you know; they cut out the tongues of horses; they were barn burners and it was only justice that a mob should lynch them one night; fill in with suitable and horrid details—also add that the priest must have had quite a confessional the next week and so on. All this comes to one free for living in Souwesto; I imagine that in Kentucky or Colorado or Georgia there are similar stories. I've even heard of famous criminal families putting their story on the stage to defray legal expenses (somewhere in the train-robbing country in Kansas?). Well.

Then you meet a local minister who writes a book counter to the grisly version which by now has become enshrined in a penny dreadful called *The Black Donnellys*. According to the local minister the family were not quite so black; in fact, according to him they're almost innocent; not quite, but they had a door anyhow, were the subjects of a great deal of slander and lies and we tend to see them through their enemies' eyes. Aha, a double point of view! A mystery! One starts doing one's own research; their priest's nephew tells a version in which the Donnellys are handsome and aristocratic; a farmwife says that people who knew Mrs. Donnelly say she was coarse; an old lady remembers her as an evil giantess. The Now it's this way and Now it's that way—never stops.

What emerges from all this is a saga-like play structure in which you simply can't get through everything in one evening. It's a vortex; structural devices such as the Mass, the catechism, the newspaper fall in and are devoured by acid; the Donnelly family become something they could never have possibly been to those who knew them (knew them!)—

magnets you could write about forever. In the case of this individual play there had to be an introduction to their difficulties with land — the territorial imperative — the father's fall (the murder or manslaughter of Farl) and their survival up until the first invitation by their community to get the hell out. That was all you could do in one evening. I can remember how images fell into place; for instance, the villain confesses through a wheel and is caught in a wheel at the end of the play.

On thinking over this very rich material it was decided that what could be fun to do was to look at a section of the story for a turning point (recognition): once this was discovered — Donnelly's refusal to leave Biddulph when his barn burns down — the rest followed mathematically. Behind one was, of course, a vast play that tried to do everything, just as tellers of the story tell you everything, but of course give you only the impression that there were some insects once who got squashed; any contact with the material at all leads one to detect monstrous lying, dignity, evil, brilliance, entrapment, pride, in short a tragic situation of great mystery and depth. Seven sons — my God! some of them good, some of them bad? All of them bad? All of them — what? So the individual play here was conceived in desperation as just a start; there were predictable howls from those who saw their favourite Gothic novel laughed at; don't make them into saints, was one cry. I wonder how they saw themselves, I reply — as devils?

Probably my parents have a lot to do with interest in drama. When you see that your own family is interested this certainly spurs one on. I think the muse of drama must be a pretty tough old bird by now, so I won't bring her on the scene. When a play really works, the effect on an audience (the poetry hitting them directly, the laughs in the right place, the silences filled with tension, the feeling of group pleasure and articulation) is irresistible; you just have to do this again.

I write about the family with side glances at society and history. My favourite answer at these hot-seat sessions theatres in this country seem fond of having after the first run-through (the preview audience) is that I'm just interested in telling a story. I don't write about anything (dianoia); I just tell stories (mythoi). For purposes of examination I could riffle through the plays and come up with something like family problems; the ones in the Rider Haggard story in *Listen to the Wind* are beyond the call of duty—what a family problem was there! All you're really saying is the plays are about stories. Just vaguely *Three Desks* might be about intellectual working conditions; but to me at the time it was the three desks and the way they got moved about that appealed to me.

Whatever the style is called that blasts the box-set-with-lighting concept apart is the style for me. After watching producers struggle so disastrously with the change of set that divides the central act of *Killdeer* I determined never again; so anti-illusionist from now on in. Also when one counts up the cast of the *St. Nicholas Hotel* and discovers that there are eighty people involved, the answer becomes apparent: multiple casting, *play* theatre, where the actors can be anything and everyone. Once you have actors chanting things it seems to me that this music and sound pattern leads to a production where there are no holds barred. My ideal is an Eskimo solstice celebration I once read about in which in one big underground igloo the whole community gathered and put on their annual us-against-winter play; masks, chanting women all sitting on a bench, but swaying and miming; men being crows, animal marionettes entering by invisible means, and total audience enjoyment. That's a style I'd like to reach up to.

I would describe my plays as quirky, odd, weird, unsuccessful, successful, mixtures of sad and humorous, odd contraptions. The characters I like best are the evil ones, although I certainly wouldn't want to live with any of them for very long. But although Madam Fay is my choice for likes and Bethel is very amusing to me, in the end it's the marionette character Apple Butter that is my favourite. After all, I made that marionette and he's beyond dislike or like. He and Rawbone are the ultimate in what you'd like a friend to be. Reasons for preferring evil characters are the usual: they look more interesting, just as people say that Hell looks more fun than Heaven. It depends who's drawing it, of course; in Bosch, the Eden certainly has as much weird stuff going on as the Hell. Maybe I'll come up with some new concept of goodness.

I dislike characters who somehow give unexpected difficulty to director and actor; I said, unexpected. I'm not fond of the Executioner in *One Man Masque* and the Hangman in *Killdeer* and the good students in *Ignoramus*— well, Beatrice is fun, but the others are part of the vexing problem of how you get across culture without being prep school and bluestocking.

I'm interested in Keith Turnbull's idea of a theatre company devoted to poetic drama—the word as opposed to self-expression, playing willpower games with each other. If I told you my dearest wishes I feel that then the sap might somehow go out of them, but I would like to do a play about Americans in a Canadian setting; I would also like people to commission plays about themes; I'd like to be given a free hand in a TV studio. I'd like to do a movie. I keep seeing things they could do in both media and I keep getting no satisfactory answer to my questions of "Why not?" But I'm also quite content, when I think of the rampant mechanization of TV and movie, to stay in the side street of drama with its minority audiences; over the years I'm convinced you do get a large audience, but they've all had a chance to choose whether they wanted to come to you or not. One film fact in our town that has interested me has been a couple of movies made by Greg Curnoe using an old camera that only does 16 to the second instead of 24! You immediately and simply get a style problem solved. You could do *Listen to the Wind* as a movie within a movie; the inner story could be on some old camera that eventually changed into Bergman's camera at Svenskfilm studios.

Occasionally, as one summer at Halifax when the children's workshop in the morning and the adult workshop in the afternoon had gone particularly well, I could see the sort of theatre complex I'd like to belong to: it reaches into the community through a regular weekly, in the summer—daily, exercise for the imagination for anyone, young or old who can get there; out of these groups comes the audience and the actors for the plays. I think the sometimes reviled Creative

Drama can be part of this sweep into the community that a regional theatre should take. There have to be ideas and leaders; you could have a culture much more sensitive to the spoken word and to metaphor than is the case right now. When I see Romper Room on TV I clench my teeth; from experience I know you can do more with kids than that.

I would like to see Canadian colonialism finally disappear. I was recently at some drama confrontation at the Poor Alex and a poor girl staggered up and informed Mr. Phillips, the new director at Stratford, that out of 200 odd shows there, only one had been designed by a native. If only there'd be a bit more push all down the line by the community: everything is latent. After being scoffed at in the sixties for nationalism and writing plays at all, it is almost bewildering to see the influx of new plays and national seasons. Such organizations as Tarragon and Playwrights Co-op and the rest of the theatre movement in Toronto (Dupont Street, Holy Trinity and Duke Street) have finally got writers and ideas moving. More intensity? Yes, no one can make enough demands on their talent.

Not long ago I remember seeing some young filmmakers whom the Ontario Art Gallery had sent out; their animated films — done with magic marker, it seemed — were appealingly rough and primitive. Jim Anderson is the name I remember; the same day there were Eskimo films of the same quality on TV. After the slick slick slickness of the efforts at the local cinema, one longs for just rough poems. Maybe Canadians could dominate the Home Movie; what worries me about Canuck films is the sad attempt to get that polish, or the modish equivalent of it (Warhol!) into our hick projectors. We could try something else; maybe the abrupt shifting of levels you get in Atwood poems and novels. Why doesn't Kroiter make a feature and so on.

I think it's important to set down the names of the theatres where I have had a good theatrical experience; the Royal Alex — a great theatre where besides an early Amelia Hall *Merchant of Venice* there used to be many summer stock pure trash goodies, rarities such as Francis L. Sullivan in a play

about Charles Dickens that never made it to even New Haven
(*The Ivy Green*), a *Doll's House* where somebody in the
balcony shouted something at Claire Luce; a *Richard II* where
somebody shouted something at Claire Bloom; a Wolfit *Lear*
and so on. Hart House Theatre at The University of Toronto
where about ten plays still stay with me from the Bob Gill
period. Vaguely in the background of that theatre is a feeling
of the earlier Toronto of the twenties when the kind of culture
that the Victorian capitalist could underwrite must have
seemed the way ahead. That Toronto with its secondhand
bookstores all up and down Yonge Street has faded into a
quite different culture. The Dominion Theatre in Winnipeg
where Hirsch and Hendry first started their theatre; *Hatful of
Rain* had such a real set, they washed the floor of it in front of
your eyes. The Playhouse in the same city for Hirsch's
production of the *Enchanted* and *The Inspector-General*,
whatever happened to Peter Perrinchuk? I haven't quite been
able to get up fervour for some of those big new theatres west
of Winnipeg, but the Bastion in Victoria has the right
feel—oddly enough, what I remember in this theatre is not a
play, but a film of west coast bird life up and down the Pacific
Edge with the narration smoothly given by the film-maker
standing right there. Why aren't there more films with room
for a live narrator? It could be scored. The Théâtre de Gésu
in Montreal gave me Gélinas in *Tit-Coq* in its original run.
Even the way he tore up a letter and let the pieces of paper
cloud the air had style. Last of all, Stratford's Shakespeare
Theatre when it was in the tent and Guthrie was raging. You're
looking at the party scene in *All's Well That Ends Well* and the
actors sift back and forth in glamour. A mutter of thunder, the
top of the tent sighs and heaves. Circus. What a beautiful shift,
and it is a long way to bike home after the show in the dark
too. At the Avon Theatre (formerly the Majestic) Galt
McDermott's *My Fur Lady*—before he went in for fur alone.
Neighbours had kids as extras in the production and I can
remember them discussing how they would have directed the
Parliament sequence. I don't think I'd ever heard of such
aplomb.

Well, if you are going to ask questions of a playwright, I think the best place to close is to get him talking about actual theatres he's been in. If they've had any power over him, it just might be that what he is trying to do is help build a society where this fact keeps repeating itself over and over again until our whole nation loses its stiffness and becomes itself a sort of theatre. Not the sort of theatre it is now where Technology (descended from experiments with organ pipes and mechanical clocks and fountains, evidently) creates ever more horrifying and sinister spectacles; no, but a place where we ourselves, with just our bodies and the simplest of props (albeit in abundance) available to everyone, create a civilization where it finally seems true that to be wise is to know how to play.

Chronology

1926	Born in South Easthope, near Stratford, Ontario, son of James Nesbitt Reaney and Elizabeth Henrietta (Crerar) Reaney.
1932-39	Elementary education at the country schoolhouse, Elmhurst School, near home.
1939-44	High school education at Stratford Collegiate and Vocational Institute in Stratford, Ontario.
1944-48	Attended the University of Toronto, majoring in English Literature. First book of poetry and short stories published.
1949	Received his M.A. in English from the University of Toronto and won the Governor-General's award for poetry for his first volume, *The Red Heart*.
1951	Married Colleen Thibaudeau, poet and fellow student at the University of Toronto.
1950-60	Taught at the University of Manitoba.
1952	First child born, James Stewart.
1954	Second child born, John Andrew.

1956-58   Two-year sabbatical in which Reaney worked on his doctoral thesis, "The Influence of Spenser on Yeats," under the supervision of Northrop Frye. Received his Ph.D. in English from the University of Toronto and published his second book of poetry, *A Suit of Nettles*, for which he won his second Governor-General's award for poetry. Wrote "The Rules of Joy."

1959   Third child born, Susan Alice Elizabeth.

1960   Moved with his family to London, Ontario, where he became a member of the English Department at the University of Western Ontario. *The Killdeer*, *One-Man Masque*, and *Night-Blooming Cereus* produced in Toronto.

1962   Awarded his third Governor-General's award for the publication of *The Killdeer and Other Plays* and *Twelve Letters to a Small Town*. *The Easter Egg* premièred in Toronto and London, Ontario.

1963   *Names and Nicknames*, produced in Winnipeg.

1964-65   *The Sun and the Moon*, produced in London, Ontario. Three marionette plays, *Applebutter*, "Little Red-Riding Hood," and "Aladdin and the Magic Lamp," produced for the Western Fall Fair at London. Wrote "Let's Make a Carol" and "The Shivaree."

1966   Directed his own play, *Listen to the Wind*, in London, Ontario. Wrote "Ignoramus."

1967   *Colours in the Dark*, premièred at the Avon Theatre, Stratford Shakespearean Festival, Ontario. Developed the Listeners' Workshop in Alphacentre. *Geography Match* produced starring students from a neighbouring school. Wrote *Three Desks*.

1967-68   Moved with his family to Victoria, B.C., for a sabbatical year, during which time he began writing *The Donnelly Trilogy*. Also wrote "Don't Sell Mr. Aesop" and "Genesis."

1973   *Sticks and Stones*, the first part of *The Donnelly Trilogy*, produced at Tarragon Theatre, Toronto, after an intensive workshop for it in Halifax. Wrote "The Greek Alphabet."

1974 *St. Nicholas Hotel*, the second part of *The Donnelly Trilogy*, produced at Tarragon Theatre after Halifax Workshop. Received the Chalmers award for the Best Canadian Play of 1974.

1975 *Handcuffs*, the third part of *The Donnelly Trilogy*, produced at Tarragon after Halifax Workshop.

1976 Travelled with the NDWT theatre company across Canada presenting the entire *Donnelly Trilogy* on successive nights in theatres from Halifax to Vancouver. *Baldoon*, written in collaboration with Marty Gervais, produced with NDWT at Bathurst Street Theatre, directed by Keith Turnbull.

1977 NDWT Theatre Company toured Ontario with *Baldoon*. Première at the Hart House Theatre in Toronto of new play, "The Dismissal," produced by NDWT in co-operation with University College and directed by Keith Turnbull.

Selected Bibliography

Primary Sources

PLAYS

Applebutter and Other Plays for Children. (*Names and Nicknames, Ignoramus, Geography Match,*) Vancouver: Talonbooks, 1973.

Baldoon. (In collaboration with Marty Gervais). Erin: Press Porcépic, 1977.

Colours in the Dark. Vancouver: Talonbooks, 1969.

The Donnelly Trilogy. (*Sticks and Stones, St. Nicholas Hotel, Handcuffs*.) Erin: Press Porcépic, 1977.

The Killdeer. Toronto: New Press, 1972.

The Killdeer and Other Plays. (*The Sun and the Moon, One-Man Masque, Night-Blooming Cereus*.) Toronto: Macmillan Company of Canada Ltd., 1962.

Listen to the Wind. Vancouver: Talonbooks, 1972.

Masks of Childhood. (*The Easter Egg, The Killdeer, Three Desks*.) Toronto: New Press, 1972.

Selected Poems. Edited by Germaine Warkentin. Toronto: New Press, 1972. (Dramatic verse.)

ARTICLES, THESES, AND RELATED WORKS

Alphabet: A Semiannual Devoted to the Iconography of the Imagination. Vols. 1-20 (1960-71). (Edited by James Reaney.)

"Book Review of W. B. Yeats' *Explorations* and Joseph Hone's *W. B. Yeats 1865-1939.*" *Canadian Forum* 42, No. 504 (1963), pp. 235-36.

The Boy With an R in His Hand. Toronto: Macmillan of Canada, 1965.

"Cycle." *Canadian Drama/L'Art dramatique canadien* 2, No. 1 (1976), pp. 73-77.

"An Evening with Babble and Doodle: Presentations of Poetry." *Canadian Literature*, No. 12 (1962), pp. 37-43.

Halloween, Nos. 1,2,3 (1976) University of Western Ontario. (An occasional theatrical newsletter, edited by James Reaney.)

"The Influence of Spenser on Yeats." Ph.D. dissertation, University of Toronto, 1958.

"The Novels of Ivy Compton Burnett." Master's thesis, University of Toronto, 1949.

"The Plays at Stratford." *Canadian Forum* 33 (September, 1953), pp. 134-35.

"Ten Years at Play." *Canadian Literature*, No. 41 (1969) pp. 53-61.

Secondary Sources

BARR, MARY. "James Reaney and the Tradition of Poetic Drama," *Canadian Drama/L'Art dramatique canadien* 2, No. 1, (1976).

COHEN, NATHAN. "Mr. Reaney Writes a Play." *The Toronto Star*, January 14, 1960.

DUDEK, LOUIS. "A Problem of Meaning." *Canadian Literature*, No. 59 (1974), pp. 16-39.

GRAHAM, HUGH. "The Biddulph Feud." *The Canadian Theatre Review*, No. 8 (1975), pp. 88-89.

HUEBERT, RONALD. "James Reaney: Poet and Dramatist," *The Canadian Theatre Review*, No. 13 (1977), pp. 125-28.

LEE, ALVIN A. *James Reaney.* New York: Twayne Publishers Inc., 1969.

————."A Turn to the Stage: Reaney's Dramatic Verse." *Canadian Literature*, No. 15 (1963), pp. 40-51, and No. 16 (1963) pp. 43-51.

MACLEAN, GERALD M. "Sticks and Stones: The Donnellys Part One." *Canadian Drama/L'Art dramatique canadien* 2, No. 1 (1976), pp. 125-27.

MACPHERSON, JAY. "Listen to the Wind." *Canadian Forum*, 46, No. 548 (1966), pp. 136-37.

MILLER, MARY JANE. "Colours in the Dark." *Canadian Drama/L'Art dramatique canadien 2, No. 1 (1976), pp. 90-97.*

MOORE, MAVOR. *Four Canadian Playwrights: Robertson Davies, Gratien Gélinas, James Reaney, George Ryga.* Toronto: Holt, Rinehart and Winston of Canada Ltd., 1973.

————."This Play May Become Part of Our History." *The Telegram* (Toronto), January 27, 1960.

PARKER, BRIAN. "Reaney and the Mask of Childhood." In *Masks of Childhood.* Toronto: New Press, 1972.

REANEY, JAMES. *James Reaney.* Profiles in Canadian Drama Series. Toronto: Gage Publishing Ltd., 1977.

SOUCHOTTE, SANDRA. "Assessing the Donnellys." *The Canadian Theatre Review*, No. 7 (1975), pp. 131-35.

SCHNEIDER, JULIA. "Negative and Positive Elements in James Reaney's Plays." *Candian Drama/L'Art dramatique canadien 2, No. 1 (1976), pp. 98-114.*

TAIT, MICHAEL. "The Limits of Innocence: James Reaney's Theatre." *Canadian Literature*, No. 19 (1964), pp. 43-48.

————."Everything Is Something: James Reaney's *Colours in the Dark.*" In *Dramatists in Canada: Selected Essays*, edited by William H. New. Vancouver: University of British Columbia Press, 1972.

WARKENTIN, GERMAINE. "The Artist in Labour: James Reaney's Plays." *Journal of Canadian Fiction 2*, No. 1 (1973), pp. 88-91.

WATERS, ESTHER. "Crime and No Punishment." Canadian Literature, No. 49 (1971), pp. 55-60.

WILSON, MILTON. "On Reviewing Reaney." *Tamarack Review*, No. 26 (1963), pp. 71-78.

WOODMAN, ROSS G. *James Reaney.* Toronto: McClelland and Stewart Ltd., 1972.

ZIMMER, ELIZABETH. "Listen to the Wind." *The Fourth Estate* (Halifax), January 25, 1973.

Seven

JOHN HERBERT

(1926-   )

Preface

John Herbert has had a multi-faceted career as playwright, director, actor, set and costume designer, prop man, lighting, stage and house manager, critic, and university lecturer in drama. Intelligence, creativity, and an amazing fearlessness in the face of his critics, are among his many attributes.

In 1975, his most successful play, Fortune and Men's Eyes, won the Chalmers Award. Staged at the Phoenix Theatre and directed by Graham Harley, this was the first Toronto production, of a play that had achieved notable success off Broadway in 1967. John Herbert accepted this belated Canadian acknowledgement of his dramatic achievements with a mixture of humour and irony. This moment of triumph from Toronto's critics and public was hard won. So controversial is Herbert's work, and, in particular, this play, that it took the encouragement of the late Nathan Cohen, as well as an off-Broadway success, and a wait of eight years before a Toronto director would accept and produce it. By that time, it had been produced in many countries and translated into several languages.

Long a flaunter of tradition and conservatism, John Herbert has shrugged off the effects of prejudice and misunderstanding that usually accompany his work. At the 1975 "Face-to-Face" Drama Conference in Montreal, Herbert's intelligent and forthright comments were often met with anger and discourtesy. Nevertheless he continues to offer constructive criticism.

Why this unusual reaction to a Canadian playwright whose play, Fortune and Men's Eyes, has been received with such acclaim by the foremost New York critics? This is not an easy question to answer. His particular tragedy as a youth was rooted in a six-month prison sentence to Guelph Institute on charges that Herbert has deplored as unjust. In prison he was forced to pit his genius against his fellow prisoners' advances. Released from prison, he worked at a variety of jobs in places as far flung as Labrador and Winnipeg. He finally settled back in his own city of Toronto, a place for which he has a love/hate relationship. Here he studied acting and playwriting, eventually becoming thoroughly absorbed in theatre. A prolific writer of "Letters to the Editor" to Toronto's newspapers, Herbert has championed many deserving causes, particularly the weaknesses of Canada's prison system, and, more recently, the cause of liberation for homosexuals. An acknowledged homosexual himself, Herbert has struck out against injustice in their regard.

Tennessee Williams, the great American playwright, praised Herbert's courage in presenting so explicit a play on homosexuality as Fortune and Men's Eyes in 1966. The play was the forerunner of many plays on this theme on and off Broadway in the following ten years. Herbert has always been a great admirer of Tennessee Williams' dramatic genius. Simultaneously with Fortune a play by Williams opened on Broadway, The Gnädiges Fräulein. Herbert found it so stimulating that he vowed to produce it in Toronto and to play the Gracious Lady himself. In 1976 he directed and played this title role, selecting men to play all the women characters. The result was a rare artistic success. Because the play is a satire on the Broadway theatre, each character is merely a symbol of the critic, the producer, the audience, Hollywood, with the Gracious Lady representing the art form. This play was met with outrage by some Toronto critics who mistakenly took it to be a play about transvestites.

An original one-act play of his own, Close Friends, was also presented on the same program. This short drama delicately probes the emotional upheaval experienced by two male friends who face the destruction of their friendship. The play rises to a universal experience because the stress is on human friendship as well as the homosexual experience.

This is true also of Herbert's finest play, Fortune and Men's Eyes *(1966), which records with brilliance and insight, Herbert's own experiences in prison. Its emphasis is on the need people have for one another. Some review highlights give the flavour of the critical response:*

> It is consistently fascinating, a solidly effective drama, an impressive playwriting debut. —Smith, Village Voice.
>
> The production is brilliant, quick, true, rough, funny, spontaneous. —Tallmer, New York Post.
>
> It is the strong stuff of which great theatre is made. —Jeffreys, ABC-TV.
>
> Vital and thrusting, it has impact. —Bolton, Morning Telegraph.
>
> It's a good play and it's well done. —Probst, NBC-TV.

Genet's Death Watch *makes an interesting comparison with* Fortune. *Both deal with the same subject but Genet uses romanticism while Herbert uses realism; Genet's criminal is a hero, Herbert's a victim. Herbert's straight youth is gradually transformed into a confirmed homosexual in an honest portrayal that is full of pathos and indignation. The character of Queenie provides the needed comic relief. Herbert is able to catch the right mood and provide the momentum in a powerful drama. The high point in the play occurs when "Mona" refuses Smitty on the excuse that a physical relationship will destroy rather than enrich their friendship. He quotes Shakespeare's sonnet from which the title of the play is taken. The moment is unforgettable —a miraculously fresh, delicately sensitive wisdom infuses it.*

Among Herbert's other plays, none of which reached the stature of Fortune, *mention should be made of three:* Omphale and the Hero, The Dinosaurs, *and* Born of Medusa's Blood. *These plays contain some rather heightened language and melodramatic effects, the result, perhaps, of Herbert's deliberate intention to use expressionism and symbolism rather than straight realism.* Omphale *is a picture of Canadian provincial and puritan morality in which the warm relationship between French and Indian is destroyed by the divisive English Canadian.* The Dinosaurs *symbolizes the uneasy* relationship between Canadian critic and Canadian actress; the latter has chosen to pursue her career in sophisticated European theatre. The confrontation between critic and actress is devastating, enabling Herbert to express all his frustrations with the naïve and narrow taste of theatre in Canada, and ending with the destruction of the critic whom the actress refuses to rescue. Born of Medusa's Blood is more reliant on realism. Here Herbert's intent is to delineate emotional relationships among damaged people, society's so-called losers.

Herbert is now reaching the prime of his career. His past experiences in every area of theatre make him very conscious of all the elements that go into the creation of a great play. That he will surpass or at the least equal the genius of Fortune and Men's Eyes is the hope of his friends and admirers. At the present time, however, he is absorbed in writing a novel. Whether or not this will change the direction of his artistic career remains to be seen. But John Herbert has tasted both the sweetness and the bitterness of success in the theatre and it is unlikely that he will turn his back on the stage which has nurtured him.

INTRODUCTION TO THE PLAYWRIGHT

Why does anyone become a dramatist? What drives one person to dramatize life's conditions and events in a way that causes others to label him a dramatist? Does he see life differently from others? Why should he choose an assortment of characters to deliver his message, rather than taking to the pulpit or lecture stand to offer the world his opinion? Why the need for many voices in his writing when the minister of religion and the professor of language (or history or sociology or psychology) seems satisfied to speak through a single voice? Is the dramatist different?

Yes, I believe that the creator of plays is usually a person who wants to play many roles in life and so sees himself as the actor of numerous parts. I suspect, too, that this is an innate quality for the most part and may be detected early in life.

As a child I was enormously curious about everyone around me, man, woman, or child, and I felt a part of everything that others said or did. Enormous ego? Perhaps. Certainly there was a sense of self, for I never felt like a cypher, but rather as if linked to all life: animal, vegetable, mineral, mental, spiritual, and emotional. To feel was to live. To experience was to move. I equated movement with growth. When music touched me, I danced; when speech made sense to me, I answered; when the wind blew, I ran with or against it; when rain fell, I drank it or waded into it; when ice formed, I skated over it; when anger was hurled at me, I threw it back; when affection was offered to me, I burst into love, and so on, through childhood, getting bruises, colds, cuts, criticisms, kindnesses; I made friends and enemies; I was always a creature of action. When the child says something more than, "I want to win," then he moves into the creative field of living—art.

Even as a small child, I was more moved by drawings, music, flowers, sunsets, stars, moonlight, grace, love, form and order than I was by brute force, material prizes or the spilled blood of others. I felt, even then, that the bullies of the world were in love with death more than with life. To me, life was always "growing things" and I was horrified at the sight of things lost to life: dead animals, broken limbs, destructive adults, cruel teachers, hunger, poverty, crippling, and competition without compassion. I know that I was aware of these feelings in embryo as early as the age of four, when I made my first crayon drawings.

When life seemed small or mean to me, I sought a way to enlarge (or dramatize) its quality, and this urge took many shapes within my varied activities. I yearned for beauty in my existence and, when I felt that it was found, would run with the secret to share it with my family or friends. These discoveries (or uncoveries) took forms such as crayon drawings of lovely unearthly nymphs, birds and animals; a few words scratched on paper; beautiful garments out of the family trunk of costumes donned for play-acting; a handful of violets from the banks of the Humber River, gathered purely for their beauty; and many games played out in the back yard or vacant lot, wherein all actors won.

These were my first plays, I believe, for I led the other children into games demanding imagination and a sense of shared experience. I acquired a following of children, both girls and boys, that eased the pain of deprivation during those thin depression years, by releasing feelings into the open where we could make of them what we chose. We did not understand the true fascination in objective terms, but were captured by "the play" nonetheless. The truth, of course, is that we ceased to be "victims" the moment we began to tell our own stories and to make our spirits larger through adventure and romance. We entered the theatre by the stage entrance, as it were.

So, I did not discover the theatre within a building, or through the words of a book, but the theatre instead found me in the urges of everyday life. As I grew older I could not relinquish the intoxication of drinking drama from life's incidents: I enlarged every story, embellished each description of ordinary activities, told of neighbours as if they were gods or giants, saw my peer group of neighbourhood children as the inhabitants of timeless legends and became known by others in our local community as a "queer one," a "liar" and an "impossible child." I felt the dullards were fools or worse, and I incorporated my critics into my fantasies, giving them roles as dwarfs, ogres, witches, and ghosts.

I am not different today, except that I know now why men steal, rape, kill, hoard, cheat, lie, compete, accumulate, suppress, destroy, cripple, profit, win, lose, drink, drug, divorce, desert, hate, suicide, and die. I still admire only the elements of growth and beauty in humanity and I play the ugliness, which I cannot ignore or escape, against the stellar qualities of man. An artist dare not lose his childhood faiths as other more pragmatic people do, for he would cease to be an artist at the moment that profit and competitive destruction became foremost to his survival as a human creature. I have seen artists kill themselves with greed and envy, often.

servant to craft, evidence reveals that the true artist is still able to return his audience to the most basic elements in feeling and knowing, so that the techniques, however elaborate or modern, become forgotten during the final performance. There are plenty of half-baked artisans around, making plenty of money from exhibits of mean stuff which pander to the lowest octave in human experience, but they have forgotten that the artist is expected to transcend humiliation and suffering, for the act of art is an affirmation of life's importance, whereas a prostitute is in the profit business.

So, vain as it may sound, I feel that the theatre has always been within me and should I no longer feel that way, then a building called "a theatre" would be of no more concern to me than an office building or a bank building. I suspect that theatres live within us all and that we are glad when the drama of living takes on meaning for us. When an actor is a great artist, every member of the audience is experiencing his "own" life, rather than observing the actor's expression of life. I believe that the writer of plays must always be conscious of the sharing of experience, so that the "living map" he makes will provide great room for involvement of the audience's emotions and thoughts.

The opposite to this real accomplishment of communication is the manipulation of thoughts and feelings without respect for the audience's need to share in the drama. A wonderful play asks questions. Over ninety percent of the plays I see on stage are designed to tell the audience what is happening, rather than to show it so it may think its own thoughts and experience its own emotions. Close to one hundred percent of television drama manipulates the audience without an iota of respect for the watcher's need to live, share, and comprehend. We see "capsuled theatre" becoming as popular and as palatable as popcorn and boxed candy. The horror is that the producers are sugar-coating the great forces of life as gumdrops.

The very elements which the original dramatists in ancient Greece approached in fear and awe, thereby reminding us of the size and terror of being alive, are now tossed about like juggling pins as though the natural forces were now all reduced by man's ability to control them. When a man sees life as small, he must accordingly grow smaller, for even an idiot detects that the world is larger than himself and the universe a mystery, infinite in its wonder, hope and grandeur. When man ceases to acknowledge that he is a voyager, privileged to pass through this plane of existence and given the chance to study its magnificence, like all his kind before him, then he is both too big to grow and too small to matter. He destroys the drama of life. Such a man could push a button to end the world.

The following sections will help the reader to understand the eventual creation of my play, *Fortune and Men's Eyes,* written more than twenty years after the described incidents took place.

THE CUBAN SAILOR

I will tell you that I was young and you will know how long ago it was when I say that I was leaving a theatre where Leonide Massine had just danced the role of the Cuban sailor in the ballet, "Gaieté Parisienne." The theatre was the very old Victorian house called the Royal Alexandra, and it was the only theatre of any size or importance at that time in the cold, grey city of Toronto, Ontario, Canada. The visiting company was The Ballet Russe de Monte Carlo and, like many other such famous European companies, it was on a world tour that, by some gracious miracle of kindness, included the dull

Presbyterian place in which I lived. The potential audience in Toronto must have been small, because these lovely, enchanting visitors never stayed for long, and one had to keep watch in the newspapers, and on the theatre's billboards to be sure to catch the gorgeous butterflies that could colour the life and stir the imagination to some point of momentary spiritual hope for an evening, before that cold and stony city closed in again, chilling a young heart to the marrow with its relentless pursuit of money and senseless illusion of security.

Leaving the theatre that particular evening, my body and mind were alive to the point of ecstasy, and the image of the Cuban sailor, startling in his clarity and poise, appeared over and over in my mind's eye, as I shuffled slowly through the faded, dusty lobby of the Royal Alexandra with my fellow theatre-goers. He had appeared for the first time in the ballet at the top of a wide staircase, suddenly there, framed by the graceful French doors, through which all the other lovely creatures had gradually appeared, preparing the way for his dynamic presence. The legs were arched in almost full circle, the arms raised gracefully aloft and holding two small black bags, one in each hand, and the dark wicked face was tilted saucily to one side, balancing a small white sailor hat jauntily above one eyebrow. The stageful of laughing, playing dancers looked his way, but he had eyes for only the exquisite little glove seller in her pink frills and rosy tights. Like a bird preparing for the mating dance, he dipped in a slow and muscular plié, feet together, knees scissored outwards; then, suddenly, in a breathtaking leap, legs spread to his sides like wings, he soared toward us from the top of the staircase to land as lightly as a black and white feather at the glove seller's dainty, pink-tipped feet. The audience as a man, had caught its breath and so perfect was that flight that tears sprang into one's eyes from the terrible, quick knowledge that we had just experienced one of those moments in art, so complete, that our hearts ache for life's contrasting imperfections.

In the theatre lobby, my mind had wandered back to that triumphant moment of the Cuban vagabond, and without realizing what my body was doing, so that the amused giggles at my elbow reached me slowly and I came back to reality with a blush of embarrassment. I had let my limbs move into the remembered positions of the dance, and the audience around me was laughing, the faces full of disdain and disbelief. Fearfully, my gaze swept the sea of smug expressions, searching for one pair of eyes that understood, but all that met me were solemn countenances. Every woman seemed to be wearing a Persian lamb coat in either black or grey, and every man seemed to be garbed for funeral purposes in black or grey suits and homburg hat. I hurried quickly through and past them, the first seeds of hatred shooting into the soil of my uneasy relationship with Toronto society.

The cold of the night air helped to cleanse away my recent humiliation in the theatre lobby, and hunger for food took over quickly, as it does in the very young when health is good and hope springs quickly back into the head and stomach. I was suddenly aware of the bleak ugliness of the area in which Toronto's only live theatre was located. Across the street was an old, rusted iron fence, beyond which were railroad tracks and a line of dull, red-brown freight cars which seemed to sit as sullenly as the great warehouses and office buildings surrounding the railway yard. There was not a light anywhere, and the forbidding shadows of King Street seemed to say that live theatre and laughter had no business being here at all. There was only one restaurant and it was a fly-specked, counter-and-stools sort of place where you could get a warm roast beef sandwich with cold, soggy gravy for seventy-five cents and a thin cup of coffee for which it was criminal to charge a dime. I always went here after a show, however, because there was a chance that performers from the Royal Alex would drop in for food after their night's performance.

The owner, who seemed to do everything himself, from cooking in the kitchen to serving at the counter, was a tall, quiet, brooding European with a disturbing air of disdain for, and detachment from, all of his customers except the strange, exotic creatures from the theatre. I always wondered about his past and longed to talk to him but never had the courage, so would, instead, simply mumble my order for a sandwich and coffee, then wait quietly, smoking cigarettes, until he would deliver the soggy, lukewarm food in his own good time.

He seemed to watch the door for that moment when the performers would stroll in, chattering and laughing and moving lightly in their own special world of shared understanding.

How he changed when they finally did arrive! A smile would break across his cloudy countenance, like the sun reaching through a storm, and his movements became quicker, lighter and, to me, amazingly alive, in contrast to his ordinary shuffling gait. He would then serve bottles of soda pop in a manner that convinced the onlooker he believed the containers to hold champagne. The dancers or actors would laugh with him and share in some special delight which I instinctively understood but could not be part of. Now, looking back, I suppose he, like many Europeans, knew and loved the theatre, and he did not know that I was not just another one of the stupid, skeptical Torontonians who bought tickets to stand in the lobby, looking at one another, instead of attending the theatre to see a play or dance. Who could blame him?

I was fearful and timid at that time, and dressed in the manner that Toronto habits dictated, which was the careful art of hiding oneself as thoroughly as possible under a modest bit of dark flannel or Harris tweed. I worked in an advertising office of the largest department store in town and all the rules of the place stressed conformity in most things, so I walked about in a grey-green Harris tweed jacket, grey flannel trousers, brown brogues, white shirt and quiet, printed necktie. There was always some well-groomed watchdog in the office who would not hesitate to warn a junior employee that his haircut was dangerously past the two-week mark. So, to this strange, dark, hirsute restaurateur, who prowled his small café in long, oily ringlets of hair, and with silk shirt open at the throat to reveal a mat of curly, black chest hair, I must have seemed a typical member of Toronto's buttoned-down Anglo-Saxon society.

How could he know that my whole being ached to be a part of the world to which he had shown homage by hanging the walls of his little restaurant with autographed photographs of the many artists who had played the stage of the Royal

Alexandra in his time and eaten a meal in his restaurant? I looked around at the fly-specked surfaces of the pictures and took a little comfort for myself in the recognition of faces I, too, had seen on that stage and sometimes at closer range in this restaurant: Nazimova, who had played the mother in a production of Ibsen's *Ghosts;* Elissa Landy, who had cavorted in a production of *Blithe Spirit;* Tamara Toumanova, who had blazed across the Royal Alexandra stage in Stravinsky's *Firebird,* blinding us by her brilliance and beauty; Ruth Draper, the great *monologuiste,* sending that rich voice in warm waves throughout the auditorium while moving in the grandeur of tragic queens and heroic peasant women.

One evening I saw Tallulah Bankhead, young and exquisite in the photograph on the wall but bloated and loud when I watched her on the stage. That was one to remember. At the end of her performance in *Private Lives* with Donald Cook as leading man, she was given curtain call after curtain call, the ovations growing to hysterical proportions, unusual in staid Toronto theatre manners. Why? Sadly, the audience was full of gaudy homosexuals, most of whom were unaware that they were watching an actress in decline, a once-brilliant player being a clown for her own amusement or, perhaps, out of her disrespect for the audience. Whatever the reason, she had behaved badly on stage, tossing her great golden mane of hair in front of her leading man's face at every possible opportunity, and cutting across his lines with her bellowing and brassy outbursts of lines or laughter so that his character faded like a damaged watercolour drawing, as the evening progressed. The hysterical homosexuals loved her for her domination of the stage and her errant disregard for the right of others; she was helping them to express their suppressed desires to hit back at a world which insulted and despised them daily. They needed her, so they loved her, and the tragic loss of her art was nothing to them so long as she would parade her aggressive femininity and indulge her hungry ego. I hated the play and I despised the performance, personally, but I was just as much in awe as anyone there of that powerful, explosive presence known throughout the theatre world as "Terrible Tallulah."

As the noisy adulation subsided, Miss Bankhead stepped regally to downstage centre and, touching her eyes gently with a handkerchief, made a short curtain speech in which she thanked the audience for its reception and said that she "loved Toronto" and that she would "never forget this marvellous, marvellous evening," finishing with "Good night, my darlings!"

The incident was truly affecting, and we all exited quietly as though someone very special had reached out to say we were loved. It was the final evening of the play's performance, so she would be moving on to the next city of the tour. About a dozen people turned into the alleyway leading back to the stage door and dressing rooms, and I went with them. Dozens more stood about in groups on the sidewalk in front of the theatre, waiting for one last look at the famous image. The little old man who was always there, guarding the stage door, allowed us into the tiny foyer, through which the performer had to pass in order to reach the street.

We did not have to wait long in this case; first a tall white-haired woman carrying a fluffy white dog and a briefcase of black leather stepped out from the backstage area, measuring the waiting crowd with a cold and withering glance. She passed us by, silently, and then Tallulah hit the foyer all golden like a lioness, wearing a beige suit and carrying mounds of luggage, slung over her own shoulders, arms and wrists. Every piece was made of beautiful bleached rawhide and initialed in gold letters, and she stood swinging them all as though we were blocking her passage to Valhalla. The body was short, strong and graceful and the legs exquisite. I was startled by her shortness of stature and the daintiness of her feet. The head was huge, or so it seemed, as one might expect of a person six feet tall, and the eyes unforgettable in their knowing blueness and radiant intelligence. The heavy, half-moon lids seemed to warn us that the eyes could shoot fire, if necessary, and the thick, golden hair rippled over the square, aggressive shoulders like molten sunlight. At close range, she was a stunningly beautiful woman, and the puffiness of cheek and the pouchiness of eye took nothing from her fantastic presence. She seemed to have been drinking, for there was a weaving abandon in her manner. A rosy-cheeked girl of the private-school variety rushed forward from our waiting group to ask for an autograph. Tallulah held onto her luggage. "I've got no time for any autographs. I've got to catch a bloody plane in five minutes."

With that she started for the street door, only to find herself being blocked by a tall effeminate young man who was bleached blond and carefully made up so that he looked "cupie-doll" pretty.

"Miss Bankhead?" he gushed, "you were absolutely divine." She looked him over calmly from curled head to sandalled toe and said, "You're not bad yourself, darling!" With that she was away, racing down the lane to the street, incongruously carting all her own luggage, legs moving rapidly in a long, firm gait. We followed, hypnotized, to the street, where an airport limousine waited to whisk the visiting glory away to further conquests. The black car pulled away, its mysterious golden cargo moving on with the terrible burden of having to complete the legend of "Tallulah. . . ."

The visage on the restaurant wall was delicate and lovely and must have been photographed at about the time that Miss Bankhead played *The Lady of Camellias* in London, England, where Augustus John painted her portrait, providing her with one of the possessions she prized all of her lifetime.

The door burst open and the Ballet Russe de Monte Carlo entered in full strength, like a flock of tiny, brilliant birds, chattering gaily in a language I could not comprehend. My mind questioned itself, "French? Italian?" and my own ignorance depressed me as I watched the café owner's face light up happily as he greeted them graciously in their own tongue, and perhaps his, too. I felt terribly alone as I watched them move with fire and grace, touching one another easily, laughing, and showing the rose which the host had placed in a narrow, graceful vase on one of his ugly, hard-topped tables. I discovered that the rose was for the prima ballerina. The troupe encouraged the little "glove seller" to sit at the table and appreciate the flower. "How beautiful they all are!" I thought, and I could find no solace in my plate of lukewarm beef and thin gravy. My personal pain was too intense to sit any longer at that counter. Yet I did not want to disturb the owner of the restaurant who would have to come down front to the cash register while I paid my cheque. I counted my silver to see whether my pocket held the correct amount of change. Then I slipped quietly to the cashier desk to lay my money on the glass top. One last glance toward the group of dancers and I realized that no one noticed me in the slightest degree; I was not of their world. I slipped out into the cold and desolate silence of Toronto's King Street.

I was seventeen years old and over six feet tall, and the size of my feet, the gaucheness of my clothing and the thinness of my body all seemed to separate me from that party of graceful, fiery, laughing creatures who welcomed the beautiful Cuban sailor.

THE GOOD CITY

Society seems to teach us to become liars and hypocrites, to present an image that will protect us, no matter what our true selves may be. This calculated image-presentation is often called "respectability." If we can respect these carefully calculated lies, how then could we possibly respect or love truth? Either I was very naïve when I began my adult life in the city of Toronto, or very stubborn. I still am not sure which way it was. Whichever, I suffered the same consequences for my honesty.

My first steady job, other than those I worked at part time while attending school, was in the advertising department of the T. Eaton Company, on the sixth floor of its main building. The time was 1944 in the last years of the war, and I had been told by the business manager that my employment was temporary because there would be skilled men, then in the armed forces, who would be returning to their old jobs. It was an uneasy time for a teen-ager to go to work because the future held uncertainty for him at best. However, I felt I would learn something about advertising before the end arrived, and probably find another job. Because of the feeling of insecurity, I found myself determined to get something more out of life in downtown Toronto than was promised for the future by my job.

The city seemed very glamorous to a boy from a suburb near the country. I loved the bustle and excitement of the central section of Toronto. There was limitless variety, it seemed. One could go to the Royal Alexandra one evening to see the American Ballet Company or the Sadlers Wells from England, or to the Casino Theatre on Queen Street, where some good and bad clowns held forth against the death knell of vaudeville. There were two or three on the circuit at that time who later became famous, one a top Hollywood film comedian. These funny men were backed by a chorus of thirteen or fourteen girls, called Casinoettes, who were unconsciously funnier. No two of them were the same size or shape, and the effect was closer to a carnival "Ten-in-One-Tent. " They were lively and colourful, however, and that is all I asked of the theatre at the time. I applauded the Casinoettes as wildly as I would the Ballet Russe de Monte Carlo's prima ballerina.

Then I began to meet people of all kinds and sorts a city breeds. Sometimes I would go out for the evening with a person or two from the advertising office; another time I would go alone and chance to meet someone new. I found myself sitting in restaurants late at night, smoking and drinking numerous cups of coffee, talking to characters who seemed fabulous and fascinating to me. Occasionally I would miss the last car to my suburban home, Mount Dennis, and would sit in an all-night restaurant, Bowles Lunch, at Queen and Bay streets, until the first streetcar of the morning could take me home. It was on one of these late sojourns that I had my first encounter with the Toronto Police Force. Life is often a mixture of comedy and tragedy, and we never know which face will be shown us for certain.

Though I was terribly frightened, my first experience with Toronto Police was very funny, and I was able to look back, years later, and laugh at my own folly. Eventually, however, my first foolish act of walking, by my own will, into a Toronto police station, led me to tragedy.

It was the wee hours of the morning, and I had missed the last Dundas-Runnymede streetcar that would have taken me to Keele Street and thence to Mount Dennis. I was walking away slowly from that familiar corner behind the old City Hall and feeling disappointed about having missed the car. I was tired this night and would like to have reached home. It was near pay day for me, so I was, as usual, close to being broke. I was just resigning myself to the need of putting in time over a single cup of coffee until morning when I found a large navy-blue body blocking my way on Queen Street. It was my first encounter with a Toronto constable.

"You got a home, Mac?" he queried, not too sweetly.

"Yes, I have," said I, matter-of-factly, secure in my feeling of citizenship.

"Then what the hell are you wandering the streets for at this hour?" He came on strong.

"I just missed my Runnymede car." I excused my presence on his beat.

"So take a taxi or something," he advised.

"I haven't enough money," I answered, and there left myself wide open, making the terrible mistake of telling the kind of truth that one later learns to avoid. I did not know, then, that there was a law for the rich and another for the poor.

"How much have you got?" he asked, and, "let's see it." So, I removed the pitiful handful of coins and streetcar tickets from my pocket for his inspection. "You got a job?" he asked, looking me over very coldly and professionally. "Yes" I said, "I work right here," and I indicated the T. Eaton Company building beside us. "Oh yeah?" said the protector of the public. "What do you do there? Sell perfume?"

His hostility for no apparent reason shook me and I found myself trembling. "I work in the advertising office on the sixth floor."

"I thought so," said the astute man. "A goddam queer!" I said nothing, and tried to conceal my shock and fear. "O.K.," said he, like a local version of a storm trooper, "go down to Dundas Street station and turn yourself in."

"How do I do that?" asked the ridiculously dumb child. "And where is it?"

He looked at me, with a smile for the first time, and gave me his instructions.

"What do I tell them?" I said, nearly crying.

"Tell them I said you were a fucking queer," he counselled, and with those kind words to carry me, I stumbled along Bay Street to Dundas, where I turned east, bracing myself to face the boys of the Dundas Street police station (now defunct).

I told my story to the night sergeant as respectfully and impersonally as possible, under the circumstances, and he looked at me with utter disbelief. Finally, after a long silence, he said, "Wait here! I'll be right back." He hurried away, returning with an army of police officers. I began to pray quietly to myself. "Now, tell these guys what you told me," the sergeant instructed. I launched delicately into my tale, and was rewarded for the performance with some of the loudest and longest laughter I've ever heard, except in the theatre during moments of cruel comedy. When they had exhausted the joke, the night sergeant said, "O.K., Nellie, on your way, and don't let any of us see that sissy face of yours downtown again." "I work downtown," I answered fearfully. "Well don't! Get a job in Timbuktu or you'll wish you'd never been born." On that happy note, I left for my home in Mount Dennis almost a little wiser than I had been at birth.

But I have had a way since childhood of thinking things over, afterward, and sorting them out to a result. As I dwelt on the experience, I discovered that there seemed a sort of injustice about the whole procedure. I asked myself many questions. "Was it my fault that I had an appearance often described by others as sensitive-looking or aesthetic? Did I have less right than other people to live and breathe and walk downtown? If we were fighting and protesting brutality in Germany, could we condone it in uniform at home? Were these men not brutes who were taking advantage of their size, as bullies do in a schoolyard?" And so on, for days, I thought persistently.

At last, I decided that I had the same right as any other citizen who was living within the confines of the law. I set the incident aside, and went on about my life as before. It was many weeks before there was reason to be reminded of the experience. I had made a friend of a musician who lived on Wood Street near the Maple Leaf Gardens. We often attended concerts together at Massey Hall or Varsity Arena (the Promenade Symphony Concerts) and then would go for coffee afterwards. I always walked him to his home before heading for the streetcar.

One night, just after leaving him, I was on my way along Bay Street, toward the City Hall car stop, when I passed a police officer. I was a few steps past him when I heard his voice calling: "Hey, there! You were told to keep off the street." I felt a terrible temptation to run, but did not. Some kind of anger and resentment came welling up from within, and I found myself walking toward him.

"There's no curfew in this city," I said. "This isn't Germany or Occupied France and I'm not wearing an armband or anything like that. What do you want with me?"

"Don't give me any of your goddam lip," advised the noble officer of the law.

We were arguing my rights to ordinary citizenship when a police car pulled alongside us.

"Anything wrong there? Need any help?" inquired one of the officers in the cruiser.

"Nah," said the brave policeman. "Just a sassy-mouthed fruit, telling me about his rights."

"Yeah?" said the beefy-faced officer on the street side of the car. "You want to take him for a ride?"

"Good idea," said my first friend, grabbing my upper arm in a vise-like grip with his big meat hook. "Get in there, Nellie!"

He shoved me into the back seat of the car and climbed in after me, giving me a solid belt in the ribs with his elbow as he sat. "Where are you taking me?" I asked, and I was really frightened now.

"To the station," said the humourist in the front seat. "The gas station." They all three laughed at that cunning sally, and drove to a very familiar spot, for me. . . . They parked the car in a lane beside the T. Eaton Company warehouse building, which I passed every morning on my way to work. There was an alcove, a few feet square, hidden on three sides by Eaton's building. The fourth side was the opening to the alleyway, now blocked by the police car.

"Get out," one of them said, and I did so. The three climbed from the cruiser and surrounded me, in the dark corner.

"Which way is home?" one asked me.

"West," I said, "to Mount Dennis." "That's north," another said, and pointed northward along the alley way. "Do you want to go?"

"Yes," I said.

"Then get running for it, you fucking freak!"

So I did, but it was futility, like a bad dream, where one wants to reach a goal but instead runs madly in one spot unable to escape. They tossed me from one to the other of them, punching me in the chest and head and stomach, slapping my face and stamping on my feet. I began to shout, but it was an isolated area, where no one would have come to my rescue. Finally I was on the ground and saw a foot raised to kick my face. I became cunning surprisingly fast. "I've got your license number," I shouted. "I've got your license number," I sobbed in despair. Then I saw legs running from me, and heard an engine start quickly and the car raced madly out of the alley.

I slipped into complete unconsciousness, feeling only beautiful grateful relief, before the blackness came.

I awoke to cruel white daylight and voices all around me, saying a variety of things, such as "I guess he got drunk and passed out," and, "No, I think somebody beat him up. Look at his face." and "Maybe we should call the police." That brought me to, quickly. "No!" I shouted. "No police. I'm all right. I'm sick. I fainted." I made a dozen excuses to the crowd going to their jobs, and crept out of the alley, my head beating a tattoo of pain and fear. I found my way to Wood Street, and upstairs to my friend's rented room. I was afraid to face my family in that condition.

I was ashamed, somehow, and could not bring myself, until weeks later, to tell him exactly what had happened. Somehow I feared it might turn him against me. Oddly enough, I wanted to be respected and respectable. "What in hell happened to you?" he asked while getting some water for me.

"I was beaten up in an alleyway," I answered. "I was unconscious all night."

"Who did it?" he demanded.

"Oh, a bunch of bums," I replied, and didn't feel that I was telling him a lie. Because he was a friend, he asked no more at that moment but, instead, began to make coffee, so I could live another day.

It should not be difficult for the reader to imagine how short a step from the last experience was required to bring me into a Canadian prison. Because the entry into jail was the most traumatic event of my early life, I tell it in the third person. I was aged twenty at the time.

THE SISSY

The desire to maintain an identity within the institution of prison is very strong in all individuals and manifests itself in hundreds of small, particular ways—different with each, depending on the person. The most extreme example that I saw was a boy who came in, convicted of having impersonated a woman for immoral purposes. He claimed that he had been on the way home from a costume party when he saw a police cruiser following him. He had accepted a ride in another car offered by the driver, a married man, who thought the boy was a prostitute. When the police stopped the car and took the driver and passenger from it, the man was so frightened that he agreed to anything and everything the police said or advised. Subsequently, the police charged the boy with the homosexual equivalent of prostitution, "gross indecency," and he was convicted, on the spoken evidence of the two policemen and the "victim." The boy says that he did not tell them that he was not a woman until they all reached the police station, on the chance that he might be treated more carefully as a woman and perhaps let go before arrest was completed.

In any case, he was very feminine looking—blue eyes with black lashes and arched brows, a fine complexion, a sensuous mouth, oval face, and black curly hair. Although he was very tall, his frame was slender and feminine too, narrow shouldered, wide-hipped and long legged. His hands were long and elegant and his legs very straight. He walked lightly like a top fashion model, even in prison clothes. Somehow he gave the impression of being a "haute-couture" model, forced to impersonate a boy.

The day that he walked into the mess hall for the first "jug-up" it was pretty obvious that a problem existed and that the future would hold some interest. As he was spotted by the other inmates, a murmur went over the room which increased to such proportions that there was open whistling and catcalling.

This, of course, set up a situation where he had either to live up to that first entrance or go down to ignominy. The guards were already planning his downfall, if one could judge by their remarks and faces—full of hatred and disapproval. Yet it seemed that he was only being himself. He smiled rather shyly as he approached a table, but the excitement was too high to quiet completely, and the rest of the meal was feverish with unrest. His saga could only have been played out by a most unusual individual. The sequence of events that followed helped to shape his life in prison and perhaps forever afterward.

As each "hippo" tried to corral him, the boy submitted passively, then asserted himself by claiming his independence and openly spitting in the eye of the bullies who abused him. He moved on, walking a veritable tightrope of human relations, dismissing and despising those men he did not like and openly befriending and bestowing his favours on those that he cared for, whether they were "big time" or not. He seemed afraid of no one, answering the guards quietly and intelligently, but very bravely when they brutalized him. When he was taken to shower with the others, he covered his genitals with his hands, turned his back on everyone and showered in the far corner of the stall. The other boys made such a fuss when he was naked that it was ruled he should be taken to shower alone, and that became established ritual, where he would be seen going through the corridors, escorted by a guard, after everyone else had bathed. This twosome, no matter which guard, was dubbed "David and Bathsheba," and all of the boys would call out from behind the bars as they passed. "Let me change places with you, David. I'll trade you my short time." (Short time is the part of sentence left to complete. The inference being, too, that the guards are serving life sentences and therefore are never free.)

He was allowed to spend a very brief time in a dormitory, but his presence became so disturbing that they put him in a cell alone for most of his stay. It was at the very end of a corridor, where the guards and politicians had to pass through to the next corridor by the unlocking and relocking of a door. Oddly enough, though he did not conform, many politicians liked and admired him, and would toss contraband fruit, candies, and cakes through the bars to him.

There was a guard who had been in Europe and liked theatre and opera and who was on night duty. The guard used to give the boy tailor-made cigarettes so that he could stand and talk to him about plays and operas. But the others never stopped trying to subdue him.

At clothing change, he was purposely given a monstrous assortment of ill-fitting garments, which looked ludicrous on his tall, thin body, but the next day they would be changed like magic. He worked in the tailor shop and would slip parts of his clothing into the sewing machine while still wearing them, and always finished the week with clothing that fitted better than that of anyone else. He shaved the soles of his shoes until they were as thin as a Spanish dancer's, flushing curls of leather down the toilet each night. As he would be caught in each of these tricks at one time or another, he would be shipped upstairs to the tower for a diet of bread and water, where he would lie on the hard bunk like a siren on a rock at sea and sing sad songs of love, heard and encouraged by other inmates of the tower.

The guards hated his courage; they beat him, insulted him and tried to humiliate him at every turn, but he moved on through the dull grey world of the prison life—smiling, singing, flirting, laughing, challenging. He became a kind of "star," and though he had many enemies among the inmates there were more who showed appreciation and even respect.

Finally they found an excuse to whip him. He had been trying to see the doctor, but on this particular day the line for the hospital was full and he was told to go on out to work. When the work party reached its destination, he said to the guard, "I can't work today. I really am very ill." It happened to be a guard who loathed the boy and could not hide his animosity. He repeatedly asked the boy only one question, knowing that the boy knew the consequence of a wrong or negative answer: "Do you refuse to work?" He thundered it over and over at the boy until he got the reply, "Yes, I do. I'm sick." He was hurried into the superintendent's office, where the story was told by the guard only. "I'm sick," the boy interrupted. "You've just broken another rule," said the superintendent, "by speaking before spoken to. Take him to the hospital, and if he passes the test, I order corporal punishment."

The doctor put a stethoscope to his heart, said that it was strong, and the boy was fastened into the whipping machine and thrashed by a guard wielding a piece of cowhide strap. They made him, finally, scream for God and his mother, then threw him into an isolation cell to cool off. He came out of the machine fighting wildly and had to be physically subdued before getting locked up. In the morning he was unconscious, with a temperature of 104 degrees, and they did take him to the hospital, where it was discovered he had pneumonia and was almost dead.

When he survived this ordeal, nothing could stop him. He got cold cream from the hospital, supposedly for chapped skin, and made eye mascara from a mixture of soot off the window sill of his cell and the cold cream. He used a carpenter's pencil to accent his eyebrows, made up his cheeks and lips with a lipstick given to him by a boy who had begged it from his own sister on visiting day. He cut the toes and heels out of his shoes to make them look like sandals and put the laces from his boots together to make Roman sandal cords that would wind up as high as the shins on his light-coloured wool stockings. He rolled up his trousers to show his foot gear to advantage and rolled the sleeves of his shirt to below the elbow. If the guard forced him to roll them down, then the next day he cut them off at the same place, so that there was nothing to roll down. He set his hair in curlers made of toilet paper and achieved fantastic hair styles that finally resulted in the order to shave his head.

The next "jug-up," he appeared with small Grecian curls drawn all over his skull with the black carpenter's pencil. He became a frightening goddess of freedom; the whipping had only succeeded in liberating the spirit completely.

It was at this time that some government people from Ottawa saw him as he passed in the line-up of prisoners, moving through the corridors. The visitors were being taken on tour by the head of the reformatory, an ex-army colonel who looked and spoke like the British officers in old colonial movies. As the visitors giggled in disbelief, the outraged colonel called the guard to "yank that thing out of the line and bring it here." Standing gracefully before the enormous, red-faced colonel, the boy looked like a drawing from a Grecian vase. "Do you know what you look like?" the colonel raged. "Do you know what a Golliwog is?"

As coolly as though being questioned in a classroom, and very politely, the boy replied, "The only one with which I am at all familiar is that in the musical composition for piano by the French composer, Charles Debussy—The Golliwog's Cakewalk." The Ottawa audience roared with laughter and the colonel ordered the guard to take "this thing away for a haircut." (So cleverly was the drawing done the colonel thought it to be real hair.)

There is a point when nothing much more can be done to punish a creature. Since he has survived, he is to a degree accepted and considered incorrigible. This was pretty much the circumstance of the boy's situation around Christmas time of that year, and probably explains why his final and complete act of defiance and rebellion was possible within the confines of a reform institution. It is traditional at the Christmas show in that and most penal institutions for boys and men to take the roles of women in performance. Sometimes it is in a play or a musical or chorus line, but for this particular concert the conveners had, for some reason, decided that there would be only one such act. The popular choice among the politicians and "hippo" inmates was a boy younger than the one whose story I am telling; but for some reason the guard who was in charge of that portion of the show, and also of the orchestra, decided that the "black" one would be the solo performer, rather than the younger blond boy who had become the new "starlet," in a modest way.

The "black" one was foolish enough to think that he had been chosen because he could sing and would look right in female garb. Not until rehearsals began did he find that he was to become the chosen "fool." The two songs selected by the guard in charge of the orchestra were of the type that would be sung by little girls of twelve—or even less. They were very silly and would seem grotesque being done by even an attractive, clever female *chanteuse*. He went along with the plan, seemingly, throughout rehearsals, giving them all as much fun at his own expense as they had bargained for. He lisped the songs awkwardly and sang the written lyrics religiously. The guard was licking his lips in anticipation of the concert and the fool's "public humiliation."

The boy received a fresh surprise on the night of the performance. There was make-up, but no wig to cover his shaved head. The dress was an ordinary black street dress, but it was wrapped in a piece of beautiful black satin. He insisted that they lock him into the little dressing room alone to get ready, and only let him out in time for his performance. When they opened the door, prepared to laugh, they were met by a striking figure in dramatic black evening dress. The lines of the street dress had been twisted, pulled and changed to seem to be an elegant cocktail gown, and the piece of black satin was twisted around the head into a Parisian headdress more glamorous than any hair piece could have been. The make-up had achieved the exotic countenance of a Maria Montez or a Gloria Swanson, and the smile was in the best tradition of Hollywood cheesecake—assured and inviting.

The orchestra was being conducted by an inmate, a very clever musician who liked the boy, which was the only stroke of luck. Just before going on, the boy said to the guard and the prisoner-conductor in a husky whisper "You'll have to slow the tempo and follow me, because I've developed laryngitis.

Pianissimo too, please." The guard was so thrown by the boy's appearance that he nodded his head as one being given orders by a famous performer.

The boy had been rehearsing privately in his cell, and had changed all of the lyrics to the songs, and went onstage, microphone in hand, to give the audience a lazy, assured Dietrich-like parody of love in a reform institution. The inmates went mad with pleasure and stomped and applauded deafeningly. The performance was capped by the boy's taking a cloth rose from a garter high on his leg and tossing it into the lap of the colonel, who sat with his wife in the front row. It was truly a remarkable triumph, as arrogant as it was vulnerable and as hated by the prison authorities as it was loved by the men deprived of their freedom.

As his time to leave the institution drew near, a change came over him—so imperceptible that many would not have noticed. He still seemed to go through each day as though life in a prison was one long glass of champagne, but a new sadness and some secret fear had crept into his eyes, possibly related to his thoughts of returning to society and new battles. Before he left, a grey, almost white streak had grown into his hairline on one side above the brow, and to me it seemed a kind of scar in that midnight hair.

The day of departure is a strangely sad one at best. There is no real reason for joy once it has arrived, and his case was no exception, though he smiled at everyone and particularly at those people he liked least. But on the last long trip along the corridor, on the way out, the farewells are strangely heartbreaking, and as he passed the barred cells and dormitories, crowded with familiar faces shouting all kinds of wishes, his face was streaming with the only tears that had been seen on it during his internment. He had learned something about the price to be paid for freedom and, armed with only that piece of wisdom and the white scar in his hair, knew that the battle to live had only begun. They gave him six dollars to get started.

Editor's Note: The following one-act play, a confrontation of John Herbert with himself, should provide the reader with an insight into the years that followed, finally shaping the character and personality of the ex-prisoner who became one of Canada's outstanding playwrights.

VARIATIONS ON A SCHIZOID INTERVIEW
A ONE-ACT PLAY

Place: John Herbert's room

JOHN: Now, are you comfortable, Mr. Herbert?

HERBERT: Don't be ridiculous. I've never been comfortable in my whole life and I don't intend to begin now.

JOHN: You make communication very difficult.

HERBERT: That's the whole point, isn't it? When you're dead, it will be much easier. You may have a neat little stone which simply says, "Here lies . . ."

JOHN: I almost wish I hadn't started this.

HERBERT: Well, it was your idea. I don't give a damn what the public thinks, as you ought to know by now.

JOHN: That's your pose and people are getting pretty bored with it.

HERBERT: Now you're on the right track. Keep it up. You're actually communicating. However, you are wrong about the pose.

JOHN: I've been checking over your history before doing this interview, and I say your attitude of indifference to public opinion is a pose. Nobody writes plays and is disinterested in the public.

HERBERT: Let me qualify that by saying simply that the general public's approval is not worth having. A small minority of the population maintains a real interest in live theatre. Plays are written for those who go to the theatre.

JOHN: Then you admit to caring what they think about you and your work?

HERBERT: Not much, frankly!

JOHN: That strikes me as being a perverse attitude, since you do need an audience.

HERBERT: Who says so? An audience exists. It needs to be entertained. A play can be formed and performed with actors and a director, and be an experience, but an audience without a show is just a mob of people.

JOHN: Are you daring to say that the artist is more important than the audience?

HERBERT: You're damned right I say so.

JOHN: You have an outrageous ego, haven't you?

HERBERT: An artist without an ego is a sailor without a ship.

JOHN: A playwright without an audience is only a man talking to himself in the dark.

HERBERT: Bullshit! If a writer believes in himself and in the existence of an audience, the listeners come into being. They may exist in another country or even in some future century, but the writer believes in his audience or he would not even begin work. The problem here in Canada is the sad fact that people make lousy, dumb, negative audiences.

JOHN: Aha! Now I've got you. Canadians go in droves to hear Shakespeare and Shaw.

HERBERT: Bullshit encore! I've sat with them for years at Shakespeare, Shaw, Ibsen, Chekhov and Strindberg, and they hear nothing. They are there to watch themselves watching Shakespeare, Shaw, Ibsen, Chekhov and Strindberg. Canadians are insular. They don't let much into their heads unless it smells of easy satisfaction for them. Thought is a suspicious stranger to them, and feeling is a foreigner. The farthest they can or will go is to ballet and opera, which is pretty safe stuff. One can enjoy either without much mental energy.

JOHN: Celia Franca wouldn't like that remark too much.

HERBERT: That's nonsense. She understands the nature of her choice in art, or she could not have done so well by it. Dancers need very good feet.

JOHN: You are saying that dancers don't have to be intelligent. You insult them and their audience.

HERBERT: Don't impose those easy Canadian judgments on me, please. I am saying only that a dancer will not succeed without good feet, whereas a writer can work without any, if he still has his head. I think Karen Kain of the National Ballet to be one of the most intelligent dancers I have seen. Every movement she makes is filled with thought and feeling. She rises well above her beautiful feet, and reminds me of Tamara Toumanova in this way. Some actors hereabouts should take lessons in communication from Miss Kain.

JOHN: You always return to a negative.

HERBERT: Oh, no; I'm very positive that most of the actors I have seen on stage in Toronto in recent months need to have Karen Kain's respect for stage technique. She cannot, of course, pass her intense feelings on to them: those are uniquely her own. I guess that I am weary of watching sloppy, cold-hearted actors telling audiences little mundane things that hardly matter at all. We did not retain the high-placed Godwalk from the original theatre of ancient Greece and the reason is now clear. The Gods had to be played by actors who understood the deep primal urges of life. I see none of that size in Canadian performances. They seem to despise magnificence.

JOHN: Well, that, of course, is your domain, alone.

HERBERT: Please don't ask me to suffer your cheap Canadian sarcasm. I've had enough of that national disease to last me a lifetime.

JOHN: You seem to be permanently infected yourself, a terminal case in fact.

HERBERT: Just a case of fighting in kind.

JOHN: Fire with fire, as it were?

HERBERT: Not really? More a case of fighting mosquitoes with a fly-swatter.

JOHN: You're sure to miss every time, then.

HERBERT: It's the gesture that matters in the final accounting.

JOHN: I can't stand you, Charlie Brown, when you talk as though you will write history.

HERBERT: Look, Lucy, I made history, and that's a damned sight more difficult. If I had topped the Canadian high-jump record in the World Olympics, everybody here would acknowledge it.

JOHN: Well, everybody's writing plays now and they're all in training to take next year's prizes. You had your jump.

HERBERT: But that's just my point, stupid! In any other country in the world, a writer who had become known in a hundred countries and been translated into forty languages would have been offered the chance to further his career. Why, even Jean Genet, with his sensational temperament and equally shocking past, was caught up by the top theatrical directors, producers and critics at the start of his life as a playwright. That was more than twenty years ago, and without the wisdom and belief of Paris literary and theatrical figures, who would know of Genet? They rose to his first one-act piece.

JOHN: Well, you can't blame Canada for its innocence and youth. Toronto is not Paris. The young must grow.

HERBERT: Who is faulting this fool place for its ignorance and youth? I'm complaining about its destructiveness and negativism. It has behaved as if it hoped the high-jumper had sprained both ankles in his effort and would never jump again, let alone top his previous record.

JOHN: You are overly sensitive to honest criticism.

HERBERT: Shit! I know the difference between intelligent criticism and wanton axe-swinging. I have read everything written by Stark Young, Kenneth Tynan, Brooks Atkinson, Jean Paul Sartre and LaJos Egri.

JOHN: I'm sorry to say that this interview is becoming as uncontrolled as all of your other chances to react reasonably.

HERBERT: I am trying to recall an interview which offered me the chance to be reasonable. There may have been one.

JOHN: You didn't treat any of the Toronto hosts with much courtesy. Do you recall that first CBC television interview in 1967, just after you returned from your play's opening in New York? Shameful behaviour!

HERBERT: I wasn't ashamed. That's what CBC asked for. I refused to give it to them. When that painted alcoholic middle-aged male idiot they chose to question me asked slyly about my sexual nature, his eyes fairly glinting with suppressed malice, I simply told him the truth.

JOHN: You didn't cooperate with him.

HERBERT: Untrue! I answered his questions more openly than he expected. I said that I went to bed only with persons that I liked very much, then asked him what his bed rules were.

JOHN: You knew that would shut him up.

HERBERT: Only if he was gutless, which he proved to be. Cowards can bully but they won't fight.

JOHN: What did you accomplish finally? They edited that section out for the shown program.

HERBERT: Of course. Very astute of them. The interviewer was revealed as a fool. CBC meant that role for me and not for him.

JOHN: Your paranoia is monumental.

HERBERT: Just a healthy sense of self-preservation!

JOHN: You know something, Herbert? The more I talk to you, the less I like you.

HERBERT: So what? I'm not out to win any popularity contests. Every radio announcer in Toronto is begging to be loved and admired. I think it makes them appear ridiculous. In between their pathetic bids for approval, they sell soap and second-hand cars like crazed carnival barkers. Go interview one of them if you want typically Canadian thoughts and values expressed. I get paid in small royalties, no big residuals. Every actor I meet lately recounts to me his income from commercials as if he expects to be respected. I find that pathetic. I waited on tables but I didn't brag about it.

JOHN: Persons who live in the nebulous, risky arena of public life often have to make compromises for the sake of survival and, yes, money.

HERBERT: I've heard of Richard Nixon.

JOHN: We're not really getting anywhere, are we?

HERBERT: You have insisted on travelling backwards. All interviewers ask that.

JOHN: What about tomorrow then?

HERBERT: It will be shaped by yesterday.

JOHN: You are maddening. I just gave you the chance to move forward.

HERBERT: You did not. You asked me to make either promises or prophecies, and I believe in neither one.

JOHN: Do you believe in anything?

HERBERT: Only this moment and myself in it. There is no life except that.

JOHN: Then I've been wasting my time?

HERBERT: And mine!

JOHN: Why did you not tell me that?

HERBERT: You were too busy with all those other questions.

JOHN: You don't feel they matter?

HERBERT: Not much!

JOHN: And what of your answers?

HERBERT: Not important!

JOHN: You surprise me. Why not important?

HERBERT: Your questions and my answers will not alter the larger situations.

JOHN: Does anything matter to you?

HERBERT: Oh, emphatically, yes!

JOHN: May I presume to ask "what?"

HERBERT: Work.

JOHN: That's all?

HERBERT: That's everything to me.

JOHN: What about play?

HERBERT: It's all the same, if one cares.

JOHN: Are you writing a play?

HERBERT: No, I am not.

JOHN: Then you are not working now?

HERBERT: Indeed I am.

JOHN: At what then?

HERBERT: A novel.

JOHN: Why a novel?

HERBERT: It's a happier kind of work than to do a play.

JOHN: In what way?

HERBERT: One can use all of one's powers without worrying about areas to be provided for the work of others.

JOHN: It sounds ungenerous.

HERBERT: I'm hoping my readers will not feel so.

JOHN: Is the process so much happier than for a play?

HERBERT: Much, and simpler too.

JOHN: It has always appeared to me that a good novel was more complete than a good play.

HERBERT: I was speaking of the period after the writing as being simple. One sends his manuscript to a publisher and the answer will be a simple "yes" or "no." There need be no begging of producers, searching for directors, casting of actors and waiting for audience. The work of a novelist goes out, mysteriously, into the void. At present, this method enchants me. One's work may become less sullied. The artist like a Garbo can watch himself travelling from a distance, so that all wonder is not killed. It transports my spirit to think of others, curled in a chair, or on a bed, sharing thoughts with me.

JOHN: So you will not write more plays?

HERBERT: Not without great desire or reason.

JOHN: Are there no subjects or ideas which you encounter more suited to the stage? You once saw life as theatre.

HERBERT: I am more private now. Yet once in a while there is a particular happening which seems so suited to a drama. Only last week I was . . . ah well, I shall turn the scene towards thought rather than action.

JOHN: But maybe it belongs in a play.

HERBERT: No more than in a book.

JOHN: How can you be sure?

HERBERT: The incident I saw represented aspects of the Canadian nature which I have already spoken of in my last three playscripts.

JOHN: That sounds as if you had only one theme with which to work.

HERBERT: Perhaps I have and it is the one I have used in everything I wrote: poems, stories, one-act plays and the three long plays. I suppose it is my song.

JOHN: What was the incident?

HERBERT: It has truly haunted me for I saw terrible things alive within that short, unexpected incident or accident of everyday life. It was a warm spring day, almost like summer, a week ago, and I was walking on Yonge Street, happy to be among many moving people. Spring always makes me restless and somehow optimistic. I may depress you. Do you want me to go on?

JOHN: Can it be worse than what is past?

HERBERT: The horrors of the world do not have to happen to us to be horrifying. Sometimes we only have to see them.

JOHN: I'm depressed before you finish, but go on anyway. It's too late to forget.

HERBERT: I promise it has laughter in it too.

JOHN: I will try to be hopeful.

HERBERT: Good! So, as I said, the day was warm and friendly, and I had the urge to drop into a bar for a cold drink. Sometimes a bar feels companionable and promising, as no other place in society's edifices. In the bar there was a table near the one I took, and it was surrounded by noisy, merry young men in their twenties, of that type who come from upper-middle-class homes.

JOHN: How did you judge them that way?

HERBERT: They spoke reasonably well, were all in the kind of health suggestive of lifetimes of good food and family care, and they were dressed in the height of youthful fashion, clothes worn being of good materials and finely cut designs. And they were spending money rather too freely and unconcernedly to not have known where to obtain more. They all wore very expensive boots, which looked to be new. Perhaps they had gone shopping together for them that very afternoon. The boots were in the current fashion, with very high heels, deep platform soles and of leathers and suedes in mixed textures and colours.

JOHN: There is nothing wrong with men being handsomely dressed. You would admire those platform shoes on an actor on stage in a Greek comedy.

HERBERT: Wait, please! I was enjoying their enjoyment in their own hair, health, and habiliments. Permit me my story. As in a good scene in a play, at the peak of their happiness, a man entered the bar in faded working denims, carrying a tin lunch box and limping. I saw that the man had a very bad club foot, which was supported on a grotesquely high platform sole, perhaps of six inches in depth. He had a pale, haggard face and one could see the marks of much drinking written over its early torments.

JOHN: You may stop now. I know what's coming.

HERBERT: You started me off this evening, so you will hear me out; then you can seek all the distractions you want. I'll be brief.

JOHN: Get on with it, then. A crippled man entered.

HERBERT: Yes and he sat and ordered his beer like any

other man, hoping to relax and enjoy an easy hour or two of the distant companionship one feels in a bar. He had settled himself comfortably, lunch pail under his chair and cold beer glass in hand, some strain easing away from his worn countenance, when the table of young heroes discovered his presence. The handsomest of the youths, all fair skin, hair and dimples, leaned toward his fellows, whispering something to them, so they all turned to gaze at the lone drinker. He discovered their eight bright eyes turned on him like so many blue lamps, shining new, and his own weak, faded, veined windows looked back defensively, disturbed.

JOHN: You're stacking the cards in favour of the sad, old drinker with the club foot.

HERBERT: I shall identify with whom I choose, and I think of him as "The Worker," as opposed to "The Playboys." My story is a true one. It happened and I can only tell it with my voice.

JOHN: I can't win with you, it seems.

HERBERT: Maybe you fight for vague things. Some things are terribly real to me, and for a very long time. I shall always be able to remember last week's spring promise, and the loss of it. Let me not keep you too long. Let's finish. The Worker stared back at his audience and said with some hostility, "What the fuck are you apes gaping at?" The dimpled fair youth leaned toward the man very gracefully and replied, staring pointedly at the club foot, "Why, sir, we were just admiring your platform shoe. It's in the height of fashion, isn't it?"

JOHN: Well?

HERBERT: Well, what?

JOHN: Is that all?

HERBERT: Isn't that enough?

JOHN: You promised there was laughter too.

HERBERT: And there was; all the young men roared with hilarity at the cleverness.

JOHN: I don't understand what it had to do with you?

HERBERT: The look on the Worker's face echoed feelings very familiar to myself. He was past anger, accustomed to cruelty and injustice, and filled with deep contempt for his critics. He lifted his glass to them, without expression in his face of any kind, and said, "To your continued good health, gentlemen!" then his eyes dismissed them. There is no one I have ever seen that I admired more.

JOHN: Except yourself. Good-night!

HERBERT: Except myself. Good-bye!

Curtain

Chronology

1926	Born in Toronto, October 13, son of Claude Herbert Brundage and Gladys Reba (Kirk) Brundage.
1932-43	Educated in public schools in Ontario. In 1942 wrote his first play, "A Marshmallow Drama."
1943-44	First job as an artist in the advertising office of Eaton's Department store, Toronto.
1946	Served six months in Canadian prison reformatory, Guelph Institute.
1946-55	Worked at a variety of jobs: tobacco shipper, construction worker in Labrador, carnival spieler, builder on Winnipeg Dam, store clerk in Chicago, artist for ads, private club waiter in Toronto. Attended night classes at Art College of Ontario (1947-1949).
1955-58	Studied at New Play Society School for Drama in Toronto.
1958-60	Attended the School of the National Ballet of Canada.
1960-62	Artistic Director of Adventure Theatre, Toronto. Wrote and produced two plays, "Private Club" and "A Household God" (1962).
1962-65	Artistic Director of New Venture Players. Adapted a play by Dumas, "A Lady of Camellias," 1964 production. Wrote *Fortune and Men's Eyes*, 1964. Workshop production at Stratford Festival, 1965.

1965-70	Artistic Director and producer of the Garret Theatre Company, Toronto. Wrote "Born of Medusa's Blood," "Closer to Cleveland" (1967) production, *Close Friends* (1970), adapted Buchner's play, "World of Woyzeck," 1969 production. *Close Friends* produced in 1976. *Fortune and Men's Eyes* produced off-Broadway in 1967 at the Actors Playhouse, Sheridan Square, New York City.
1968	Awarded Dominion Drama Festival's Massey Award, which he refused.
1969-70	Summer School lecturer in Drama; Ryerson Polytechnical Institute, Toronto.
1972	Wrote ballet biography, *Belinda Wright and Jelko Yuresha*. Summer session lecturer in drama, York University, Toronto. "Born of Medusa's Blood," produced. Wrote the play "Omphale and the Hero."
1972-74	Actor, set and costume designer, prop man, lighting, stage and House Manager for New Play Society, Toronto. Dancer for Garbut Roberts Dance Drama Company.
1973-76	Summer School lecturer in drama, New College, University of Toronto (1973-76), and lecturer in writing, Three Schools of Art, Toronto, full semesters (1975-77).
1975	Received the Chalmers Award for his play, *Fortune and Men's Eyes*, as the Best Canadian Play produced in Toronto in 1975.
1975-77	Associate Editor of *Onion*, arts newspaper, issued twice a month in Toronto.
1977	Engaged in writing a novel, *The House That Jack Built*, published serially in *Onion*.

Selected Bibliography

Primary Sources

PLAYS

Beer Room. In *Some Angry Summer Songs.* Vancouver: Talonbooks, 1976.

"Born of Medusa's Blood." *MS.* Toronto, 1972.

Close Friends. In *Some Angry Summer Songs.* Vancouver: Talonbooks, 1976.

"Closer to Cleveland." *MS.* Toronto, 1967.

The Dinosaurs. In *Some Angry Summer Songs.* Vancouver: Talonbooks, 1976.

Fortune and Men's Eyes. New York: Grove Press, 1967; in *Open Space Plays*, London: Penguin. 1971.

"A Household God." *MS*, Toronto, 1962.

"A Lady of Camellias." Adaptation from A. Dumas, fils. Toronto, 1964.

"A Marshmallow Drama." *MS*, Toronto, 1942.

The Pearl Divers. In *Some Angry Summer Songs.* Vancouver: Talonbooks, 1976.

"Private Club." *MS*, Toronto, 1962.

"Omphale and the Hero." *The Canadian Theatre Review*, No. 3 (1974).

Some Angry Summer Songs. Vancouver: Talonbooks, 1976. (Four one-act plays.)

"World of Woyzeck." Adaptation of a play by Georg Buchner. *MS*, Toronto, 1969.

ARTICLES

"My Life and Hard Times in Cold, Bitter, Suspicious Toronto." In *The Toronto Book*, edited by William Kilbourn. Toronto: Macmillan Company of Canada Ltd., 1976.

"Report of Conference, 'Face to Face'," *Canadian Drama/L'Art dramatique canadien* (Fall, 1975).

"Tepid Theater in a Cold Climate." *The Village Voice*, (New York) 1967.

"Theater Seen." *Glitter* (March-June 1975).

BIOGRAPHY

Belinda Wright and Jelko Yuresha. London: Kaye Bellman, 1972.

Secondary Sources

ADILMAN, SID. "Savage Realities of a Penitentiary Riot." *The Telegram* (Toronto), May 28, 1971.

ANTHONY, GERALDINE. *John Herbert*. Profiles in Canadian Drama. Gage Publishing Ltd., forthcoming.

"Author of Hit Play Is Barred from United States." *New York Times*, October 6, 1967.

BERGER, JENEVIA. "John Herbert, A Man Who Doesn't Rest on His Laurels." *Tribal Village*, October 21, 1969.

BRYDEN, RONALD. "Theatre." *The Observer Review* (London, England), July 14, 1968.

CARSON, NEIL. "Sexuality and Identity in *Fortune and Men's Eyes*." *Twentieth Century Literature* 18, No. 3 (1972), pp. 207-18.

COBB, DAVI. "You Think It's Easy to Produce a Play?" *The Telegram* (Toronto), January 6, 1968.

COHEN, NATHAN. *Canadian Writing Today*. London: Penguin, 1970.

———. "Catching Up with Fiction." *The Toronto Star*, September 16, 1968.

———. "When *Fortune and Men's Eyes* Opened." *The Toronto Star*, September 7, 1967.

EVANS, RON. "Theatre." *The Telegram* (Toronto), October 20, 1967.

"Film's Shooting Remains at Old Prison on Plains." *Quebec Chronicle Telegraph*, November 24, 1970.

KAREDA, URJO. "Whatever Happened in This New Effort by Toronto Playwright?" *The Toronto Star*, December 30, 1972.

KRETZMER, HERBERT. "Moving, Frightening, Funny and a Hard Look at Life." *The Daily Express* (London, England), July 19, 1968.

LA GUARDIA, ROBERT. "Diary of Three Motley Days in a Quebec Jailhouse." *After Dark* (Montreal), May, 1971, pp. 35-40.

LANKEN, DANE. "A Movie That Could Shake Our Society." *The Saturday Gazette* (Montreal), November 7, 1970.

LYNCH, MICHAEL. "That Man's Scope." *The Body Politic*, No. 10, (1973). (1973).

MEZEI, STEPHEN. "Born of Medusa's Blood." *Performing Arts* 10, No. 1 (1973), pp. 21-22.

MESSENGER, ANN. *Dramatists in Canada*. Vancouver: University of British Columbia Press, 1972.

MICHAEL, FRANK. "Structure Distorted, Style Disparate." *The Canadian Jewish News*, January 5, 1973.

NAEDELE, WALTER. "Prison Life Is More Than Just Bars," *The Evening Bulletin* (Philadelphia), June 13, 1968.

PRITCHETT, OLIVER. "The Power Politics of Homosexual Life." *The Guardian* (London, England), July 21, 1968.

RUBIN, DON. "Garret Theatre's Trio of Plays Makes for an Interesting Evening." *The Toronto Star*, November 8, 1968.

SHORTER, ERIC. "Canadian Convict Life Shown in Play." *Daily Telegraph* (London, England,) July 12, 1968.

SINGER, SAMUEL. "Herbert Play Depicts Life in Prison." *Philadelphia Inquirer*, June 3, 1968.

SMITH, MICHAEL. "Theater Journal." *The Village Voice*, March 2, 1967.

"Week in Theatre." *The Stage* (London, England), June 18, 1968.

WHITTAKER, HERBERT. "'Medusa's Blood': Lots of Insult, Little Drama." *The Globe and Mail* (Toronto), December 14, 1972.

————. "Toronto's Jack Brundage Has a Winner." *The Globe and Mail* (Toronto), March 4, 1967.

YOUNG, B. A. "What Is a Play?" *The Roundhouse* (Chalk Farm, London, England), July 24, 1968.

Eight

MICHAEL COOK

(1933-)

Preface

Michael Cook, like his fellow countryman, Tom Grainger, had to leave school early in life to go to work as a labourer, and he therefore came late to the writing of plays. After a twelve-year stint in the British Army, followed by a three-year course in drama at Nottingham University, Cook, aged 33, began to write radio plays. That year, 1966, he emigrated from England to Canada settling in St. John's, Newfoundland, where he directed plays for Memorial University. His first radio play was accepted by the Canadian Broadcasting Company and he plunged into the writing of short radio plays, averaging about three a year for CBC. Three years later he founded the St. John's Summer Festival of the Arts.

In 1971 Cook wrote his first full-length stage play, Colour the Flesh the Colour of Dust, which has been performed in St. John's, Toronto, Ottawa, and Halifax. Two years later he wrote another Newfoundland play, Head, Guts and Soundbone Dance, presented in St. John's, Montreal, Calgary, Regina, and Fredericton as well as on national CBC-TV. There followed two short plays, Quiller, and Tiln, produced at St. John's and in Montreal. Cook was then commissioned by Festival Lennoxville to write two full-length plays. He wrote Jacob's Wake, produced at Lennoxville in 1975, and completed "The Gayden Chronicles" in 1977. The Centaur Theatre in Montreal commissioned him to write a one-act play and he wrote Therese's Creed which Centaur Theatre produced in 1977.

Michael Cook has become nationally known in Canadian theatre within a very short time. He has been writing stage plays for only five years and it is obvious from his eleven plays *that he is rapidly developing his own style. Like John Coulter and Tom Grainger, he is an immigrant to Canada. His attempts to catch the nuances of Newfoundland speech, the tone and atmosphere of Newfoundland life, have been increasingly successful. But whether he will eventually settle for Newfoundland drama or seek his inspiration in his own past personal experiences in Britain, Europe and the east it is still too early to predict. So far he has opted for Newfoundland plays exclusively. Of the nineteen radio plays and the eleven stage plays he has written in the past five years, three stage plays have become nationally known:* Colour the Flesh the Colour of Dust, Head, Guts and Soundbone Dance, *and* Jacob's Wake. *The first and weakest of his plays,* Colour the Flesh the Colour of Dust, *is set in St. John's in 1762 and records the historical event of the transfer of political power from British to French and back to British rule. The Newfoundland people ride with the tide, easily changing their allegiances with successive transfers of power. Politics fails to touch them essentially. A large cast of soldiers, politicians, harlots, fishermen and ordinary folk people the play. Yet it remains artificial in its setting, characterization and dialogue.*

But Cook's next stage work, Head, Guts and Soundbone Dance, *triumphantly catches the spirit and the subtleties of speech of the Newfoundland fisherman. A powerful folk play, it assumes the qualities of myth, exposing the beliefs, hopes and fears of past generations of Newfoundlanders. The play reaches its tragic climax when Skipper Pete gives the shocking reason for his refusal to save a drowning boy: "The sea wanted him, Old Molly. She took him in her good time. She marked him down . . . She touched him the day he was borned." The fatalism in this play reminds one of Sean O'Casey's* Riders to the Sea, *and again of the power in Greek Tragedy. Michael Cook himself has said that in the Newfoundland outports " . . . the elements of a great civilization survive . . . whose life experience is essentially Greek, profoundly tragic . . ." In* Head, Guts and Soundbone Dance *he has caught and held this experience, while at the same time portraying the jealousies and cruelties of men toward each other.*

Jacob's Wake *is Cook's most powerful play to date. A family conflict play in the genre established by* O'Neill's Long Day's Journey into Night, *Tennessee William's* Glass Menagerie *and* David French's Leaving Home, *it reveals a live, unforgettable Newfoundland family confrontation. Each member establishes his own individual identity as the play develops. Skipper, the old patriarch, has spawned a family whose weaknesses, dishonesties, cruelties, and madness grow beyond control. The dialogue is natural, the suspense admirably built up. Only the ending seems a mistake in a play that relies totally on realism throughout. There is a sudden change to fantasy in a symbolic ending with the old dead skipper suddenly appearing at the door and charging the family to leap to their posts. Cook's unexpected conclusion offers the theatre-goer cause for reflection.*

The future looks bright for Michael Cook. Each succeeding play improves on the last. His imaginative hold on the Newfoundland scene, his talent for realistic Newfoundland dialogue and characterization, his own Anglo-Irish background, provide him with the tools necessary to fashion a body of drama revealing the unique qualities of a race of people set apart from the Mainland, rich in their own traditions.

I think I was five. Or was it six? I remember it distinctly. It was a bright summer's day somewhere in rural Buckinghamshire, England. I had laboured secretly for weeks, writing furtively by candlelight in my small room high in the attic of the old Georgian house inhabited by my uncle on my mother's side. The house was surrounded with great lime trees, planted by Calamity Brown, so my uncle said. The branches tapped urgently at the leaded panes as I laboured, urging me on.

I had also bribed, bullied, and cajoled the other members of my Anthroposophical Kindergarten Class into participating in the tragedy, for that is what it was. A five-act play portraying the vicissitudes of infant life. There was to be a garden party at the school. The place was thronging with mothers and fathers and uncles and aunts and sisters and brothers and their future lifetime associates. We were to put on a play. Oh yes, I knew what they expected. Some boring little scene from history, sweet little Mary Crewe lisping her way through Elizabeth's coronation, or the odious Bertram Tuck strutting to Agincourt on his bandy legs. Well, they were going to get a shock. A three-and-a-half-hour exposé of the kindergarten view of the adult world, a bitter brew of frustration and hate with a few furtive fecal asides thrown in for good measure. It was 1939. And the shock waves the play would generate would be compounded a few days later by the Declaration of War.

Ah! How nice if it were true. How lucky to have stored away somewhere some anecdote confirming direction and destiny. If only G.B.S. or somebody of that ilk had patted me on the head and said kindly, "You will go far little man." Unfortunately everyone thought I was destined to be a bank manager at best or a travelling salesman at worst, and for myself, I had no idea who I was, where I was going or what talents I possessed, if any, which might be utilized in some future existence at twenty or thirty or at any age whatsoever.

To be honest, I always wanted to be a poet.

This was, in part, a smokescreen.

My mother, whom I do not remember, had been by report a fine pianist. My father was an accomplished watercolourist in the gentle, melancholy English style, and his own dramatic

gifts, whimsical, of Irish extraction, were manifest in his gift
for caricature, at which he was a master. Granted different
circumstances, he could have become a brilliant political
cartoonist, but it was not to be. The Irish Connection (my
grandfather), spendthrift, loquacious, inheritor of the gentleman's tastes but without the inclination to work for the
means, had reduced the family of seven to dire straits and
when he was bodily thrown out of the house by his sons, the
pattern of my father's life had become clear.

By day he laboured as a draughtsman. At night he painted
and dreamed. As he grew older, the washes grew more
abstract, the colours more vivid, the landscapes shifting and
changing as if he was wrestling to break down all he knew of
form, in his art and his life, and start anew. He was a good
man. I think it was for him that I wrote "the bravest people I
know are the ones who endure."

But as I've said, I determined at a comparatively early age
that I wanted to be a poet. This helped to allay the onslaught
of instruction which everyone seemed to think would surely
develop some hidden talent somewhere in either music or
painting. It seems in retrospect that my interest in words was
purely defensive. I was also a splendid liar, a gift which is
much misunderstood by parents and child-trainers who in
their rigid pursuit of truth destroy the soul. The American
people have had much to endure, but surely nothing has been
more catastrophic for the American imagination than the
stuffing of every child's head with the example of the
wretched George Washington who never told a lie. Nixon rode
to history on the back of that myth.

Lying and poetry. Not much of a future in that, and in fact,
as it soon became apparent that I was pretty deficient in
almost all academic pursuits, confrontations with school
authorities grew, and my poor harassed father, by now into his
Second World War, must have considered that he had a
delinquent on his hands. The upshot of all this was that my
schooling was arrested, abruptly, at the age of fifteen when I
was thrown out, and I was at last able to be free. Free in this
instance meant the discipline of physical labour, and off I
wandered in pursuit of something or other until it became

obvious, even to me, that I was ill-equipped to handle life in any capacity. And so I joined the army for twelve years, in which institution I stayed in a semi-retarded state, fed, clothed, bustled here and there about the globe, in a womb-like trance observing as in a dream the colour and corruption of humanity.

I still toyed with poetry.

As my father had found his skill with caricature and cartoon to be valuable personal aids in wartime, so now did I find that a few lines of doggerel could work wonders, if written with the right amount of impudence and deference for superiors, and pure filth for one's peers. I learnt for the first time that words are power. And power in this instance meant survival, allowing for a protective shield which warded off the worst excesses of an often brutal and savage and violent life. A life, however, not without light. There were even warm friendships, much riot, and endless opportunities for learning the true meaning of absurdity.

I have gone through this preamble in an attempt to find out myself why I began to write plays. I don't honestly know. I also feel acutely embarrassed when called upon to discuss my own work in any context. The plays should say it all, and who really gives a damn for the peculiar circumstances which divert the most unlikely candidates into egomaniacs convinced that they have something to say which isn't just of value — every living thing is of value — but which craves form and demands attention, whilst at the same time howling like a demented canine for privacy? The writer's schizophrenia is reinforced by the practical demands of survival. He or she needs publicity and exposure. Yet the mechanics of such displays are agonizing, an expense of spirit in a waste of shame.

I remember, still with horror, an interview conducted after the televised performance of *Head, Guts and Soundbone Dance*. For three hours under the merciless lights, the interviewer and I bandied words and phrases, sweating Ping-Pong players; he attempting to score with forehand smashes and I presenting a flat, bland bat. It was all wrong. The questions were wrong. The answers were wrong. I didn't want to be there. Whatever the viewers thought of the play, they didn't want to listen to someone who supposedly had written the damned thing acting as critic and guide through this supposedly unfamiliar terrain. The critics were enraged and gleeful, pouncing on the interview, not the play or its production. Urjo Kareda, then of *The Toronto Star*, shouted his disapproval, gobbling up this writer like a defenceless snail.

It's frequently the same with tape-recorded interviews, made with a view for later publication. The writer, in insensitive hands, is edited, tailored and moulded to fit the interviewer's concept. One may be forgiven for becoming slightly paranoic at this moment in time, for the country seems to abound with manic figures brandishing cameras, tape recorders, pens, and notebooks, all seeking to publish definitive views of Canadian artists whether the artist wills it or not.

And there's the rub.

Whether they will it or no, the artists need it.

It is not surprising that those in the performing media develop distinct personas. Quick-change artists by trade, they lug these other beings about, one to fit every conceivable occasion. If you're Dylan Thomas or Brendan Behan, harassed to the point of pain, then you get, and stay, drunk until the performer takes over, kicks the artist aside and, like the goat at the Killorglin Fair, presides over the chaotic celebration of sacrifice. Unlike the current Killorglin goat, however, the artist is not turned free at the end of his Misrule. The sacrifice is played out to the end.

It's a dangerous game.

An attractive, and necessary and potentially ruinous affair with the self. Overt onanism.

And to compound it all, there is fear.

Not fear of flying.

Fear of failure.

Talking about the work just finished always gives me a tight feeling at the back of the throat, a sick feeling in the stomach. It's dead. Finished. Done with. The exhilaration I feel when I've actually finished a new play is always short-lived. What next? The question crops up unasked, uninvited, over dinner, rediscovering the children after days or weeks of abstraction, watching, with Madonna, the caplin roll onto the beaches, to spawn and die. One of creation's mysteries. Lightning flickers through the mist and the fish in their millions panic in the fluorescent waves. It's not death that causes the panic. It's the waves that will send them spinning and floundering onto the beach before they've spawned. And Madonna rushes up and down, seeking out the females, throwing them back in. And the question rises. What next?

Failure or success, the manuscript that lies by the side of the typewriter has ceased to be the reason and justification for your confirmation as playwright. Oh, you can rewrite it, and rewrite it. But the mainspring has gone. It takes another idea. Another play. The assurance that you can start and finish another one. What next?

Talking about the past, then, increases that fear, adds to uncertainty. And the true analysis of self, the workings of the soul, takes place in private, in the dark of the mind, washing dishes, digging the garden, hammering fence posts. And in plays. If anything slips out here, it will be by a process of oblique reference, avoiding all the central questions, attempting to talk as I would to a friendly visitor, over a cup of tea or coffee, in the kitchen.

Why did I begin to write plays?

Because I felt a compulsion to dramatize myself? Perhaps.

I still do it. I'm doing it now.

And that I suppose, explains the fear, and the foolish vulnerability. Perhaps there will come a time when I'll create a universe of characters from whom I can be completely detached. Like God. Or Robertson Davies.

But of course, it goes beyond self, spreads out into all areas of one's experience. I think in a series of images, dramatic scenes, and circumstances. It sometimes horrifies me that even with my best friends, half drunk, some recess of the mind is blocking out the situation and storing away the dialogue, or at least, selecting and editing and expanding upon the dialogue and situation and setting. I used to question my own sincerity until I came to live in rural Newfoundland. My neighbours know what I do. Craftsmen themselves, they respect the craft of other people, particularly if they labour with honesty. When they stop for a chat over a cup of tea or a beer, or just over the fence, they are aware of the nature of my response, which frees them to respond in an equivalent way, with imagination and freedom. The mythology, the history, the tall tales and the true, are gifts from them to me. Their response to the plays that incorporate much of their material in many ways is always direct, not always approving, but often warm and, when they are approving I feel that I have fulfilled my function as an artist, joining with them in a celebration of life and the imagination and ideas that sustain it. They understand the ritualistic necessity of change and interchange, of recreation.

As one friend and neighbour put it: "When I wants to build a boat I goes to the woods to cut the lumber. Ye just can't take any tree, ye has to be selective, big old spruce with a bow in her for the knees, and straight fer for the planking and so on. And we cuts her down and hauls her down and puts her through the sawmill and makes a boat of the trees. They's still trees in a manner of speaking, but they is something else." There it is. Editing, selection, craft, recreation, the tree living with a new identity, form and shape. And so, as I've said, I don't bother about that kind of use of people anymore. Of course, plays, unlike the boats my neighbours build, can sink much faster, and often do in this country, which still has a fairly minimal response to the theatrical needs of the community, still suffers in large part from that dreadful hangover which began in the seventeenth century, the divorce of the theatre from its roots, the people themselves.

I suppose though, that there are currently advantages in the situation. With one or two exceptions, most plays run for a brief period, then are lost in time as the frantic search for newer and better plays goes on. The onus is upon the playwright to keep producing. I doubt if many playwrights in this country have pipe dreams of having a major international success, of achieving any degree of financial security from the theatre. To some extent, then, we are freed from Mittyism, and must concentrate upon producing, must have in fact, a fierce belief in what we are.

And in any event, I am not a popular playwright, in the accepted sense of the word. I doubt if I ever will be. I like confrontation in an age that seeks reassurance, not uncertainty. I like to challenge and to shock and to reach as far as possible into certain levels of experience and consciousness which are perhaps as painful to some as they are rich and joyous to me. One of the paradoxes in me as a person is that knowing this, I'm still acutely sensitive, far too sensitive, to criticism by the very people whose opinions can be signposted in advance. I expect I'll learn one day. It is of greater satisfaction to find that actors and directors become really excited by my work. It elicits a high energy response from them, a clear-cut commitment, and a physical involvement which a lot of contemporary scripts seem to avoid. In a sense I suppose my work is populist, if not popular.

Enough of this kind of self-analysis, though. It's enough to say that I write about people I know, including myself. They exist in a peculiarly Canadian reality—as I do myself. And they pain and they suffer and they use humour as a weapon or an escape, and they find it difficult to love. Not unnatural. And they pursue—the people anyway—a staggering path toward God!

My first play was a woeful attempt at what used to pass for drawing-room comedy in the fifties. I'd directed a few of them by then, in the Army, for garrison entertainments. I showed it to an acquaintance of the family, then Reuters Far East Correspondent in Singapore. He kindly suggested that I give up all thoughts of writing and make a career in the Army. It was an interesting time for me, I realize in retrospect. I read omnivorously and had opinions about everyone, from Shakespeare to Beckett, which were not impeded by the workings of intellect. I suspect that some of them were—as personal intuitive responses to work and words that excited me—more valid than later critical responses filtered through the more formal process of a college education acquired when I left the service. I've always had a deep distrust in my own head, of intellectual responses. I have had the feeling, whether correctly or not, that my work would change utterly, and a terrible boredom would be born.

When I directed *Hamlet* in the Arts and Culture Centre in St. John's, I was anxious to minimize his intellectual agony—confusion perhaps is a better word— and concentrate upon the disruptive excitement generated in an overheated brain by the circumstances with which he was confronted, an excitement that was already present before the play commenced. I saw Hamlet as a man of immense physical energy, of raw animal power trapped by birth and breeding and intellectual attainment into a life style he didn't want in the first place, a frustrated playwright, adept at self-dramatization, confronted with a plot and a series of characters not of his own making. My actor would be a volcano, violent, cunning, explosive, enjoying himself hugely on several of the most traumatic occasions, and moving towards resolution only when he had come to terms with his own nature, with nature herself. I would like to have cut "To be or not to be" altogether, but left some of it in under pressure!

I suppose that one of the reasons that *The Tempest* is my favourite play of Shakespeare's is its sublimation of intellect to the process of the supernatural, itself an intuitive response to the process of science, and its concentration upon the world of nature as it exists within and without us, to the imaginative illumination of the dark and glowing soul of men. *The Tempest* is a play for any time. Prospero, the prophet and seer, returns to the world of reality, which was death, and leaves to us the world, the island. But how can Caliban hear the voices in the trees, go gathering berries in the glades? The hope of his nature, that intuitive response to the natural world which alone would refine the animality, has been denied him. Rivers rot. Forests die. The seas—Miranda with nothing to protect her—are raped. We have become either dumb or deformed. Prufrock and Caliban are brothers. I have a strong urge, every time another astronaut is to be launched from anywhere—Russia or America—to beg Mission Control to keep the purpose of the journey a secret. Give the astronaut a sealed package of orders, not to be opened until he's well past the moon. Then let him open them, with every television set in the world waiting to hear what the instructions are. And they would be: "You are to find God."

It would be difficult for me to state specifically what playwrights or plays have influenced me. Theatre has influenced me. I think that's it. My tastes are pretty haphazard, as they are in most things. I'm also self-conscious about reaching for any identification, knowing that in some bored critic's mind there'll be instant fuel to feed in the next review or general feature. I've already been accused of aping Synge and O'Casey and on one occasion even George Bernard Shaw, God help us. One of the nicest things about being a writer, or any artist, is learning from your companions, whether they've been gone a thousand years or are your peers. We have, as a community, a sense of tradition stronger than race, place or time, and struggle to give something tangible to each other. I forget the context but I remember the poet, Masefield, and the lines about our function here: "But gathering, as we stray, a sense/Of life, so lovely and intense/It lingers when we wander hence,/That those who follow feel behind/Their backs, when all before is blind,/Our joy, a rampart to the mind."

I have, on occasion, deliberately taken images, sometimes ideas, from fellow playwrights living and dead. I don't think they'd mind. It's part of that ritual of sharing again. I certainly wouldn't. I remember vividly a line from the film, *The Magnificent Seven*. Eli Wallach plays a superbly villainous bandit in charge of a band of marauding guerillas terrorizing a village. Confronted by the villagers' hired protectors, led by Yul Brynner, he wonders at their motive. There's enough for all, he says, we could share it. "After all, if God didn't want them sheared, he would not have made them sheep." It's a great line. Years later, writing my one-act play *Tiln*, I converted it to: "If God had meant lamps to be lit, he'd have hung them in the Garden of Eden."

I have favourites of course. I like Shakespeare and Marlowe and Jonson (Can't stand Dryden) and Webster, some of Ibsen, particularly *Brand* and *Peer Gynt*, and Strindberg, and Williams and O'Neill, and Behan and Beckett (I think *Endgame* is the finest English-language play I've ever read, but then it was first written in French) and *All That Fall* is possibly the supreme height of the radio dramatist's art; I like Osborne and Arden David Rudkin and Albee. Of my contemporaries here, I like Ryga, Freeman, Gurik, Reaney, and Tremblay. I like Hardin too—he has a rare mythological sensibility. The list can go on and on. The only remarkable thing about it is the huge gaps and the people left out. If there is anything consistent in the list, it's that none of the playwrights are afraid of language or emotion or the earth. I don't know why; perhaps it's a by-product of the celluloid and closed world of television, but we seem to be scared of richness, of poetry and rhetoric, of supercharged emotional responses, of the reality of pain and joy as it is lived by all of us.

The most successful plays in Canada, not necessarily—in fact, frequently not—Canadian are those which do not disturb sensibilities, people's images of themselves. A little laughter, a little pain, sentiment, not sensibility and, above all, plays which conform to the mode and style of other cultures, notably American or English. I don't believe that this success can be judged in terms of the potential majority of theatre audiences. It's an essentially middle-class response, dominated by the attitudes of Theatre Board Members and similar governing bodies who look at a packed house for yet another Neil Simon play and say, "This is obviously what the audience wants," but never take time to find out where that audience comes from and how representative it is of the community the theatre is supposed to serve.

One of the sadder occurrences in Canadian theatre in the past few years has been the splintering of theatrical energies. Our major theatres as a rule steer blindly along the same traditional course, while all around them, other groups, practicing Passe Muraille style theatre, collective creations, haphazard and clumsy but passionately devoted traditional companies surviving on shoestrings in rural communities, seek to serve, rediscover, and communicate with the people who have been denied theatre and images of themselves for centuries. I have always felt that such a state of affairs is not, as it's currently popular to say, indicative of a healthy state of affairs. It's just the opposite.

A healthy theatre is one of such diversity, yes, but one in which each unit communicates, shares, interchanges, bound by a common philosophy, funded from a central budget, each recognizing the essential function and need of the other. With such a system we could embrace even Stratford. With such a network of communication, bound by common ideology, it would be possible for an actor playing a season at Stratford as say, Richard III, or Angelo, to move to Newfoundland at the end of the season and spend six weeks recreating the life of the fishermen of Joe Batt's Arm. Unfortunately, we have that ancient, worn-out class struggle between establishment and workers, in the very art form which alone of all art forms has within it the possibility of creating bloodless revolution and reform, of bonding and binding the country into a cultural unity such as existed in Elizabethan England. For centuries, too, our theatre has neglected its history, its mythology, and above all its people, afflicted with a strange self-destructive disease, similar to that which the Aztecs must have had when confronted by the rapacious Cortez. One of the prevailing attitudes militating against the formation of such an indigenous theatre as I, and thousands like me, dream of is the attitude of many critics.

"The great mass of Canadian plays," they chortle, "are appallingly mediocre." Fine. Quite true. Many of them no doubt are appallingly bad. However, the vast mass of Canadian people don't get the chance to trot off to New York or London and make invidious comparisons. The vast mass of Canadian people don't read plays. Until some of our critics have been to the remoter parts of this hungry country and seen how a starved audience reacts to a clumsy and amateurish troupe putting on some appalling melodrama, they will never learn what an audience response is, or what the basic needs of the people are, or what the real purpose of theatre in this country should be. And it is not to mount a production which will have a huge success on Broadway; no, not even one that might bring down the St. Lawrence Centre, like the facile *Trelawney of the Wells*, but plays which, however mediocre, relate and have meaning for the people hungry for images of themselves, hungry for theatre, for entertainment, for anything that is alive. For every Shakespeare there are fifty lesser playwrights. All of them being seen and performed. That is what creates an audience sensibility, an audience's own critical judgment, an audience's sense of participation and progress. If such playwrights had not been performed in Elizabethan England, then Shakespeare's progress itself might have been damaged, if not destroyed. The same is true of the Irish and Spanish Renaissance. And yet here, certain members of the critical gallery, watchdogs of excellence, of what constitutes good theatre, would deny material which, if not high art, is at least relevant to Canadian theatre, while condoning wretched mediocrity, if not actually applauding it, everywhere else.

The whole question of criticism in this country must be reviewed by every concerned member of the theatrical community and the audiences alike. What responsibility does an editor of a major newspaper have for the competence and qualification of his theatre critics? Or doesn't he care? It's an important question and one that needs to be examined. As does the whole wretched business of dishing out luncheons to critics, free tickets, free drinks, treating them like potentates. They, surely, like the artists they review, should be working craftsmen, who are paid to do a job of work. Their responsibility is awesome. Their integrity must not be in doubt, if they are to be respected. The necessity for them is not at issue. But certainly when the issue of mediocrity is raised, we should examine carefully the quality of the person raising the question.

It is true that we must seek excellence. It is true that standards must be continually raised. But these aims must go hand in hand with a healthy over-all dramatic picture. It is the quality and diversity of theatrical productions which make decisive critical standards possible, which make it possible for a critic to speak to a self-educated audience. This is the goal.

Enough of that.

Strangely, a lot of the central ideas from my plays come from lines in poetry. My poetry. That, too, has never seen, nor is likely to see, the light of day, but it frees me to experiment with words and images that form associations which mould themselves finally into a dramatic picture.

> *I have been listening to the pearled*
> *and fishy parables of the sea,*
> *to the screeching sermons of desolate gulls,*
> *to the scuttling cantos of crabs:*
> *have broken salt with Noah wise men*

who hung their Jonahs from the yardarms
of sailing barns,
scattered black ash and burning alms bowls
across Golgothas of grey seas
I have been sucked down dreaming
into the green and screaming darkness
drifted with bladderwrack and the black seed
of sea moss amongst bones, and wrecks, and
reptiles
and mad-mouthed enigmas of forgotten
empires.

When I came to Canada in 1966 I was unemployed.

I directed a play or two for the university, but soon discovered that there was no market for any prospective stage scripts, of which I had half a dozen by that time, and so I set about converting them into radio scripts. I've always been fascinated by radio as an artistic medium. It's one of the last refuges of poetic drama. It is, in the context of the confined television and theatrical world of which I've been speaking, one of the last refuges of the imagination. You can dispel the unities or hold to them absolutely. You can use sound as it exists in reality—rarely possible on the stage. You can drop a word into the blind eye of the listener and wait in silence for it to spread ripples like a stone in a pool. I've written about twenty plays I think in the last nine years for radio, ranging from the mediocre to the good. One or two I think, are very good, but alas, too true to the form demanded by the medium to be adapted back to the stage.

One of the saddest things about writing for radio is that it is a one-shot thing. There's your hour or your hour and a half. Two or three months or even more work. And then it's gone. You turn the set off. Silence. The play is finished. It's ephemeral. Never to be published. Never to be heard again.
to it. Some of their finest work has gone into it. That's another thing that's indicative of the general critical response to

In a sense, radio is still—despite everyone's mourning its loss with the demise of Andrew Allan—the real repertory of Canadian theatre. Every writer in the country has contributed theatre in this country. It's ignored by every paper, by pretty well every critic. Who listens to radio? Well, we all know who listens to radio. It's the people in the rural communities. It's the people who prefer the spoken word to the visual image. It's the people who haven't lost the capacity to sit and listen and concentrate. Both they, and the people who write for them, are quietly ignored. And the luckless programmers and producers for the Canadian Broadcasting Corporation spend fifty percent of their creative energies fighting for the lives of their programs, their actors, their writers.

Once again we're behind, of course. In the States, radio drama has found a new lease of life. There's a vast educational audience clamouring for material. In Great Britain, after a period when they thought all was lost, it's come back in full swing, finding to its astonishment a huge audience. In Germany radio drama is reaching a new peak.

I'm preaching again, but with reason. Radio has kept half the writers in this country alive. And, unlike its rival, television, has defined itself as a specific art form. TV still flounders along, committed to politics and the documentary, with occasional fearful bows in the direction of plays. Fearful because few producers have yet been able to match technology with the art of theatre. Fearful because, at the switch of a button, millions who've never been exposed to a play will be confronted with something other than soap opera and dreadful sitcoms and will immediately complain. Fearful because they haven't yet developed the stamina to absorb the complaints and push boldly on. And the writers are fearful, too, knowing that in the editing room their script might become a travesty of the original, a new work of art created by the director.

The medium will hopefully triumph, but it is in its infancy, whereas radio came of age with Tyrone Guthrie's "The Squirrel's Cage." I'll continue to write for it, despite the lack of feedback and that sense of satisfaction that comes from a known participation. It is artistically satisfying. It also, very practically, helps to provide a livelihood. It's a good year when I can make five thousand dollars from my plays. That's a bad year for an actor or director, and unheard of for theatre management. Something has to be done about allowing playwrights in this country sufficient to live on with dignity, without stress of having to seek other work.

Colour the Flesh the Colour of Dust is the first play of mine to see the light of day in Canada. I don't know what to say about it, really. I think it reads better than it plays. Once again, the stumbling block, I think, in terms of response to it, is that it deliberately mixes caricature with character, Dickens-like. I still don't know why I shouldn't do it. The reality of caricature is the moral force behind it. In that play both the Merchant and the Magistrate are caricatures representing dual forces of evil, usury, corruption, greed. Their success or failure depends to a large extent on the force and comprehension of those qualities and the force with which they're played. It's episodic in structure. I don't think that goes down too well anymore. It contains some of the best lines I've ever written, but a few good lines don't necessarily make a good play. If I appear to be ambiguous in my feelings about it it's because I have become confused myself. People either loved it or hated it. Keith Turnbull, who directed the play at the St. Lawrence Centre, loved the play but grieved that he was unable to fulfill its potential, basically because of the working conditions and the nature of the company involved. I think it would make a great film. Unfortunately, everybody seized upon the historical aspect—it is based upon the one historical incident of the French capturing St. John's in 1762 and its recapture six months later. If it's historical, the argument ran, then the substance must be authentic, documentary. But I have, after all, written a play. It's like asking—and I'm not making this comparison for any other purpose than to make the point—Shakespeare to be more accurate with regard to Henry IV or V, or George Ryga not to tamper with the life and times of Paracelsus.

I'm not sure about that play. I once toyed with the idea of turning it into an opera. The mind boggles.

I like *Head, Guts and Soundbone Dance*.

I'm fascinated by what people do with their hands. The way they move. I wanted to incorporate many of the fisherman's basic activities into a play, net-mending, splitting fish, making tea, making a killick . . . I reasoned that these things, dying things, would be as fascinating to the audience to whom they were relevant as they would to those not familiar with them. Once again, various people made a mistake setting it in a specific time. The only thing relevant to time was that the world they inhabited was gone. And the Old Skipper had retreated, yard by yard to his stage head and there re-created, kept it alive, in his head, with his hands, with his loyal and confused crew.

It had, I believe, a confused production in Montreal. The truth of the situation was revealed when Sean Mulcahy, who had seen the production, came up to me in St. John's and said, "I like it." "What?" I said. "The play. *Head, Guts and Soundbone Dance.* I've just read it. That's not the play I saw in Montreal." Well, that's the way it goes.

The nicest reaction, for me, came from a friend who was in a bar down on the Southern Shore of Newfoundland. A fisherman walked in, turned off the hockey game and turned on the TV production of the play. The whole bar watched in silence and spent the rest of the night in animated discussion of it. The language, I was assured, was a matching facsimile. Walter Learning did a fine production in New Brunswick, with Henry Beckman as Skipper Pete and Sean Sullivan as Uncle John. He put them to work in a fish plant in Campobello before rehearsals started. The results were startling.

These old Skippers were gods, you know. Some were benign. Others were despots. And they lived for water. For fish. For the challenge of the sea. The challenge of manhood. While I was writing this I had a conversation with a neighbour of mine. We were down on the beach. I'd just come up from bringing the boat ashore, for her summer clean-up. I said, "Didn't I see you fishing this morning?" He's seventy-six, lives by himself now. Son's gone. Wife gone. Home gone. He was resettled from twelve miles down on Ireland's Eye Island. He replied, "Makes me sick to look at'n," he said. "The salt water. I turns the other way now." "Sick," for him, was heartsick.

Jacob's Wake is difficult for me to talk about. It's still very close. I only finished the last rewrite some six weeks before Festival Lennoxville produced it in the summer of '75. I threw just about everything into that, including an apocalyptic end-of-the-world scene, with the Old Skipper upstairs coming down as a ghost to lead the broken family into death. The family in this case, I suppose, being a little more than a family. The Old Sealing Skipper upstairs, his son, Winston, living on welfare, a man of critical sensibility and conscience trying to drown his despair in drink and sardonic wit; his three sons, a politician, a bar-owner, and a religious maniac, and his wife, Rosie, the real power, dominant, yet rarely forceful, secure, without confusion, mother-image constant in the face of disaster, relying upon instinct not intellect—there I go again—to hold her family together. And Aunt Mary, Winston's sister, prim, old-maidish, a schoolteacher, struggling to preserve her dignity in a disruptive house. Outside, the storm becomes a living thing, which threatens and finally engulfs them all.

I suppose one of the germane ideas for the play comes from E. J. Pratt, whose evolutionary vision informs most of his major poems about Newfoundland, or the sea. There is a point at which man's cupidity or greed, or simple desertion of the instinctive laws of nature that bind each to each, will result in disaster. "The Titanic" for instance. As Pratt writes it, the iceberg had been born thousands of years before, a neolithic monster waiting for a time of challenge, when it became the avenger, and the teacher. And again, in the ice floes, he creates a powerful image as the men, agents of man's greed, his stupidity in ignoring all the warning signals, become caught in a terrible storm and one, in death, is bonded in brotherhood with his victim, the seal. He is found with "his teeth fleshed in its frozen heart."

My ending then is deliberate. It's not for me to say whether it works theatrically. I like to use the theatre. I like to risk and challenge an audience in all the ancient ways. What's wrong with a ghost? What's wrong with enraged nature? Are we so secure and smug that we believe neither is possible? And in any event, what's wrong with the sheer enjoyment of the theatricality of the thing? I like lots of things happening on stage too. I enjoy what I do. And I enjoy movement and vitality and surging on the stage which are the only things which give point to silence, to the moments of contemplation at which time we share the crisis and the catharsis which makes the tears flow, which brings the release.

Jacob's Wake is also close to me because, of all the plays I've written, it's the one that is most closely based upon people I know.

I have about six plays in my head that are waiting to be written, though God knows when they'll get done or if they'll see the light of day. Currently, I am going to have another crack at what is laughingly called historical drama, which means simply that I have a diary-to-hand, written by the last person to be hanged in St. John's after being whipped through the fleet. I'm not going to give away any more than that.

It'll be a large cast.

I like large casts.

I like colour and excitement and movement and light, as I've said. I was once asked by a director to restrict myself to small-cast plays if I wanted to get produced in this country.

"Why?" I said. "What size company is the Royal Winnipeg? What size the Canadian Opera Company? What about Stratford?"

Why should I restrict my imagination to suit the size of a director's budget? If it doesn't get produced, fine. I'll write another. I can't tailor my art to suit the requirements of others, not in the initial stages at least. All I know is that I have to keep writing plays. And more plays. All I know is that I love theatre with a passion. It is life and breath to me.

I also love my home and my wife.

That makes me a lucky man I suppose.

Some men are born at home.

Others spend all their lives in search of it.

I spent thirty-four years looking for one.

When I came to Newfoundland I found it.

Instinct again.

I know I shall have to leave it spasmodically, but I'll always come back. It is the source of my imagination and the seat of any joy I have ever found.

Chronology

1933	Born in Fulham, London, England, of Anglo-Irish parents.
1940-48	Educated at various Catholic schools. Expelled 1948.
1948-49	Farm labourer.
1949-61	Enlisted in Regular Army and served 12 years, in Korea, Japan, Europe, Malaya, Singapore. Directed and wrote entertainments.
1961	Farm worker; painter; processor of ball bearings.
1963	Primary school teacher. Attended Nottingham University Institute of Education. Drama, art, and English studies.
1966	Directed and wrote entertainments. Occasional actor. Wrote radio plays, short stories, autobiographical novel (unpublished). Graduated. Teacher, Comprehensive School. Emigrated to Canada and in December settled in St. John's, Newfoundland.
1967	Directed plays for Memorial University, St. John's. Wrote first radio play for CBC. Appointed Specialist in Drama, Extension Service, Memorial University.
1969	Averaged three radio plays a year for CBC. Founded St. John's Summer Festival of the Arts. Acted and directed continuously.
1970	Appointed Lecturer, English Studies, Memorial University, St. John's.
1971	First full-length stage play, *Colour the Flesh the Colour of Dust*, performed at Dominion Drama Festival, directed by author. Became a Canadian citizen.
1972	*Colour the Flesh the Colour of Dust* performed at National Arts Centre, Ottawa, by Neptune Theatre Company. Toured Maritimes.
1973	*Head, Guts and Soundbone Dance* performed at Dominion Drama Festival. Purchased by CBC for the première of the Opening Night Series on television. Produced at Saidye Bronfman Centre, Montreal. Adapted for radio.

1974   *Colour the Flesh the Colour of Dust* produced by St. Lawrence Centre, Toronto. *Head, Guts and Soundbone Dance* produced by Theatre New Brunswick; produced by Theatre 3, Calgary. Appointed Contributing Editor, *Canadian Theatre Review*. Appointed Assistant Professor, English Department, Memorial University.

1975   Commissioned to write the play, *Quiller*, which was premièred in St. John's. Commissioned by Festival Lennoxville to write full-length stage play, *Jacob's Wake*. Performed July, 1975. Commissioned by Dalhousie University to write play for Drama students. Wrote and produced "Not as a Dream." Extended leave of absence from University to concentrate on writing.

1976   Commissioned by Festival Lennoxville to write full-length play. Completed first draft. "The Gayden Chronicles." "Not as a Dream" performed in Halifax. Commissioned to write one-act play for Centaur Theatre, Montreal. Wrote *Therese's Creed*.

1977   *Quiller* and *Therese's Creed* produced at Centaur Theatre, Montreal. *On the Rim of a Curve* produced at Newfoundland Drama Festival. Senior playwright at the Playwrights' Colony in Banff, Alberta. *Head, Guts and Soundbone Dance* produced at the Globe Theatre, Regina, Saskatchewan. Wrote and had produced in workshop at Banff School of Fine Arts a new play, "All the Funny People Are Dead." Awarded a Canada Council Grant to tour Europe in order to investigate the European market for his plays. Attended as an Observer the meeting of the International Theatre Institute in Stockholm. Gave a reading of his plays at the Canadian Cultural Centre in Paris.

1978   Plans to undertake a collective collaboration with the Mummers Troupe of Newfoundland of a new play, "The Sealing Play," with the intention of touring coast to coast in the spring.

Selected Bibliography

Primary Sources

STAGE PLAYS

"All the Funny People Are Dead." MS, St. John's, 1977.

Colour the Flesh the Colour of Dust. Toronto: Simon and Pierre Publishing Co. Ltd., 1972.

"The Fisherman's Revenge." MS, St. John's, 1976.

"The Gayden Chronicles." *The Canadian Theatre Review*, No. 13 (1977).

Head, Guts and Soundbone Dance. Portugal Cove: Breakwater Books, 1974. Also in *The Canadian Theatre Review*, No. 1 (1974).

Jacob's Wake. Vancouver: Talonbooks, 1975.

"Not as a Dream." MS, Toronto, 1976.

On the Rim of a Curve. In *Three Plays*. Portugal Cove: Breakwater Books, 1977.

Quiller. Toronto: Playwrights Co-op., 1974. Vancouver: Talonbooks, 1976. Also in *Cues and Entrances: Ten Contemporary Canadian One-Act Plays*, edited by Henry Beissel. Toronto: Gage Publishing Ltd., 1976; and in *The Blasty Bough*, edited by Clyde Rose. Portugal Cove: Breakwater Books, 1976.

"A Special Providence." MS, St. John's, 1976.

Therese's Creed. In *Three Plays*. Portugal Cove: Breakwater Books, 1977.

Three Plays. Portugal Cove: Breakwater Books, 1977. (*Head, Guts and Soundbone Dance, On the Rim of a Curve, Therese's Creed.*)

Tiln. Toronto: Playwright's Co-op., 1974. Vancouver: Talonbooks, 1976. In *Encounter*, edited by Eugene Benson. Toronto: Methuen Publications, 1973.

RADIO PLAYS

"Apostles for the Burning." TS, CBC radio, Tuesday Night, 1974. Berlin radio, 1976.

"Ballad of Patrick Docker." TS, CBC radio, 1972.

"The Concubine." TS, CBC radio, 1969.

"He Should Have Been a Pirate." TS, CBC radio, 1967.

"Ireland's Eye." TS, CBC radio, 1976.

"Knight of Shadow, Lady of Silence." TS, CBC radio, 1976.

"Love is a Walnut." TS, CBC radio, 1971; Earplay, University of Wisconsin, 1973.

"No Man Can Serve Two Masters." TS, CBC radio, 1967.

"On the Rim of a Curve." TS, CBC Tuesday Night, 1977.

"Or the Wheel Broken." TS, CBC radio, 1968.

"The Producer, the Director." TS, CBC radio, 1976.

"There's a Seal at the Bottom of the Garden." TS, CBC radio, 1973.

"Tiln." TS, CBC radio, 1971.

"A Time for Doors." TS, CBC radio, 1970.

"To Inhabit the Earth Is Not Enough." TS, CBC radio, 1971.

"Travels with Aunt Jane." TS, CBC radio, 1974.

"The Truck." TS, CBC radio, 1970.

"A Walk in the Rain." TS, CBC radio, 1968.

"Walk into the Unknown." TS, CBC radio, 1972.

ARTICLES

"Christopher Pratt: A Personal Memoir." *"Vie des Arts* (Summer, 1977).

"Head, Guts and Soundbone Dance Interview." *The Canadian Theatre Review*, No. 1 (1974), pp. 74-76.

"Ignored Again." *The Canadian Theatre Review*, No. 10 (1976), pp. 87-91.

"The Need for a Canadian Repertory." *Performing Arts Magazine* (Spring, 1977.)

"St. John's Newfoundland." *The Canadian Theatre Review*, No. 2 (1974), pp. 125-127.

"Trapped in Space." *The Canadian Theatre Review*, No. 6 (1975), pp. 117-20.

"Under Assault." *The Canadian Theatre Review*, No. 7 (1975), pp. 136-38.

Secondary Sources

ASHLEY, AUDREY. "Acting of Neptune 'competent' but 'Colour the Flesh' is 'pretty dull.'" *The Mail-Star* (Halifax) October 18, 1972.

FISHMAN, MARTIN. "Michael Cook: A Playwright in His Own Right." *Canadian Drama/L'Art dramatique canadien* 2, No. 2 (1976), pp. 181-87.

LISTER, ROTA. "Interview with Michael Cook." *Canadian Drama/L'Art dramatique Canadien* 2, No. 2 (1976), pp. 176-80.

Nine
DAVID FRENCH
(1939-   )

Preface

*One of the new breed of young Canadian writers, David French
is still in the process of discovering himself as a writer and
playwright. A modest young man, he is faced with the problem
of surpassing or even equalling the quality of his own first two
plays which were instant hits in Toronto:* Leaving Home *(1972)
and* Of the Fields, Lately *(1973), which won the Chalmers
Award for the Best Canadian Play of 1973.*

*The process of maturing takes time, especially when one is a
playwright, and French is still in this evolutionary process, as
he himself is the first to admit. A self-taught man (he spent his
early school years in sports and did not go on to university or
playwriting school), French has learned by extensive reading,
and by writing more than fifty one-act plays, the fundamentals
of a traditional realistic play. Given a subject with which he can
empathize, he has control of dramatic techniques, and is able
to produce a solidly good play. This is true of his first two
plays, which embrace the autobiographical drama of his home
and family relationships. But in* One Crack Out *(1975) French's
technique (of a slick con-game) unwittingly took precedence
over the theme of universal man who loses self-confidence.
The popular movie hit* The Sting, *immediately came to mind,
with its combination of wit and melodrama. But in* One Crack
Out *melodrama prevailed.*

*In his family plays French developed realistic characters,
eloquent language, true speech patterns, the spirit and flavour
of the Newfoundland family, the significant structure of
parental and filial relationships, acute tension relieved by the
comic spirit, dramatic conflict, suspense, and a fine weaving of
plot and subplot into a quite perfect whole. His first two plays*

234

achieve a richness in their delineation of the Mercer family. French has intimated that he plans a third Mercer play to complete the trilogy.

Leaving Home treats of parental domination in an archetypal family of opposing forces, mother and children vs. father. It is, in a sense, the re-creation of French's own displaced Newfoundland family moving to Toronto but never relinquishing the ties with home. Writing this play served as a catharsis for French. Besides the vivid recollections of his own family, he had the support of the genre of past family confrontation plays of major quality such as Long Day's Journey into Night, Death of a Salesman and the more recent Broadway success, The Subject Was Roses. In all of these plays the father is pitted against the sons and mother, in a collapsing family goaded toward self-destruction. The family enclave, which should support and strengthen its members, seems instead to cripple and destroy them. The audience can easily identify with these family conflicts at the core of this play. The proud, inarticulate defeated father demanding his patriarchal rights; the rebellious and confused sons seeking their independence; the loyal and loving mother attempting to keep the peace but in reality creating a barrier between sons and father. French does not try to determine who or what causes family disintegration, but allows the play to speak for itself.

Of the Fields, Lately is a continuation of this theme, concentrating on Ben's return to the family for a relative's death, only to discover that his own father is dying. Death is the theme —the death not only of Dot and Jacob but the death of communication, of love, of family unity. David French uses Tennessee William's technique from The Glass Menagerie by having his central character open and close the play talking directly to the audience and thus distancing the drama into a play of memory. Ben opens the play by speaking to the audience of the wall that separated him from his father. He ends the play by telling the audience that he never did get any closer to this man. Again French does not interpose any reasoning here but allows the play its own echoes and answers.

One Crack Out builds melodramatic suspense with hustlers, hookers and con men in the subculture society of a poolroom.

Fantasy, sentimentality, naturalism, and realism are combined in eleven short, rapid episodes with quick blackouts to achieve the fluid movement of film. Like the father of the Mercer trilogy, Charlie is the victim causing hypertension, violence, love, and compassion. Somehow this play does not come together as one unique whole. Yet French's intent was to emphasize human weakness. Perhaps the forthcoming movie version will strengthen this intent.

Bill Glassco, the artistic director of the Tarragon Theatre in Toronto, has been a great help to several young Canadian playwrights. He will work with them until their plays are polished, tightly constructed, and ready for production. French has often acknowledged the insights Glassco has given him into the complexities of stagecraft. As he continues to develop his talents, it is the hope of those who know and appreciate David French's work that he will continue to apply his personal experiences to the broader, more universal aspects of life, as he has done in his first two plays.

I was fifteen when I first decided to become a writer. Not a bookworm by any stretch of the imagination. If I cracked a book, it was usually over somebody's head. I was part of a local gang and considered a good athlete, playing soccer, baseball and hockey for my school. The only books I read were either school books or some detective thriller somebody might give me at Christmas. At home there were only two books, the *Bible* and *The Book of Common Prayer*.

Anyway, this is what happened: I was sitting in my eighth grade classroom, two days before graduation, and I was fooling around as usual. The teacher, Mr. Bean, told me to shut up, take a book from the bookcase, sit down and read it. I did, and my world changed. The book was *Tom Sawyer*, and as soon as I'd finished it I knew I was hooked: I wanted to be a writer. I lost interest in sports, gangs and the life of the street. I haunted the library all summer, reading everything by Twain and about Twain that I could lay my hands on. Then two years later I discovered Jack London and ran away to sea for the summer. I was very impressionable, to say the least.

I started publishing poetry and short stories in my high school yearbook and also in *The Canadian Boy*, a monthly paper put out by the United Church of Canada. From fifteen to seventeen, I wrote for *The Canadian Boy*, making anywhere from fifty cents to a dollar for each piece. My biggest kick was getting a short story published in a hardcover anthology of prose and poetry by the youth of Canada. The book was called *First Flowering*, and I received two copies of the book but no money. But I was only sixteen, so just correcting the galleys was payment enough. Somewhere in the back of my mind I hoped to write novels one day. I never thought of plays, though. I don't think I'd ever seen one.

My first encounter with theatre was the high school shows and the Earl Grey Players' productions of Shakespeare that toured Ontario schools. I remember sitting in the front row of the Harbord Collegiate auditorium one night, watching my first Shakespearean play—*Twelfth Night*. As soon as the Duke began his monologue in the first scene, I burst into laughter and had to dig my nails into the palms of my hand to control myself. To a working-class kid who had spent most of his life in the streets, it was very foreign and very effete. At least that particular production.

I wanted desperately to become a member of the Drama Club. By my third year in high school I had a dual ambition: to write and to act. I didn't mind telling people I wanted to be a writer. At least I'd shown some talent for it. But my secret dream was to be an actor, and not even my closest friends knew that. I thought they'd all laugh at me.

I mentioned before that I was quite impressionable, and by this time in the mid-fifties James Dean had already died on a highway in California and I fancied myself the new James Dean. I even tried to comb my hair like his and play the bongos. There must've been a big boom in bongo drum sales at that time, because a million other kids all had the same fantasy.

My big drawback was I was painfully shy, so the fantasy never got beyond pasting pictures of James Dean in my biology book, along with Brigitte Bardot. So year after year slipped by and others got parts in *Thunder Rock* and other plays while I twisted with envy in my seat in the dark auditorium, castigating myself for being a coward, for not stepping forward to audition. I hadn't the courage to risk being laughed at. What I hoped would happen was some astute teacher would spot a potential James Dean brooding in the classroom and force me on stage. That never happened, of course, and I left high school in 1958, vowing to myself to become an actor and not having the slightest idea how you went about it.

I read somewhere that the sons of American TV executives often started as mailboys, so I went down to the CBC and got the job. I figured it would be an ideal place to meet actors and producers and watch plays in rehearsals. It was, but I'd often become so engrossed in a rehearsal that I'd miss my rounds. Then in September I read in *The Toronto Star* an ad for the Al Saxe Studio. Saxe was a former member of the famous Group Theatre in New York, and the year before he'd come to Toronto to teach. The ad said acting-playwriting courses. So I phoned and made an appointment, and early one rainy evening I went downtown to the brick coachhouse where he lived and worked.

I cursed the rain for spoiling my James Dean haircut, lit a fresh cigarette, dangled it from the corner of my mouth and went in. A voice from upstairs called out that he'd be right with me. And then he came downstairs, this short intense man with a thick head of white hair. He stopped on a dime and stared at me, and I hoped he saw the strong resemblance to James Dean. He must've seen through my ridiculous pose, but he didn't look it. He just kept staring at me, sizing me up. Then he smiled and asked what I wanted. And as soon as he said that, I lost what courage I had. "I ... I want to be a playwright," I stammered.

"That's good," he said, "only the trouble is you're the only one wants to be in that course, and I just can't afford to teach one student. I'll tell you what. Why don't you go into the acting class? You can learn a lot about writing plays from acting."

So I rushed into the acting class, which is where I wanted to be in the first place. I was immediately terrified, and surprised, to see ten other James Deans waiting to be discovered. I remember hiding in the corner at the back of the studio for the first three weeks, ducking down every time Al looked around for a student to stick in some improvisation. Then one night he sent me on stage with a woman, and the first line I made up got a laugh, the laughter continued, and at the end of the skit an unprecedented thing happened— *applause*. From then on, let me tell you, I sat in the middle of the front row, waiting for Saxe to call on me.

After two years at Saxe's studio I took off for California and spent the summer at the Pasedena Playhouse. There was talk about a scholarship for the following year but I turned it down and came home and began to make the rounds. After six months of haunting the corridors of the CBC, I landed my first part: the lead in a half-hour drama. But at the end of five years I knew acting wasn't for me. There wasn't enough work, and I was far too nervous and self-conscious. I also knew there was more inside me than could ever be satisfied by acting. So I quit.

I had written my first play when I was twenty-three. At the time I was obsessed with a girl in Montreal. I'd been involved with her for close to two years. Every week or two I'd hop on a bus and drive to Montreal and come back to Toronto very depressed. She was much younger than I but very beautiful, talented and crazy, and I suffered from the delusion I could save her from the mess her life had become. But in the end I had to walk away to save myself, and on the bus back home that last time, I became so low that for the first time in my life I thought of ending it. I couldn't sleep, so I just stared out the window at the snowy fields and the moonlight, and an idea slowly began to form itself.

When I got back to Toronto I stretched out on my floor with a pencil and a pad of paper and wrote a one-act stage play about a young man who tries to commit suicide but decides at the last minute he wants to live. I wrote it complete in that pad over an eighteen-hour period and discovered that I'd written away all thoughts of my own suicide. I typed the play and sent it back to the CBC in Montreal. They bought it, and that was my first play and my first sale. It had been so easy, I thought to myself, I'll be rich, I'll turn out one a week. As it happened, it took me another year before I sold another.

I wrote a number of others that sold. All half-hours. But I never really wrote for television, I only *sold* to television. They were all one-act stage plays with one set and two or three characters.

Now that I had given up acting and had decided to go back to my first ambition, I set about learning to write with a singlemindedness of purpose. I knew next to nothing about craft, except what little I'd picked up as an actor, so I started to learn it with as much seriousness as someone studying medicine or architecture. Devouring all the books on craft, reading and analyzing plays. And, of course, turning out play after play of my own, none of them very good. What I was doing was feeling my way slowly, modestly experimenting with different themes and forms. Most of it was influenced by

Tennessee Williams or the Theatre of the Absurd. An occasional pseudo-poetic piece or realistic play. In other words, I still hadn't found my own voice.

I knew I wanted to write but I didn't know for sure where my talent lay. I was still searching. I wrote plays for two more years and then quit. I was getting no real satisfaction from it and thought maybe I was meant to be a novelist. So the next year and a half I wrote a novel, *A Company of Strangers*. It didn't sell. Then I moved to Saskatchewan for most of the next two years, spending the summers in Prince Edward Island. In both places I wrote almost nothing but short stories, all of which came back from the magazines with almost predictable regularity. By this time I was quite frustrated and desperate. I was 32 and afraid that what I felt inside me would never get out.

I'd gone east to Prince Edward Island in the summer of 1971 and I was living in a tiny rented cottage overlooking St. Peter's Bay. I wrote a short story inspired by a classified ad in one of the Charlottetown newspapers—an old widower who advertised for a wife—and set the story in the village where I lived. That was all I'd done that summer and I was feeling more than a little guilty.

It was the first of September, the leaves were already turning, and I was so broke I couldn't affort to rent the cottage, let alone leave the island. So strictly out of economic desperation I set the typewriter back on the little arborite table in the kitchen with the intention of knocking off another hated one-act play that I might possibly sell to the CBC in Montreal. It was the quickest and only way I could think of to bail myself out of the predicament.

Then came the problem of subject matter. I knew the things I wrote best were the things I knew best and felt deeply, the things that *had* to come out of me or I was in trouble. At the time I still had a lot of unresolved conflicts inside me about my family and I knew I would always be in a turmoil unless I could come to terms with all that.

For years I'd tried to write about my family in one form or another: two chapters in my unpublished novel, an unproduced short film script, two or three unpublished short stories. But always as a disguised Ontario family. And the reason for that was because I didn't think I could capture the Newfoundland dialogue. I couldn't, for instance, even tell a verbal story with an accent. And because I hadn't made a concentrated effort to do it, I didn't know that I heard it inside my head.

This time out I decided to be true to my family background. As a simple exercise I typed a few fragments of remembered conversations and was surprised to hear my father's voice on paper. I wrote a few more scraps and they got better. I then started the play. It had one set and three characters: father, mother and son, Ben. The working title was *The Keepers of the House*, from a passage in Ecclesiastes, I believe. Eventually it became the play *Leaving Home*.

As usual, I never mapped anything out. How could I when I didn't know what was going to happen? Oh, I knew that Ben would leave home at the end of the play, but that's all. That was the point of light to aim towards at the end of the dark tunnel. But what would happen in between I hadn't the slightest idea. If a writer does map his play out beforehand, that presupposes he knows his characters well enough to determine what they will do, ten, twenty pages down the road, what fork they will take. I didn't know that yet. I had to become acquainted with them. Sure, I intended to write about my family, but I knew from past experience that the characters would end up just being *based* on real people, not carbon copies. There would be other character traits I would invent or discover in the writing, and those parts I couldn't anticipate. The way I often create a character is to use a real-life model, but also to make the characters composites of more than one person, project a lot of myself into each one, plus whatever I know about people from my experience and observation. So I preferred to feel my way along, letting the objectives or wants of each character determine the dramatic action and conflict. It seemed to me the only organic way to work.

I typed the title page and began. By the bottom of page one,

Ben told his mother he wanted to leave home, and that stopped me. It was too sudden, almost coming out of left field, and too arbitrary for dramatic action. And once again I ran up against the same old obstacle that had stymied me in the past, the lack of a strong catalyst. I cursed and walked away from the typewriter—and ran right back because the simple idea had suddenly occurred to me crossing from the table to the coffeepot on the stove that if there was another son and he was also leaving home for some reason—a *shotgun wedding?*—that might be the central event to set off the powder keg. The marriage would also give Ben the excuse he needed to escape the father who was devouring him. He could pretend to be moving in with the two kids to help them out financially.

So far, so good. I began the play again with the two kids coming home from school and the mother, Mary, preparing supper for her husband, who would soon be home from work. I established the fact that the wedding rehearsal was that night, the wedding the next day. Then the father came in and I had a problem. I wanted Jacob to be on the offensive as soon as he stepped in the door, to establish the conflict with his older son, Ben. Otherwise it would again be too arbitrary. So I began the play a third time, with this additional fact: the night before had been Ben's graduation from high school. My own graduation had been in November, so I decided that's when I'd set the play. Ben was now going to university, Billy was still in high school, and Ben had neglected to invite his father to the graduation, a deliberate omission that sorely hurt the man. That gave Jacob a grudge right from his first entrance and he was not a man to forgive or forget easily.

Three days later I knew I was in a bind. The play was already eighteen pages long and I'd hardly started. There was no way it could fit the prescribed thirty pages of a half-hour TV show.

I walked down to the beach, trailing my dilemma. Should I just continue it and say the hell with being broke? Hadn't I been in similiar situations most of my life and survived somehow? Still undecided, I walked across the bay to pick up my mail and found a letter at the post office. It was from David Peddie, producer of the To See Ourselves TV series in Toronto, asking me to adapt a Hugh Garner short story for his series. I did the job in a week, made $900 and was solvent again. The economic pressure had vanished but not the inner and most important one. Nor my growing sense of excitement.

I went back to the play with a vengeance. Don't worry about length or form, I told myself. Nor whether it'll ever be produced. Just get it down on paper. That was hard enough. It looked as though it might develop into a full-length play, and that was a challenge, a test of whatever craft I'd learned over ten years of hit-and-misses.

When I sat down to the play again, I realized it made little sense, and certainly not good dramatic sense, to be marrying Billy off without the bride-to-be showing up. After all, it was *her* wedding too. Mary would naturally have invited her to supper before they all trooped off to the wedding rehearsal. The introduction of Kathy would undoubtedly add more conflict and thus more density to the play, and I was not against that. I now had to give some thought to her character and background, and one of the ideas contained the source of more conflict: What if Kathy were Catholic and Billy Protestant and Billy had turned Catholic to marry her? That would surely upset Jacob, who came from a background where the Knights of Columbus and Orangemen often murdered one another.

I started over for the fourth time, making all the necessary adjustments—i.e., slipping Kathy into the play long before she appeared, planting the fact that she was coming to supper. But I hadn't thought much about her yet, which is why as soon as she stepped inside the front door I was stumped.

At this point in the play I sensed the need for a complication. If the forthcoming wedding was the catalyst, something now had to happen that would lead sooner or later to a blowup in the family. It was also apparent to me that the meat of the play dealt with the relationship between Ben and his father, and if Ben was using his younger brother's marriage as an excuse to slip out from under his father's shadow, then it followed that an obstacle had to at least threaten the possibility of escape. That pointed logically to the wedding being called off. Not likely, I thought. The young girl was pregnant and Billy hadn't much choice but to marry her. If she wasn't pregnant, of course—right. If she wasn't pregnant . . . What if she had a miscarriage? That was believable. I'd known several girls that had happened to and I knew the circumstances.

I wrote the scene between the two kids, which proved to be the most difficult scene in the play to write. I kept writing it, worrying it like a dog with a bone. There was no problem from Billy's point of view. I knew what he wanted, which was to get out of marriage and stay in school. Unlike Ben, he was quite content to live at home.

But what about Kathy? For the life of me I didn't know how she felt about the wedding. I kept trying to write the scene in the hope the character herself would suddenly tell me. She had to want the wedding to happen or there was no scene and probably no play. But why would a seventeen-year-old girl want to get married? I didn't know and the reason I didn't know was simple, though I should have known better. I just hadn't gone into her background enough to look for a possible answer. When it struck me that I could draw a parallel between her and Ben, I knew I had the answer. She wanted to leave home as much as Ben did and for the same reason: to escape one of her parents. In her case the mother. Father dead.

Now that I knew what Kathy wanted and why, the scene was written without too much difficulty. Then I moved on to the long supper scene. No one, except the two kids involved, knew about the miscarriage yet, so that lent dramatic irony to the scene.

Suddenly the front door burst open and in marched Kathy's mother, Minnie, a character who simply invited herself into the house and into the play. I was quite grateful she showed up. I could now show the audience why her daughter wanted to escape her clutches, instead of telling them.

But I still had to create her. I still couldn't see her clearly in my mind. How did she feel about the wedding, for instance? I could sense that Minnie would be a formidable opponent if she, too, wanted the wedding to happen. Sooner or later it would come out that there was no reason now for the wedding to take place, but if both she and Kathy, and Ben, for his own selfish reason, wanted it to happen, the sides might be evenly matched in a battle of wills.

But why would Minnie want her daughter married off? Especially if she was a widow and Kathy an only child? You might think she'd at least want the girl at home for company, if for nothing else. Well, I thought, she might want her daughter out from underfoot if she had a new boyfriend and wanted to be alone with him. That made sense. Finally I decided to make her a bawdy, middle-aged woman, recently widowed, with a new lease on life. The idea of making her boyfriend the undertaker at her husband's funeral seemed to strike the right note of outrageousness for Minnie's character. But where was that new boyfriend? Why wouldn't she bring him along? She wasn't the type to let the poor guy out of her sight. So Minnie went back out the door and came in the second time followed by Harold, her silent stud, whose silence only set Minnie's character into sharper relief.

And so it went, my solving each problem as I ran up against it. Each time a problem was solved, the solution in turn would create a host of other problems that had to be solved. It is a slow and stumbling way to work, but it does offer at least one consolation and a rather important one: each character in the play will be there for a definite dramatic purpose.

The first draft took me three weeks, logging fifteen to eighteen hours a day. There were two more drafts over the winter and spring, and I don't remember a day when I wasn't eager for the typewriter and not a night I didn't resent the necessity of sleep. My characters chose to go their own way, and I just followed. If I thought I knew what a character would do a page or two ahead, which was rare, he would surprise me and do something else.

It was the most cathartic experience of my life. The more I began to understand the relationships in the family the more moved I became. There were times I couldn't see the keys of the typewriter for tears, and times I would almost topple my chair howling with laughter at the funny things those people said and did.

For the first time I managed to find the balance between comedy and tragedy that I had always wanted, and for the first time, too, I found the kind of satisfaction from the writing of plays that had eluded me for ten years.

Since then I have written two other full-length plays for the stage: *Of the Fields, Lately*, which is a continuation of my projected trilogy about the Mercer family, and *One Crack Out*, a play dealing with characters from the Toronto underworld. Each of these plays was written with the same stumbling difficulty and the same sense of discovery.

Nothing is more exhausting and exciting than looking for ways to put my own interior life on the stage. And of course, never being satisfied. Ever.

Chronology

1939	Born January 18, in Coley's Point, Newfoundland, son of Garfield French and Edith (Benson) French.
1945-58	Family left Newfoundland for Toronto where he attended Rawlinson Public School, Harbord Collegiate, and Oakwood Collegiate. Began writing poetry and short stories at 15, published in the *Canadian Boy* (United Church publication).
1958	After high school graduation, studied acting in Toronto under Al Saxe (Group Theater, New York). He also worked at a variety of jobs.
1959	Left home for extensive U.S.A. travel, ending at Pasadena Playhouse, California, where he studied acting and was offered a scholarship, which he refused.
1960	Returned to Toronto where he studied acting at the Roy Lawler Acting School. He appeared on CBC-TV as an actor in plays from 1960-65.
1962-72	Sold his first play script, "Beckons the Dark River," to CBC-TV in 1962, Montreal's Shoestring Theatre Series. Began writing regularly for CBC radio and TV: scripts were produced frequently during these years.

1972	Wrote his first full-length stage play, *Leaving Home*, produced at Tarragon Theatre, Toronto, under direction of Bill Glassco. This play has been produced by more than sixty theatre companies across Canada, as well as by CBC-TV in a 90-minute special.
1973	Wrote his second full-length stage play, *Of the Fields, Lately*, produced at the Tarragon under Bill Glassco's direction, for which he won the Chalmers Award for the Best Canadian Play of 1973.
1974	Won the Lieutenant Governor's Award in Central Ontario Drama League Festival for *Of the Field's, Lately*.
1975	Wrote the play, *One Crack Out*, produced at the Tarragon under Bill Glassco's direction.
1976	Worked on a new translation of Chekhov's *Seagull*. Also worked on the filmscript for the movie, *One Crack Out*.
1977	Translation of the *Seagull* produced at the Tarragon Theatre.

Selected Bibliography

Primary Sources

PLAYS

"Angeline." *TS*, CBC radio, Toronto, Writer's Workshop, January 13, 1967.

"After Hours." *TS*, CBC-TV, Toronto, Nightcap, Dec. 14, 1965, and Montreal's Shoestring Theatre, Nov. 29, 1964.

"Beckons the Dark River." *TS*, CBC-TV, Montreal's Shoestring Theatre, Nov. 4, 1962.

"The Happiest Man in the World." Adaptation of Hugh Garner's short story, *To See Ourselves*, CBC-TV, 1972.

"Invitation to a Zoo." *TS*, CBC radio, Toronto, Writer's Workshop, Jan. 13, 1967.

Leaving Home. Toronto: New Press, 1972: New York: Samuel French Inc., 1976.

Of the Fields, Lately. Toronto: New Press, 1975: New York: Samuel French Inc., 1977.

One Crack Out. Toronto: New Press, 1976.

"A Ring for Florie." *TS*, CBC-TV, Montreal's Shoestring Theatre, March 15, 1964.

"Sparrow on a Monday Morning." *TS*, CBC-TV, Montreal's Shoestring Theatre, April 30, 1965: TV Westinghouse Broadcasting Corp., Philadelphia, Jan. 1967.

"A Tender Branch." *TS*, CBC-TV, To See Ourselves, Toronto, 1972.

"A Token Gesture." *TS*, CBC-TV, To See Ourselves, Toronto, 1970.

"The Willow Harp." *TS*, CBC-TV, Montreal's Shoestring Theatre, Dec. 15, 1963.

"Winter of Timothy." *TS*, CBC radio, Toronto, 1968.

SHORT STORIES

"The Café." *MS*, CBC radio, Toronto, Canadian Writing Contest, August 22, 1965.

"A Change of Heart." *Montrealer*, December, 1966.

"A Day of Hookey." *In First Flowering*, edited by Anthony Frisch, Toronto: Kingswood House, 1956.

Several short stories and poems in the *Canadian Boy*, 1954-57.

NOVEL

"A Company of Strangers." *MS*, 1968.

Secondary Sources

ASHLEY, AUDREY M. "Writer Hits Jackpot." *The Citizen* (Ottawa), October 14, 1972.

BEVIS, R. W. "Sins of the Fathers." *Canadian Literature*, No. 59 (1974), pp. 106-108.

BILLINGTON, DAVE. *"One Crack Out*, French Breaks Out." Southam News Service.

BRYSON, SEAN. "Canadian Play Was a Triumph." *Evening Press and Irish Press*, April 1, 1975. *(Leaving Home.)*

COE, RICHARD. "Toronto's Theatre Scene." *The Washington Post*, June 28, 1972.

DAFOE, CHRISTOPHER. *"Leaving Home* Will Strike Home." *Sun* (Vancouver), November 13, 1973.

DUFFY, DENNIS. "A Celebration of Excellence." *Toronto Life*, December, 1973.

FRASER, JOHN. *"Of the Fields* Low Key But Brilliant." *The Globe and Mail* (Toronto), October 1, 1973.

ERDELYI, JOSEPH. "French's New Play Spotlights Pool-Hall Culture." *The Citizen* (Ottawa), May 26, 1975.

HELLER, ZELDA. "Dramatist Creates a Masterful Work." *The Montreal Star*, October 12, 1972.

HORENBLAS, RICHARD. "*One Crack Out* Made in His Image." *Canadian Drama/L'Art dramatique canadien*, Vol. 2, (Spring, 1976).

JEWINSKI, ED. "Jacob Mercer's Lust for Victimization." *Canadian Drama/L'Art dramatique canadien*, Vol. 2, (Spring, 1976).

KAREDA, URJO. "*Of the Fields, Lately* — Canadian Play Deeply Moving." *The Toronto Star*, October 1, 1973.

————. "Tarragon Theatre's Dynamic Play Quite Exceptional." *The Toronto Star*, May 17, 1972. (*Leaving Home.*)

"Lively Drama at Everyman." *Cork Examiner*, April 29, 1975. (*Leaving Home.*)

MACCULLOCH, CLARE. "Neither out Far Nor in Deep." *Canadian Drama/L'Art dramatique canadien* 2, Vol. 1 (1976), pp. 115-18.

MANN, RISA. "*Leaving Home — A Play Not to Be Missed.*" *Canadian Jewish Outlook*, July 12, 1973.

MCCAUGHNA, DAVID. "How David French Wrote His Latest Play: By Hanging Around Pool Halls." *Toronto Life*, June, 1975.

MORAN, EDWARD. "Home Bitter Home." *Show Business*, November 28, 1974.

NEARY, PETER. "Of Many Coloured Glass: Peter Neary Interviews David French." *The Canadian Forum*, March, 1974.

PORTER, MCKENZIE. "Transfixed by Sordid *Crack Out*," *The Toronto Sun*, May 26, 1975.

SISKIND, JACOB. "Leaving Home the Right Way." *The Gazette (Montreal), October 14, 1972.*

SOUCHOTTE, SANDRA. "*One Crack Out.*" *Canadian Drama/L'Art dramatique canadien* 2, No. 1 (1976), pp. 123-24.

WANAMAKER, GLENN. "Leaving Home a Dynamite Drama," *Dalhousie Gazette*, March 16, 1973.

WHITTAKER, HERBERT. "Some Fine Domestic Brawling." *The Globe and Mail* (Toronto), May 17, 1972.

Ten
DAVID FREEMAN
(1945-   )

Preface

One of the few Canadian dramatists to have had a play produced successfully Off Broadway (Creeps, 1974), for which he won the New York Critics Drama Desk Award, David Freeman is one of that new breed of young writers in Canada beginning to devote their lives seriously to the writing of stage rather than radio plays. Creeps, about victims of cerebral palsy, is a major contribution to Canadian drama. Its characters are drawn faithfully with touching versimilitude. The fact that Freeman has cerebral palsy, an affliction since birth, no doubt accounts for the painful realism. But only some innate artistic talent could achieve that dramatic quality responsible for its success.

This was Freeman's first play. It was a gradual evolution beginning with his first article, "The World of Can't," published in Maclean's Magazine (1964) when he, with other cerebral palsy victims, was being exploited by a sheltered workshop for spastics. This article brought the problems of C.P.'s to the attention of the public and it brought Freeman to McMaster University, Hamilton, Ontario. There he majored in political science and graduated with a B.A. in 1971. Since Creeps, he has written three more plays, all produced with varying degrees of success in Toronto and Montreal: Battering Ram (1973), You're Gonna Be Alright, Jamie-Boy (1974), and "Flytrap" (1976).

Freeman is still in his early stages of development as a playwright, so that it is impossible at this point to predict the direction he will take. The three plays produced since Creeps, have not equalled in quality that first one. Freeman needs time and freedom to find his own style.

In Creeps he was dealing with his own twenty years of

252

frustration and bitterness as a spastic. Such intolerable suffering was caused by the misunderstandings, fears, and condescensions of the so-called "normal" people in society. Added to this was the shocking exploitation of spastics by industry. Freeman was moved to write about this. His objectivity lent clarity to the subject; his anger provided the passion. He re-creates faithfully on stage the tragedy of spastics' lives, their fears and insecurities. Set in a workshop similar to the one in which he had been exploited, Creeps depicts with both realism and fantasy the emotional lives of its victims, their motivations, needs and private hopes. The sincerity of the characters, the truth of their situation, their individual qualities of mind and heart and spirit —all combine to make this a work of art.

Not so in his later three plays. In Battering Ram, a paraplegic is invited to stay with a volunteer worker and her daughter in their home, where he becomes the object of the woman's sexual frustrations and her daughter's fears: again the victim motif with a comment on the sexual needs of spastics, which society seems unaware of, or refuses to face. Unfortunately the tones and rhythms of the dialogue seem forced and artificial, unlike his first play. As well, there is a hard, brittle quality about these three characters which the audience is unable to penetrate. One never seems to reach the inner qualities of mind and heart. It is difficult to relate to them or to feel compassion for them. There is no real final solution to their individual problems, but only a nasty confrontation at the end and banishment for the spastic (who has the final destructive word). All this gives the impression of realism. Yet Freeman maintains that it is not realism but an eerie unreal quality he tries to achieve especially in the dance scene. This is not immediately apparent and would suggest that the play needs rewriting.

You're Gonna Be Alright, Jamie-Boy (1974) is superior to Battering Ram, but not as brilliant in conception as Creeps. Jamie is not a spastic; he is a victim with psychological problems caused by his mediocre, uneducated family, whose values are derived from television and whose petty confrontations suggest utter vacuity. Here is social comment on the lower middle class. Obsessed by the television characters of pallid drama, these plastic people assume reality for the family. In this depressing milieu, only Jamie is sensitive, intelligent, and educated. His only salvation is escape, which indeed he does at the end of the play. Here the characters are drawn with some compassion and on stage they achieve a life of their own to which the audience can relate.

Freeman's latest play "Flytrap" (1976), is disappointing. Imitative of the smart, superficial comedy popular on Broadway, it relies for dramatic effect on clever dialogue. The protagonist, as in all Freeman's plays, is a young male victim. He is not a spastic but he is dependent and unable to escape from his situation. Invited to live with a middle-aged couple who are frustrated with each other, he becomes the person in the middle. Husband and wife vie for his attention and friendship. Torn by their demands, he decides to leave, only to be prevailed upon to stay, and, as the curtain goes down on the last act, the audience is convinced that he will eventually be destroyed. The characters are too stereotyped and the dialogue too glib but the theme of alienation is convincing.

Freeman has been writing plays for only a short time, scarcely long enough to discover himself, his true dramatic style, his métier. As with so many of the new Canadian plays, we are still too close to Freeman's work to view it with any perspective. During this time he has been making use of conventional realism with a victim theme to lash out against society. His plays cannot be ignored because the message in each is a powerful one. The social consciousness pervasive in his work convinces us that he will continue to voice his criticisms of the world in which we live. What Freeman must learn is how to cope dramatically with his role as a social critic, how to use the talents he exhibited so well in Creeps.

Freeman has a sharp, double-edged sardonic sense of humour. He knows how to write astringent satire, how to change a trite expression into an instrument of combat, how to provoke uneasy laughter. His jokes are harsh and self-mocking, his drama an indictment of a crippled world. Freeman uses the cripple as a symbol for us all. The explosive quality of his indignation combined with his ability to unmask all hypocrisy should result in a continued development of the Freeman drama of satire.

Like all the good things in my life, I sort of stumbled into theatre. I had always been interested in plays and films, but merely as a spectator. I had always made a mental note that, having nothing else to do, I would try my hand at writing a play just for the hell of it. However, this wasn't my real goal. What I really wanted to be was a novelist and journalist.

By the time I was twenty-one I had published eight articles in various magazines and had written a worst-selling novel. In fact, no one ever published it. To make matters even more humiliating, they still giggle about it in the executive washrooms of Macmillan's during the coffee break.

The embryo of *Creeps* was in a *MacLean's* article I wrote on the Sheltered Workshops for the Cerebral Palsy called, "The World of Can't," in 1964. A few days after it was published, CBC Producer William Davidson approached me about writing a dramatic piece. The result was four very embittered characters whiling away one afternoon in a sheltered workshop washroom loving and hating, chastising, baiting, and comforting each other as they spat out jagged bits of broken dreams. I took it to Davidson. It was great! Tremendous! But if he ever did it, he'd be fired on the spot. The problem was that the characters weren't attractive enough. How's about a nice-looking stud in a wheelchair as the central character?

After this insulting and degrading experience, the script was thrown into a drawer and almost forgotten for about four years. By that time I had graduated from McMaster University and I was looking for a job in journalism or advertising, but receiving nothing but patronizing smiles and pats on the back. Then, one day, I happened to call my old friends, Bill and Jane Glassco. Eight years had passed since I last saw Bill. As a matter of fact, it was when he drove me home after a performance of "The Deputy" at the old Crest Theatre in Toronto. Since then, Bill Glassco, Assistant Professor at the University of Toronto, had studied in New York and was now a director in search of plays to put on at Factory Theatre Lab on Dupont Street in Toronto.

This, of course, brought up the subject of *Creeps* and Bill remarked that he would like to see it and I replied that I would bring it sometime. After that I got together with him quite frequently and, with equal frequency, forgot to bring the script. When I finally remembered, it is sufficient to say that reading it did not inspire Glassco to do a Mexican hat dance on the kitchen table.

However, he did find the situation a trifle interesting and said I should try rewriting it sometime and he would arrange a reading of it. I must admit that though that wild idea rather intrigued me, I wasn't really overwhelmed. But since the job-hunting wasn't exactly going great guns, I began to work on it just to put in time. It took me about six weeks to rewrite.

I took it back to Bill and this time the reaction was quite different. Bill got quite excited. He wanted to have a reading. As for me, I was now very interested but still not ready to give my body and soul to the theatre. I chalked it all up as a very good educational experience that would last one night and no more. It wasn't until Bill phoned a few days later to say that, instead of doing this as a one-night stand, he wanted to do a full-scale production to run about three weeks, that excitement (and panic) set in.

However on opening night I was as cool as a cucumber thinking that, well, it's over. I had a lot of fun and it was a unique experience but it's over—time to go back to the typewriter and the job-hunting. I had my hour in the sun. As for the reviews, I was really quite indifferent to them and Bill was hoping for mixed reviews at best. We knew the subject matter would disturb some people very deeply. We knew that many would walk out and some would complain, possibly, even to the morality squad, while others, the more disturbed people, would do things like make nasty phone calls and write even nastier letters.

All these things did happen as predicted. But what we were totally unprepared for was totally overwhelming positive response from critics and the equally encouraging response from the majority of the audiences. What thrilled me was that my words coming from the mouth of an actor could move an audience to laughter, tears, anger or compassion, make them comfortable or uncomfortable (the latter I like to feel is my specialty and, indeed, my duty, but more about that later). So, that in the end, they leave the theatre with something more than the casual satisfaction of having killed two hours being "entertained." The theatre bug—make that vampire—had taken a big chunk out of my jugular and my ambitions of writing the great Canadian novel faded slightly as ideas for more plays began to well up in me.

The rewriting of *Creeps* was probably the most challenging and painful of all my plays. Challenging because it was, of course, my first play and writing a play isn't as simple as I, hot-shot writer for *Maclean's Magazine*, thought. For instance, the dialogue must be natural and yet must, while maintaining this naturalness, convey certain information about the characters, important past and future events. The information must be given naturally so as not to interrupt the audience's flows of thought.

In other words, it isn't like television. You positively cannot take time out for a word from the sponsor! Neither is it like writing a novel or a film script. In these literary forms, the one relies on narrative to depict scenes, while the other relies on pictures. The play is limited and therein lies the dramatist's art. Of all writers, a playwright talks to his audience the most intimately.

The theatre-goer pays his ticket, walks down the aisle and takes a seat. The curtain, if there's one, goes up or the lights go on and the audience finds itself staring at a set. Nowadays, they'll be probably staring at that set all night, so something had better damn well be happening on that stage that is worthy of their interest! The playwright owes that to his audience, and the audience has the right to demand it of him. For most of them, one performance of a play is a once-in-a-lifetime opportunity, unlike the movies where they can probably see it again on television or a book they can keep on the shelf to read as often as they want. A première of a new play is a unique experience because no play is done exactly the same way twice. Not even with the same director. So the audience must leave feeling that they've been made love to, chastized, ridiculed, teased or even punched in the mouth—but it is essential that they must leave with something. Otherwise the playwright just hasn't done his job.

What must happen on the stage? How do you hold the

audience's attention? If it's a play essentially of dialogue, it has to be the kind of dialogue that makes people want to watch the parties involved, how they say things, what they do while they're saying them, their facial expressions, physical gestures and so forth. If it is a play of movement, the movement must be striking and interesting, as in *Creeps*, where five people struggle to make their own rebellious limbs and muscles obey, or the fight in the last scene of *Battering Ram*, which, I think, is not as disturbing and as violent in the physical sense as it is in the emotional and certainly in the erotic sense.

If it is a situation play, I find the more ordinary the situation the better. Setting the play on a distant planet and having little green men as the characters will not endear a playwright to his audience. They need something to identify with. They need to see an aspect of themselves on that stage (no matter how painful that may be) or Cousin George who lives up the street.

An ordinary situation and a dull play do not necessarily go hand in hand. A play about green men on Mars can be just as dull as, if not duller than a play about the television breaking down. The trick is to break the situation down and hold each piece under the literary microscope. Who are the people involved? What are their reactions to the situation? Why do they react that way? How will the people have changed? Or will they have changed? If not, why not? How will they feel about themselves? Who wins? Who loses? Does anybody win or lose?

For instance, I have written a play about four guys sitting in the washroom one afternoon bitching about their jobs. Too bad but nothing to get excited about. They weave rugs, sand blocks, fold boxes and separate nuts and bolts.

— Oh.

— One is an artist and another one wants to be a writer.

— So what else is new?

— This might be impossible for them.

— Oh, really (pause). Why?

— They have cerebral palsy and hardly control their limbs.

Or else take the case of a woman bringing A MAN TO HER

HOME for a visit. Within a week, the man seduces her and her daughter and then takes off. Happens everyday? Of course it does but, in this case, the man was in a wheelchair and the woman was a possessive neurotic who drove her husband to drink.

The next thing is to re-orchestrate the characters. Nobody talks the same or moves the same or thinks the same. Everybody has a way of saying certain phrases, using and pronouncing certain words over and over again, that is unique to him. In *Creeps* one of Bill Glassco's criticisms of the first draft was that all the characters sounded the same. He asked who swore the most? Who swore the least? Who was most witty? Who was the most serious? The point is that while there are many ordinary situations, there are no ordinary people. Everyone is different in some way.

I found the rewriting of *Creeps* painful primarily because I lived it. I knew every inch of that washroom and every dream and fantasy, depraved or wholesome, that every one of those four characters had. This was because I happened to be every one of those four characters, and being honest about oneself is very painful indeed. One of the things of particular embarrassment and pain to me, although people who have seen *Creeps* may be surprised, was the foul language. I am not as salty as people may think. And I was living at home at the time and my parents would be coming on opening night.

But the very subject matter demanded such honesty. The reality of it was that these were four frustrated men brutalized by their jobs and the public's desire to hide their twisted bodies from the world while it continued its fanatic pursuit of the Max Factor cosmetic version of normalcy. Such men in such circumstances do not use "nice" language. Another scene that particularly bothered me is where Michael, a severely mentally retarded teenager, is urinating in one of the urinals when Miss Saunders, the Workshop supervisor, calls to him. He whirls around to the audience with his penis exposed.

Bill and I agonized over this scene for some time. I wanted Michael to turn so that only the actress playing Saunders would see his exposure. The audience would not. Bill felt that it would distract from the honesty we were trying to achieve in the play.

I left it in; I have no regrets about doing so because, to me, the scene further emphasized the dehumanization of such a place run by people like Miss Saunders and Carson, the super philanthropists, who are absolutely void of any understanding of the need for dignity.

As it went from draft to draft, the basic theme and concept of *Creeps* did not change. The play was about freedom and having the guts to reach for it. Freedom is always close at hand, and if you want it bad enough, you'll go through hell or worse to get it. Most of all, I hope the play said that no one can give another person freedom. True freedom must be earned.

The first draft of *Creeps* was written as a half-hour television play so that what I couldn't and could do was always kept in mind. Indeed, the time was 1965 and the media were painfully aware that certain displays of honesty were no-no's according to certain puritanical officials in the Canadian government. The broadcast of "Crawling Arnold" on CBC, a comedy in which a young man seduces a social worker, brought down the self-righteous wrath of arch-conservative John Diefenbaker. The death knell tolled for This Hour Has Seven Days when commentators had the audacity to voice certain all-too-candid opinions.

So the first draft resulted in a half-hour of bland dialogue that, as I look back on it now, actually didn't say anything or go anywhere. Even then it was rejected, partially for the reasons I mentioned earlier, but primarily because of the setting: a washroom.

The most radical changes came in the second draft. Not only did the dialogue become more mature and adult but the so-called "Shriners sequence" and "Brain Speech" were added. The "Shriners sequence" symbolized how service clubs such as the Shriners and the Kiwanis, in their slap-happy eagerness to pacify handicapped adults with hot dogs and balloons, serve only to humiliate us and further damage our self-images. At certain intervals in the play, while the men were trying to discuss something serious, Shriners and clowns burst in on them with assorted goodies and generally molested them in the name of charity.

The actor playing Michael found it wasn't just a walk-on role. He found himself playing a cook, a clown, a carnival barker, and, in the U.S.A., a fuzzy-headed show-bizzy M.C. of a Cerebral Palsy Telethon. In the "Brain Speech," there would be a sudden blackout and then a solitary spotlight on Michael as a carnival barker who would begin his spiel like this:

> Are you bored with your job? Would you like to break out of the rat race? Does early retirement appeal to you? Well my friends, you're in luck. The Shriners, the Rotary and the Kiwanis are just begging to wait on you hand and foot. To throw parties, picnics. To take you on field trips to the flower show, the dog show and the Santa Claus Parade. Would you like to learn new skills? Like sanding blocks, folding boxes, separating nuts and bolts? My friends, physiotherapists are standing by eager to teach you. . . . Now. I suppose you good people are wondering, how to get this one-way ticket to paradise?
>
> My props, please.

At this point, his assistant hands him a model of a brain and a hammer and he goes on to explain how you can begin your life-long vacation by damaging the motor area of the brain.

> You will then be brought to our attention either by relatives who have no room for you in the attic, or by neighbours who are distressed to see you out on the street, clashing with the landscape.

However, he cautions that the operation is "as permanent as a hair transplant" and cannot be undone.

> Should you, however, become disenchanted with this state, there is one recourse available to you, which, while we ourselves do not recommend it, is popular with many and does provide the solution to a very complex problem. All you do is take the hammer and simply tap at it a little harder.

Then he smashes the brain and, resuming his role as Michael, falls to the ground. Seeing it on paper, I had qualms about it at first. It looked very bulky and clumsy on paper, but on stage, it is one of the most chilling moments in the play.

I have seen three interpretations of the "Brain Speech." In the original Toronto production at the Factory Theatre Lab and the Tarragon Theatre, actor Len Sedon performed the speech as a cross between a carnival barker and a song-and-dance man. He treated the speech as a snappy monologue. In Montreal, in keeping with the circus atmosphere of the Shriner sequences, the actor Robert Sime performed the speech from a trapeze. And in the New York production, actor Philip Harris Mackenzie performed the speech as "Mr. Cool," a handsome, wavy-haired mannikin doing a Bromo-Seltzer commercial with soft romantic music in the background. For various reasons, I am fond of all three.

In the second draft, there were other fantasy sequences that were finally scrapped. For instance, while Pete, the rug weaver, was told about two homosexuals caught in the washroom making love, two men walked towards each other from the opposite ends of the stage in slow motion and met and embraced in the middle. Another time Sam, a man in the wheelchair, told about attempting to make love to a girl named Thelma who was also in a wheelchair. During the struggle they fell out of bed, which brought in the girl's parents. The whole scene was acted out on a remote part of the stage between Michael and the girl and when she fell out of bed, two Shriners rushed in, handed the girl a rosary and made her pray to a huge red feather made of cardboard. Nice ideas but in the end they had to be abandoned because they distracted too much from the actor making the speech.

I think I should say something about the problems of the actors in *Creeps*. We wanted to show the many diverse ways that people can be affected with cerebral palsy. After visiting workshops, residences and schools for the physically handicapped, the actors playing the four C.P.'s picked the afflictions that were the most obvious and which they thought they could handle. In the original production Frank Moore, who played Tom, the artist, and the most emotionally disturbed of the four, walked with small, awkward steps with his arms outstretched before him for balance. Jim, the writer played by Robert Coltri, walked with a stagger like a drunk, with his knees pointing inward. Sam, played by Steven Whistance-Smith, was the simplest. He merely shifted the top half of his body from one side of the wheelchair occasionally. Pete, portrayed by Victor Sutton, had the hardest part of all, holding his left hand rigidly against his chest in a sort of clawlike shape and trying to talk with a speech impediment. Michael's movements were very erratic and he moved like a rag doll and his speech was slurred.

Actors playing the character of Pete find it the most exhausting of the roles. In the case of Victor Sutton, he developed a cyst under his armpit and an aching jaw. However, so authentic was he on opening night after the show, two kindly old ladies came up to him and told of a school in Philadelphia they were sure could help him.

There were two major changes in the New York production. The first Shriner sequence was replaced by a Telethon. In it, the actor playing Michael was a Jerry Lewis type master of ceremonies, complete with sequined sports jacket and imbecilic jokes, in charge of a television spectacular in aid of the cerebrally palsied. He would introduce three equally stupid, grinning "Celebrities" who also were eager to help.

The other drastic change was that Louis Scheeder directed the play with the emphasis on the drama of the situation, rather than on the humour. Although many people who saw the Toronto production contend the humour was essential, I feel, in the end Louis' instinct was right. *Creeps* is not really a comedy. In the New York-Washington production, I think our main problem was timing.

Not only did *Creeps* open near Christmas, but it was the time of Watergate, crime, pollution, and inflation. Such problems hardly make one receptive to a play about the plight of the cerebrally palsied. Nevertheless, I blame no one. Louis Scheeder and everyone connected with the production did their damndest to pull it off and I am very proud to have known them. I look forward to working with them again.

One of the opportunities afforded me by the Washington-New York production was working with a new director. Whereas Bill Glassco would spend weeks sitting down and going over the script with me, Louis B. Scheeder, much younger than Bill but equally competent and efficient, would say, "Do this," "Do that," "I don't like this," "I don't like that," and go away and leave me to work on my own.

Before Louis, Bill was my security blanket and I was afraid to work with another director, thinking that I couldn't work on the final draft of a play without somebody looking over my shoulder constantly giving me feedback. Now, while I still intend to work with Bill Glassco, I look forward to working with other directors as well.

The reason I have spent so much time explaining *Creeps* is that it is much more theatrical than either *Battering Ram* or *You're Gonna Be Alright, Jamie-Boy*. Its production problems are unique and more challenging than the other two. For instance, the actors in Toronto were anxious to get a first-hand experience of what it is like to be physically handicapped in public. Assuming their roles as characters afflicted with cerebral palsy, they went down to a coffee shop in the rather exclusive district of Bloor and Bay streets for lunch.

It was a rather harrowing experience for everybody concerned. They got very fast service at the restaurant and became well aware of the secret stares, grimaces and looks of pity (and contempt). For my part, it resensitized me to something I had grown up with all my life. Recalling the experiment a day or two after the play opened, actor Steven Whistance-Smith remarked, "To be physically handicapped in public is a very ugly experience."

My second play *Battering Ram* saw its beginnings when I received an urgent phone call from a highly overwrought social worker friend of mine. She had to see me right away and insisted we meet for coffee that afternoon. The story she told me served as the roots of my second theatre adventure.

A week earlier, a man with Parkinson's Disease had called her to say he would commit suicide unless she came and got him. Unfortunately for all concerned, she obeyed. Now, a week later, the man was settled in her home and every hint at leaving brought on threats of suicide. The man was in a wheelchair and, with only the social worker, her daughter and an eighty-year-old housekeeper, provided quite a problem. In addition, using the same suicide ploy, he was blackmailing her into sexual intercourse with him. My role in this situation was to be the heavy and, using my best James Cagney impression, to go and evict the intruder. Fortunately, this was unnecessary as, in the end, the man left of his own free will.

I first saw *Battering Ram* or "The Siege," as it was first called, as a one-act two-character play. The dialogue being mainly between the social worker and the man in the wheelchair. As the play progressed, the man would become more and more demanding, first of her time, and then of her possessions and, finally, of her body. In the climax of the play the social worker, driven insane by the man's determination to control her every move, would push the man down a flight of stairs and kill him.

However, as time went on, I came to the opinion that stories that ended in the suicide or murder of one of the main characters are often a cop-out. This is not to slight masterworks such as Shakespeare's *Hamlet* or T. S. Eliot's *Murder in the Cathedral*, but I often find it more excruciating to let people go on living. Besides, if you are a novice playwright, it is better to gain several years' experience; if you do feel like committing murder and assorted mayhem on stage, you can at least write it in style.

A playwright's second play is often the most important and agonizing undertaking of his career. The success or failure of *Creeps* when it made its debut on the cold night of February 7, 1971, did not affect me too much. I regarded it all as an experience and an education I would never forget. In fact, working on *Battering Ram* I sometimes felt that the failure of *Creeps* would have been easier to handle.

Success is very addictive and, not wanting the attention and the publicity to wane, I was determined to repeat history. This is, of course, ridiculous. A playwright's job is to write plays; being the darling of the critics and the theatre set should be secondary. Intellectually, I could accept this, but emotionally I couldn't. My hat's off to any artist who can.

When I first began writing *Battering Ram* I filled it with so many characters it became confusing and ridiculous. I questioned each person's reason for being there. I asked myself which of the characters were most affected by the story. The cast of ten became a cast of three. The survivors were Virgil, the man in a wheelchair, Irene, the social worker, and her daughter, Nora. In committing this literary mass murder, it was with great reluctance that I eliminated one of the main characters, a housekeeper named Hannah. Hannah was the only honest character in the play well aware of her employer's weaknesses and of Virgil's selfish schemes but feeling unable to act because of her age and station.

When I decided to make *Battering Ram* just a straight, honest story about emotional blackmail and the sexual abuse of people, I abandoned a unique narrative method also with great reluctance. I had superimposed one scene on top of another. While two characters were talking, one character would freeze, a third character would appear, carry on a scene with the second one and then disappear, leaving the original one to continue.

For instance, Irene would be having a conversation with Virgil when suddenly Virgil would freeze. Bill, Irene's late husband would enter and Irene would have a conversation with him. He would then disappear and then the original scene would carry on. It was an interesting concept and I hope I can try it again someday.

A brief word about my third play, *You're Gonna Be Alright, Jamie-Boy*. I say brief because the production and staging problems weren't that difficult or unusual. Neither were the problems of writing. In fact, it was a very easy play to write, the dialogue changing very slightly in the five drafts it underwent.

My primary reason for writing *Jamie-Boy* was wanting to break away from writing about the physically handicapped. But I realized it would be safer to write about something I knew. Then I remembered that in my family, from the time I was nine or ten, every evening was spent in front of the television. This doesn't mean we were any worse than any other family. It is my considered opinion that we have become a nation of voyeurs.

The boob tube can become as much of a habit and means of escape as alcohol or any drug. What it usually provides is an escape from communicating with other people, something that is always very dangerous. So I decided to kick the crutch out from under the main character, Ernie, by having his beloved TV set break down (a new one at that!). The result is an explosive situation in which Ernie is forced to look at himself for the first time and destroyed by what he sees.

Although it will never be my favourite, I am rather fond of *Jamie-Boy*, as it helped me get a few things off my chest. However, I concede that almost every playwright has written a play like this at one time or another. For Tennessee Williams, it was *The Glass Menagerie*; Edward Albee, *Who's Afraid of Virginia Woolf?*; and for Arthur Miller, *Death of a Salesman*. (His play *All My Sons* also falls into this category of the "family" play but it isn't as good as *Salesman* and certainly not my favourite Miller.) But the most brilliant play of this type has to be Eugene O'Neill's *Long Day's Journey into Night*.

I am often asked why I don't write about "nice" people. Why don't I write happy situations? "Nice" people, although I am sure there are many around and that they have a purpose in life, make "dull" plays. Happy situations make dull plays. If a situation is happy and the people are nice and contented with their lot, then where's the play? Besides, in real life, happiness comes in spurts and starts and no one, unless he is drunk, high on drugs, or a catatonic schizoid, is in a constant state of euphoria. The most people can hope for is contentment and, in most cases, even that isn't constant.

With the people I write about, it isn't the case of their being nice or not nice. They are not evil in themselves but rather are the victims of a sick and corrupt society. From the moment someone is born, society is constantly chipping away at his self-respect and self-image via politics, religion, big business and mass media all telling him, "You'll never make it without our help." The individual is forever being put upon by the people in these fields for profit or that their own insecurities about themselves may be pacified.

Ernie's favourite television show, "The Waltons," tells him that, in the ideal family, all problems are resolved in sixty minutes regardless of the number of TV commercials. On the contrary, as everybody knows, problems in the family or any other kinds of relationship sometimes take years to resolve and often aren't resolved at all.

Society tells Irene that giving to the March of Dimes or the United Appeal will make her a good person and that working at Sunnyville, a residence for the physically handicapped, will give her a "sense of being needed," whatever that's supposed to mean.

In this case, the height of altruism is to take wheelchair-bound Virgil Timmons into her home in order to "help him." The fact that both have deep emotional problems and bringing these problems together is like putting a match to a dynamite fuse, doesn't occur to either of them. Irene's sole motive in bringing Virgil into the home is, of course, sexual satisfaction; her own. It is also sadomasochistic in that in Irene's eyes, once having had sexual intercourse with Virgil, she will have conquered and somehow have dominion over him. Ironically, these are basically the reasons Virgil has for blackmailing his way into her home. Neither one can face these truths because they are fundamentally weak and dishonest people. But society fosters these weaknesses and dishonesties. Irene, growing up in the late forties and early fifties, was told that nice girls who thought about sex were no longer considered nice girls. Virgil, like all physically handicapped people, had it drilled into him that carnal knowledge was, on one hand, an occasion for ridicule, on the other hand, tantamount to rape.

The four men afflicted with cerebral palsy in *Creeps* are the ultimate victims of this warped, depraved thinking. Society, in its constant need to manufacture an atmosphere of stability and to give the impression that we are all living in a Garden of Eden, locks these men up in institutions and sheltered workshops. Then, in order to salve its conscience, it organizes yearly campaign drives to raise money "to help" them but really ends up as a means for certain people to get their pictures in the paper. For people like the ones portrayed in *Creeps*, nothing really changes except their image of themselves, which continues to deteriorate.

Despite all this, so far, the characters I have created are reasonably well behaved, despite a few neurotic tendencies like wrestling young ladies on the living-room rug, that sort of thing. I mean they have yet to start shooting, stabbing, strangling or decapitating each other and they probably never will. Not only do I consider such goings-on cheap attempts at sensationalism, but physical violence appalls and offends me personally, especially on stage. I am all for moving an audience but not to lose their supper.

In 1971 *Creeps* had just been opened a couple of weeks when I received a call from a friend saying that a television director from Hollywood, a veteran of the old Studio One and U.S. Steel Hour days of television, was in town and had seen the play. I was naturally very interested in meeting him.

I found him to be a personable and kind man. During dinner he praised *Creeps* to the hilt. Eventually the conversation got around to the subject of violence in movies and on television and he declared he abhorred it. He found all that bloodletting in movies totally unnecessary. He had a big argument with his friend, Sam Peckinpah, about that very thing. This conversation went on for about an hour and then he returned to the play.

"It was a helluva play, Dave, a helluva play" he said. "But what you really need to make it great is one of those four guys to get murdered at the end."

Whenever I try to write a physically violent scene, it always comes out stilted and phony. This is because, like most people, I have been more involved with emotional violence and destruction than with physical fury. This kind of turbulence has always fascinated me. It is more enduring and hence more powerful. If a character is murdered at the climax of the play, it is over for him and there are no questions with which the audience can leave. If, however, a character's weaknesses and frailties are exposed for all to see and he has to face himself honestly for the first time, the audience leaves wondering such things as how will he go on living with such a burden or what will he do now that he's liberated from the web of lies that surrounded him at the beginning of the play. The other reason I feel that physical violence is wrong for me is a sad one. Brutality is used so much on television and in the movies I'm afraid that, seeing it in one of my plays, the audience will just yawn it off and not be affected.

In my brief career as a playwright, I have learned many things about myself and about the Canadian theatrical community. When I first started, my favourite playwrights were Tennesee Williams and Arthur Miller. I loved Williams for his poetry and Miller for his realism and thought they in fluenced me. But I must admit I am more influenced by Edward Albee. Not that this bothers me in the least, for he is my third favourite. His characters embody all that is beautiful and all that is ugly with their rough, jagged, love-hate relationship with life.

On this side of the border, the playwright who most impresses me with his genius is Michel Tremblay. He is the Canadian poet of the theatre. Many an evening he has taken me on a journey to a world that one might view as ugly and warped but, with Michel's compassion, has become beautiful and human. William Fruet is another playwright I admire. His play, *Wedding in White* is one of my favourite English-Canadian dramas. Martin Kinch's, *Me?* is another piece with which I was most impressed. For this reason I am thoroughly puzzled as to why, at this writing, it has been a couple of years since we have last heard from either Fruet or Kinch. Another on my list is Hershel Harding with his *Esker Mike and His Wife, Atluk*.

When I entered theatre, I never thought of myself as a Canadian playwright, just a playwright. My own feelings were that if you wrote a good play, somebody somewhere would eventually do it and all these playwrights who grumbled about their plays not being done just because they were Canadian, simply had not written a good play. But it is true to say that *anything* written by a Canadian used to be considered inferior.

Since I began writing, the climate has changed dramatically. It sometimes seems as though any Canadian play, no matter how bad, can get produced as long as it has a Canadian theme. Over the years the small theatres have stopped developing new playwrights and have succumbed to indulging them. Consequently, plays about Newfies, lumberjack strikes, the depression, John A. MacDonald, and the evil and/or saintliness of the Black Donnellys are running out of our ears. As Myron Galloway put it in his *Montreal Star* review of my newest play, "Flytrap," which debuted at the Saidye Bronfman Centre on May 1, 1976:

> The indicators are that sooner than we had any right to expect the prospect of seeing a Canadian play will no longer be synonymous with (a) spending an evening with the lower classes wallowing in their misery, (b) being told again that

Newfoundlanders are the Canadian equivalent to the Ozark dwellers, (c) that all sensitive young men are burdened with stupid, long-suffering mothers and obtuse, drunken fathers, and being forced to the conclusion that Canada has no middle-class at all.

"Flytrap," a comedy-drama about the loneliness and alienation of a middle-aged couple, was dismissed as "too lightweight" by most critics. A radio critic, demonstrating his sophisticated talent for description and perception, dismissed it as a "blah evening," while another, though this may sound incredible, did not like it because "there weren't enough swearwords." But, fortunately, the audiences were enthusiastic. Although I admit that "Flytrap" is trivial when compared to my other works, I challenge the perception that the playwright, in order to be successful in this country, must be forever depicting his fellow Canadians as drunk, on welfare, and drowning in their own self pity. Before long, this image of Canada will begin to bore, if not insult, Canadians who will begin to welcome American imports with open arms and a sigh of relief.

There is another, more deplorable phenomenon that has developed in the last few years. Certain of my colleagues whom I admire greatly, instead of working at their typewriters, have aligned themselves with dubious organizations that are supposedly working on their behalf but whose only program seems to be obtaining monies from the government for work that never materializes. They create manifestos and are repeatedly whining to the government for support for their purposeless projects such as a "writer's colony." I am in favour of organized groups or persons to represent me as an agent or a go-between to handle business dealings with a theatre. Lord knows, there is a dearth of people in such a capacity in this country. But, in this age of inflation, shortages of jobs, and people on welfare, using the artist as a front to obtain a glorified pension cheque puts us all in a very unsavoury position in the eyes of our public. I believe that the Canadian artist should be paid by a government to produce, not to be pacified.

What I have just said will not gain me many friends. It will probably lose me a few. Canada is a great country, and theoretically, it has great potential. What is needed is a discriminating eye that will honestly evaluate new work and will not be afraid of saying the right word to help the author—even if the word is no.

Chronology

1945   Born January 7, in Toronto, Ontario, son of William H. Freeman and Dorothy (Davis) Freeman.

1951-61   Entered Sunnyview School for the Handicapped. Made his first efforts at writing.

1962   Left Sunnyview School and entered Adult Inter-fraternity Workshop. Attempted first novel.

1964   First article, "The World of Can't," appeared in *Maclean's Magazine*, July 4.

1965   First draft of *Creeps* written for the CBC-TV.

1966-71   Entered McMaster University; graduated with a B.A. in Political Science.

1971   *Creeps* first presented by the Factory Theatre Lab, Toronto (February 3). Produced also by the Tarragon Theatre.

1972   *Creeps* wins the Chalmers Award for the best Canadian play of the 1971-2 season.

1973   First production of *Battering Ram* at the Factory Theatre Lab.

1974   *Battering Ram* produced at the Tarragon Theatre. *Creeps* has its first American production at the Folger Theatre in Washington, D.C., then moving to the Playhouse 2 in New York. *Creeps* won the New York Critics Drama Desk Award. Third play, *You're Gonna Be Alright, Jamie-Boy*, produced by Tarragon Theatre, Toronto and Centaur Theatre, Montreal.

1976   "Flytrap," premièred at the Saidye Bronfman Centre, Montreal.

1977   Successful revival of *Creeps* in Toronto at Toronto Workshop Productions Theatre.

Selected Bibliography

Primary Sources

PLAYS

Battering Ram. Vancouver: Talonbooks, 1974.

Creeps. Canadian Plays Series. Toronto: University of Toronto Press, 1972. Also in New York: Samuel French Inc., 1971. Also in *The Burns Mantle Theatre Yearbook, The Best Plays of 1973-74*, edited by Otis L. Guernsey, Jr.

"Flytrap." MS, Toronto, 1976.

You're Gonna be Alright, Jamie-Boy. Vancouver: Talonbooks, 1974.

ARTICLES

"Adam and Eve." *The Silhouette*, October, 1969.

"The Good, the Bad, the Ugly." *The Silhouette*, January 25, 1968.

"How I Conquered Canada." *Star Weekly*, November 13, 1965.

"On and from the Schools." *The Toronto Educational Quarterly*, September, 1965.

"This Is What It's Like to Be a CP." *Maclean's*, September 19, 1965.

"The Trouble Bush." *The Silhouette*, January 12, 1968.

"The World of Can't." *Maclean's*, July 4, 1964.

Secondary Sources

BARNES, CLIVE. "The Theatre—*Creeps*." *New York Times*, December 7, 1973.

BEAUFORD, JOHN. "*Creeps*." *The Christian Science Monitor*, December 12, 1973.

"Channel Hopping Yields Fine Satire." *The Gazette* (Montreal), April 19, 1974.

CHUSID, HARVEY. "Freeman's New Play Lacerating." *The Toronto Star*, February 7, 1973.

CLURMAN, HAROLD. "*Creeps*." *The Nation*, December 31, 1973.

COHEN, NATHAN. "A Ferociously Funny Play." *The Toronto Star*, February 6, 1971.

DAFOE, CHRISTOPHER. "*Battering Ram* Reverberates through Theatre," *Sun* (Vancouver), February 14, 1974

"David Freeman's Growing out of *Creeps*." *The Sunday Sun* (Toronto), January 20, 1974.

"David Freeman's Heaven and Hell as a Spastic Shakespeare." *The Globe and Mail* (Toronto), January, 1974.

"David, the Man, Explains the Playwright." *Sun* (Vancouver), March, 1, 1974.

"A Determination Never to Go Back." *Time*, January 28, 1974.

"Dialogue Dazzling in Tarragon Play." *The Toronto Sun*, January, 1974.

FEINGOLD, MICHAEL. "The Truth of Creepdom." *The Village Voice*, December 13, 1973.

"Freeman's Play Bares Humanity of Spastics." *Sun* (Vancouver).

FRIEDLANDER, MIRA. "*Battering Ram's* Biting Pace Never Lets Up." *Excalibur*, February 15, 1973.

GALLOWAY, MYRON. "Freeman's Flytrap! Sly Irony Expertly Forged." *The Montreal Star*, May 3, 1976.

GLOVER, WILLIAM. "*Creeps*." *Associated Press*, December 7, 1973.

HOFSESS, JOHN. "Will Success Spoil David Freeman?" *Maclean's*, February, 1974.

"A Human Being First." *Province* (Vancouver), February 22, 1974.

"*Jamie-Boy*—A Blend of TV and Good Old Farce." *The Edmonton Journal*, March 29, 1976.

"*Jamie-Boy*: A Rare Occasion." *The Winnipeg Tribune*, March 14, 1974.

KALEM, T. E. "Inside the Spastic Club." *Time*, December 17, 1973.

KAREDA, URJO. "New Theatre's First Production Beyond Praise." *The Toronto Star*, October 6, 1971.

KERR, WALTER. "A Ring of Truth But After That?" *New York Times*, December 16, 1973.

MASKOULIS, JULIA. "Freeman's Early Play Lacks Punch." *The Gazette* (Montreal), May 3, 1974.

MCCAUGHNA, DAVID. "*Battering Ram*." *Toronto Citizen*, February 23, 1973.

"Off Broadway." *The New Yorker*, December 17, 1973.

VOADEN, HERMAN. "Man's Inhumanity to Man." In *Look Both Ways*, pp. 114-20. Toronto: Macmillan Company of Canada Ltd., 1975.

WALLACH, ALLAN. "Visible *Creeps*." *Newsday* (New York), December 5, 1973.

WASHER, BEN. "*Creeps*." *Hollywood Reporter and New York Theater Review*, December 5, 1973.

WATT, DOUGLAS. "*Creeps* Packs a Terrific Wallop." *The Daily News* (New York), December 5, 1973.

WHITTAKER, HERBERT. "*Creeps* Excellent Starter for Tarragon Theatre." *The Globe and Mail* (Toronto), October 6, 1971.

Eleven
MICHEL TREMBLAY
(1942-)

Preface

No English Canadian playwright has yet reached the kind of mythic stature in drama achieved by Michel Tremblay, French Canadian separatist, in the Québécois theatre. Well known throughout Canada (his major plays have been translated into English), Tremblay at 35 years of age has already written twelve stage plays, three musicals, four scripts for films, two novels, and a book of short stories —all this in twelve years. His work is highly artistic and very original. Tremblay was the first writer to use the actual language of Quebec's working class — joual—Quebec proletarian French, a combination of anglicisms and French that defies translation. Long detested by the French as a crude bastard tongue, it has been elevated to a place of honour by Tremblay who celebrates its richness in his plays. Defying those who maintain that French Canadians should speak Parisian French, he asks why joual is not the language of the Quebec media and the arts, as it is the language of the people.

Tremblay's deep understanding of human nature and his mastery of dramatic techniques are responsible for his position as one of the leading Canadian dramatists today although he calls himself a Québécois, not a Canadian, and his plays, Québécois, not Canadian drama. He has produced a body of authentic plays, establishing the character, nuances, values, tone, and atmosphere of Québécois family life. Tremblay enriches our understanding of this unique segment of Canada while at the same time creating a universal experience. His plays have entered the world of contemporary man. He reverses the traditional values of French Canadian

276

literature — the idealization of the family, the spiritual qualities of the wife and mother, the values of religion and the Church. He gives us instead wild, frustrated women who rebel against the injustices of lower class life; grotesque homosexuals pathetic in their corruption; the lives of prostitutes and the dregs of society; family members shouting imprecations at each other. Nothing in French Canadian theatre prepared us for this onslaught of rage, made even more powerful because enunciated in the language of the people.

Of the twelve stage plays written by Tremblay six have achieved major critical acclaim: Les Belles-Soeurs, Bonjour, là, bonjour, En pièces détachées, Forever Yours, Marie-Lou, Hosanna, and Ste-Carmen de la Main. His first great play, Les Belles-Soeurs (The Sisters-in-Law) was written in 1965. Fifteen frustrated, backbiting, bitter women people this play, which sets the tone for his later work. These shrews gather in the home of a woman who has won a million trading stamps, ostensibly to help paste them in books, but actually to steal, slander, destroy. The humour is deadly; the play's realism shocking. (Tremblay was raised in a seven-room apartment with twelve relatives. He remembers being surrounded by women, and recalling their conversations gave him the script for his play.) Tremblay saw this work as his first deliberate attack on established traditions. By reproducing the realities of Quebec family life it became for him a personal liberation.

En pièces détachées (Like Death Warmed Over), his second major work, is really a series of fragmentary situations in the life of Hélène, a waitress. Again the humour is black as Tremblay exposes the tragedy of life on "The Main" in Montreal's bars. Hélène, her husband, and family live in a poor tenement in the East End of Montreal. Hélène's retarded brother runs away from the sanitarium to seek sanctuary with his family. He wears sunglasses and speaks Engish, declaiming ironically at the end that, because of his sunglasses, he has all the powers! The characters — fashioned after relatives — are victims of greed, repression, loss of identity. This is also true of the people in his play, Forever Yours, Marie-Lou. Here we have a mismatched married couple who produce two peculiar daughters, one a country-and-western singer and the other a religious fanatic. The degradation of their separate lives merges in a kind of stream-of-consciousness dialogue. Bonjour, là, bonjour involves marginal people and incest in a large family. The highly poignant scene between father and son when the son attempts to tell his father he loves him is unforgettable. This family, symbolic of Quebec itself, lives on the borderland of a relatively stable cultural area. It is characterized by the incorporation of habits and values from two divergent cultures and by its incomplete assimilation of either culture. Hosanna switches from the family scene to the life of two homosexuals living as a married couple. Here Tremblay's portrayal of exaggerated masculinity and shocking transvestite behaviour at a drag ball reveal corrupt values which are evasions. There are symbolic implications here too of the unhappy union of Quebec and English Canada. In the end they drop these poses (assumed to impress others) and embrace their real identities. Only then can they live in peace with each other. His latest play, Ste-Carmen de la Main, is his finest work to date. It presents the liberated female, a mature woman, broad-minded, sympathetic, whose holiness is the result of her wholeness. Carmen has reached her perfection and she is ready for the kind of martyrdom she receives on the Main.

Michel Tremblay says that he lives with his characters for two or three years before he ever writes the play. When he does write, he does so objectively, as one outside the scene. This distancing enables him to emphasize with bitter humour the unfortunate weaknesses and corruptions of his own people. The characters in his plays appear over and over again so that his work, taken as a whole, is really about one family, one group of people. This microcosm suggests the greater macrocosm, Quebec.

I cannot recall why but I do remember how I first became interested in writing drama. When television was initiated in Montreal in 1952 I was a child ten years of age. From that time on, I became literally obsessed with TV. You might say I grew up in front of the television screen. I fell in love with TV drama. It was the only theatre I knew. In that first decade of CBC-TV they presented two plays a week; a short play on Thursday nights and a full-length play on Sunday nights. In that decade between my tenth and twentieth birthdays I must have seen about one thousand plays!

Television changed our life in Quebec. It was such a new toy that families stayed home to watch the entertaining programs. No one spoke to one another. Communication between relatives and friends ceased. When you were brought visiting to your aunt and uncle's home or to a friend's house you were immediately ushered into a dark area and given a seat before the TV. All conversation came to an end.

As a result of this exposure to drama, I began to take a deep interest in theatre. At fourteen years of age I attended the first of many stage plays. I wanted to see what drama was like on stage, having already understood television drama. That evening in September, 1956, I went mad about theatre. Why? I really don't know. Maybe it is the immediate connection with the people who are sitting there. It's a beautiful experience to feel the mood of the house when you are present at the production of one of your own stage plays. It is much more lively than a film and more real than a book. A novelist writes for single readers who will be reading his novel at an unknown time and place. This is frustrating for the artist. But when I write a play, I feel I am writing it for hundreds of people who will actually be at its production and I will be able to feel their reactions. Perhaps that is why I began with drama instead of the novel or poetry.

At fourteen years of age I began to write plays. These plays were, of course, copies of the TV drama I had been watching and they were not at all Québécois drama. Indeed before the play, *Les Belles-Soeurs*, written when I was twenty-three years old, I had never written a Québécois play. What I had seen on TV and stage were plays coming from outside Quebec. So I did not know you could put Québécois on stage and make of your very own people heroes. When I began to write drama, I wrote bad *French* plays because what I had seen on TV were good *French* plays! This continued for five or six years. In 1959, when I was seventeen years old, I wrote a one-act play "Le Train" and I won first prize from CBC-TV for the best play of the year by a young writer. I saw this, my first play, on television and it was a bad *French* play!

For me there are two kinds of plays—two kinds of theatre: the theatre that exists only to entertain people and the theatre which is there to say something. My conception of a good play is one with a message. I do not want simply to entertain people. A good play is like one of Aesop's or LaFontaine's fables. A good play for me has at least two levels. One level is what you see and hear; the other level is what you understand from the author's meaning. This latter is the more important level. For me a good play is not a play that tells a story. Rather, it is the meaning that the playwright is trying to convey through his characters that is all important. My plays have at least two and sometimes three levels.

Because of my conception of a good play, I was influenced by the ancient Greek theatre, which is always built around one subject. When Sophocles decided to write a play about power he wrote *Antigone*. The Greek theatre is built around ideas, not real characters. Although the characters are convincing, what they mean is much more important. I love that kind of writing.

Another technique of the Greek theatre that I admire is the Greek chorus. As a result I have built into eight of my twelve plays the Greek chorus. Since it is a theatre of ideas, what I talk about is always my people and my country. Should you merely want to entertain, and there are on stage two men and a woman, and the men are in love with the woman, there is nothing further to be said. But when you put ideas on a stage, you talk to everybody and you talk about everybody. That is why the Greek chorus is necessary. The chorus represents the people—usually the people of one city. The cities were almost countries in themselves. That is why in my first Québécois play, *Les Belles-Soeurs*, there is a chorus of women. One woman saying she is unhappy with her life is pitiful, but five women saying at the same time that they are unhappy with their lives is the beginning of a revolution. That is why a chorus of many people is important. When you write for a chorus it is not one plus one plus one, but it is two multiplied by four multiplied endlessly. A chorus does not add; it multiplies the impact.

Although I love Shakespeare, Molière, and Chekhov, I was not influenced by them. In fact no dramatist influenced me after the Greeks until the twentieth century when I discovered the plays of Samuel Beckett. In Beckett I discovered a purity that was brand new in the history of theatre. That despair which I was exposed to in *Happy Days* — what he did with his characters living after everyone else is dead, writing in everyday words, talking about the end of the world in colloquial language — touched me very much. When I read or heard Winnie in *Happy Days*, trying to read what is written on a toothbrush, to me it was one of the most powerful things theatre had produced. This woman, who is there on the sand alone after everybody is dead, trying to read what is printed on her toothbrush . . . and when she can read one word she is overjoyed. So it is *Happy Days*! It is desperate but in a way it is also beautiful in its despair. I never read or see a Beckett play without experiencing a lift. It is not depressing. No playwright wrote like that before him and he has 2500 years of theatre behind him. This is what is so beautiful about Beckett.

For me the easiest part of writing is the dialogue. Yet it is the part I like least. I do not sit down and plan the blueprint for a play. My usual procedure is to simply think about a play for a few years, for example *Ste-Carmen de la Main*. I thought about that for four years before I wrote one word. When I finally wrote it, it took me seven weeks. What I enjoy is the characterization of an idea. I never tell a story so the plot is not important. In fact not one of my plays has a real plot. Who cares about the women trading stamps in *Les Belles-Soeurs*? Who cares about the four people talking to themselves in *Forever Yours, Marie-Lou*? It is what they say and mean that is significant. There are no scenes in my plays but the entire play is so constituted as to form one whole.

My characters are very meaningful to me. Before writing a play I think about my characters for weeks and months on end. I live with them. And when they are ready to say what I mean, what I have to say, I simply sit down and write. So there are no real obstacles in the building of my plays because I never think in terms of building. I never sit down at my table and say, I mean this or that. I never plan to have this character enter and meet that one, so to speak. Instead, all the groundwork is done in those two or three years of thinking and living with my characters. So when I finally begin to write, the play and the dialogue move naturally along. Because dialogue is comparatively easy for me to write, I am not confronted by any real obstacles. The actual difficulties are met in the years of thinking out the play before I ever put it on paper. At night during those years I go to sleep with those characters in my head. I talk with them. And when they are ready to talk, they do talk through me. In a way I know I am talking through them. But when I write it is they who are talking through me. I know them so well that they hold the pen. All the thinking was done before. I know they will say what I mean, but it is they who are saying it.

I most often write about the family because I want to put a bomb in the family cell. I hated what the family did to me and what the institution of the family did to the people of my country. In the family I include the presence and importance of outsiders, for it is the outside influence of society that make or breaks the family unit. Society decides what the family should be. The members of the family do not decide. A family has unwitten laws to obey, rules to fulfill, and these rules are decided by outsiders. What society asked of the family in my experience was bad. This is what I talk about in *Forever Yours, Marie-Lou*. The four characters in that play are obliged to be the family, the family cell. They hate each other but they have to live together because the laws of society governing families have so ruled. Of course they don't realize that. Therefore they hate each other instead of hating society. This is what I wanted to say: Instead of yelling at each other until the end of the world, it would be so much easier to yell at society and to find something new—something much more fulfilling.

I also write about underprivileged groups because the people of my country, Quebec, have been for 300 years an underprivileged group. This implies politics. When I wrote *Les Belles-Soeurs* in 1965, I wrote, without knowing it, a political play. I talked about an underprivileged group. And talking about an underprivileged group is a political choice I unwittingly made. Today I understand that all my plays are in a sense political. I talk in my plays about people who ached for 300 years because of another group. In Quebec it was because of the English people of Canada.

In my plays I also discuss societal differences. I write about people who disguise themselves in the way transvestites do. These are the people on the fringes of society. I do not mind describing the fringes of society because my theatre is not a realistic theatre. I am not a realistic playwright. If I choose to talk about the fringes of society it is because my people are a fringe society. We are six million French-speaking people in a North America of three hundred million people. So we form a fringe of society. And in this fringe of society in which I was raised I decided to make my point. When Mrs. Belanger or Manon speak of their problems, they speak about Quebec. I do not mean that they are Quebec or symbols or images of Quebec. But their problems with the wider society are political problems. Because they are the fringe group in society, this society in a way hates them. But they want to be happy and they want to be somebody. Hosanna is a man who always wanted to be a woman. This woman always wanted to be Elizabeth Taylor in *Cleopatra*. In other words this Québécois always wanted to be a woman who always wanted to be an English actress in an American movie about an Egyptian myth in a movie shot in Spain. In a way, that is a typically Québécois problem. For the past 300 years we were not taught that we were a people, so we were dreaming about being somebody else instead of ourselves. So *Hosanna* is a political play.

Twenty years ago if you wanted to be a writer or an actor in Quebec, you had to go to Paris, France, to study for two or three years. Then you came back with a foreign accent and only then could you be an artist. But you were not an artist when you talked like a Québécois! And the Quebec culture was mostly a sub-French culture, the only culture possible. My play, *Hosanna*, deals in a symbolic way with the problems of Quebec. Although *Hosanna* concerns two homosexuals, one an exaggerated masculine character, the other a transvestite, it is really an allegory about Quebec. In the end they drop their poses and embrace their real identity. The climax occurs when Hosanna kills Elizabeth Taylor and at the end he appears naked on stage and says he is a man. He kills all the ghosts around him as Quebec did. We are not French but we are Québécois living in North America!

Of the twelve plays I have thus far written I like best *Forever Yours, Marie-Lou, Bonjour, là, bonjour, Ste-Carmen de la Main*, and "Damned Manon and Sacred Sandra." I do not remember creating a character I did not like. I may feel some contempt for a few characters like Lisette de Courval in *Les Belles-Soeurs* but I don't hate her. I know she is wrong but there is something pitiful about her that makes me like her. This is true of my other characters also. The characters I love most are Hosanna, Manon in *Forever Yours, Marie-Lou;* and Manon in "Damned Manon and Sacred Sandra."

There is a character whom I admire but I can't say I really like her. It is Carmen in *Forever Yours, Marie-Lou* and *Ste-Carmen*. I admire her because she is so right. Unfortunately because she is so right she is a cold character. She dares to say she is right and has discovered truth. She is the only real heroine I ever created, but because of that she is not very warm. She is too right. She knows what the others need and she wants to give it to them but not in her life. She is a singer and in *Ste-Carmen* she discovers that the people need to talk about themselves. She therefore decides in her song to talk about them. She gives it to them in her songs, not in her life. I killed her after her first song because it is a revolutionary song, which she doesn't realize. She is killed because she is dangerous. I admire her but I do not love her as passionately as I do her sister, Manon, or even her parents in *Marie-Lou*. But I could not create a character without really loving the character. I love them all.

My career as a playwright has spanned a brief twelve years. During that period of time I have written twelve Québécois plays. These plays constitute a saga or cycle: "The Saga of Les Belles-Soeurs." All my plays are written about the same characters. When I wrote *Les Belles-Soeurs* I was twenty-three years old. Now I am thirty-five. When you create a character and you discover it is a good character, I don't know why you cannot take the character humbly back to the people and say: "Hey, I do need Carmen again. May I take her and put her in another play?" This is what I've done and as a result I have twelve plays that go together. "Damned Manon and Sacred Sandra" is the final point I wish to make. It is about the trip of religion and the trip of sex. Religion and sex are mixed in this play. At the end you see that these two trips are one and the same trip.

Having talked in my plays about the family and politics, about the fringes of society, about sex and religion, I have nothing more to say at the present time in drama. For the next few years I will not write for the theatre. Because I am still young, and still living, seeing, experiencing new things, it is possible that in a few years I may be inspired with new ideas to bring to drama. In the meantime I plan to write a novel. Actually I would like to write a huge novel about the war years in Montreal. I would like to write about a street without men in 1942, when all the men were on the other side of the Atlantic fighting and the only men who were in Quebec were old men or young boys. I would like to describe that society of women in Quebec in 1942.

Québécois theatre is presently passing through a crisis. A few years ago everbody in Quebec loved the theatre and everybody went to see Québécois plays. It was beautiful, Now the Québécois people are tougher. At that time we said nasty things to them. We told them how they were, what they talked about. Now, alas, they want to be entertained and it is a bit depressing for the serious playwright. Do they still want Québécois theatre? I do not know. Perhaps they are tired of being hammered on the head constantly. But there are times when the good playwright has to be a doctor and give medicine, to make the audience swallow things it does not want. I see this as my role in theatre. This is what I have to do. Let us hope there will be an early end to this syndrome.

There are still some Québécois writers whom I love and respect. People like Michel Garneau. I really love what he is doing in Quebec theatre today. He makes his points in a very subtle but passionate way and in a low key. This is a brand-new approach for a Québécois because in my theatre people yell. But in Michel Garneau's plays everything is mild. It is beautiful, too, that someone is still telling the Québécois who they are and what they need but in a low key.

Chronology

1942   Born June 25, in a poor section of East Montreal. Son of a linotype operator, Armand Tremblay, and Rheauna (Rathier) Tremblay.

1955   Won a scholarship to a Montreal classical school for high I.Q. children. Annoyed by the exclusive character of the school, returned to public secondary school.

1959   Became a linotype operator. Wrote his first play, "Le Train."

1964   "Le Train," wins first prize at a Contest for Young Authors on Radio-Canada television.

1965   Wrote, with several others, "Messe noire," produced at the Gésu by le Mouvement Contemporain, directed by André Brassard.

1966   Published a book of short stories, *Contes pour buveurs attardés*. Wrote the play, "Cinq," produced at the Patriote by le Mouvement Contemporain, directed by André Brassard. Play was enlarged and rewritten as *En pièces détachées* and produced at the Théâtre de Quat' Sous in 1969. Presented on TV as "Beau Dimanches" in 1971, 1972; in English in 1973 in Winnipeg (translated by Allan Van Meer).

1968   *Les Belles-Soeurs*, written in 1965, produced at the Rideau-Vert, directed by André Brassard.

1969   Wrote and had published his first novel *La Cité dans l'oeuf*, Editions du Jour, Montreal. Wrote adaptation of the Aristophanes play, *Lysistrata*, at the National Arts Centre, Ottawa, and at Théâtre du Nouveau Monde, Montreal. *La Duchesse de Langeais* produced at Théâtre de Quat' Sous, Montreal; "Trois Petits Tours," on Radio-Canada.

1970   Wrote an adaptation of Paul Zindel's *The Effect of Gamma Rays on Man-In-The-Moon Marigolds*, produced at Théâtre de Quat' Sous, Montreal. Collaborated with composer, François Dompierre, on a musical comedy, "Demain matin, Montréal m'attend," produced at Jardin des Etoiles, à la Ronde, Montreal, and in 1972 at Théâtre Maisonneuve, Place des Arts, Montreal. Wrote *Forever Yours, Marie-Lou*.

1971   *Forever Yours, Marie-Lou* produced at the Théâtre de Quat' Sous, Montreal. Wrote *Hosanna*.

1972   Wrote scenario and dialogues for André Brassard's "Françoise Durocher, Waitress," for Radio-Canada. Adapted four one-act plays of Tennessee Williams into "Au pays du dragon," produced at Théâtre de Quat' Sous. Adapted Paul Zindel's "Et Mademoiselle Roberge boit un peu" for production at Théâtre Maisonneuve, Montreal.

1973   *Hosanna* produced at Théâtre de Quat' Sous, Montreal, and at the Tarragon Theatre, Toronto. *Forever Yours, Marie-Lou* translated into English by John Van Burek and Bill Glassco and produced at the Tarragon. Adapted Dario Fo's "Mistero Buffo" for Théâtre du Nouveau Monde, Montreal. *Les Belles-Soeurs* produced in Paris at L'Espace Cardin Théâtre, and in English at the St. Lawrence Centre, Toronto. Collaborated with André Brassard on the film, *Il était une fois dans l'est*.

1974   Wrote *Bonjour, là, bonjour*, which was produced at the National Centre of the Arts, Ottawa, and at Place des Arts, Montreal. *Il était une fois dans l'est* shown as an official entry in the Cannes Film

	Festival. *Hosanna* produced at the Bijou Theater on Broadway.
1975	Wrote "Surprise, surprise," produced at Théâtre du Nouveau Monde, Montreal, and by Toronto Arts Productions, Toronto. Wrote scenarios for the films *Le Soleil se lève en retard sur la Rue Belanger* and *Parlez-nous d'amour*. Collaborated with André Brassard on *Le Soleil se lève en retard*.
1976	Wrote *Ste-Carmen de la Main*, produced at Théâtre Port-Royal, Place des Arts, Montreal. *Forever Yours, Marie-Lou* produced at the Arena Stage, Washington, D.C., with the first all-American cast. Collaborated with composer Sylvain Lelièvre on the musical comedy, "Les Héros de mon enfance," produced at Théâtre de la Marjolaine. Wrote the play, "Damned Manon and Sacred Sandra." Lived temporarily in Paris where he began work on a novel. (Returned to Quebec after the Parti Québécois victory in the provincial election.) Won the Ontario Lieutenant Governor's Medal for his contribution to drama.
1977	*Hosanna* successfully revived in Toronto. *Forever Yours, Marie-Lou* produced at the Lennoxville Festival of the Arts. "Damned Manon and Sacred Sandra" produced in Montreal. *Les Belles-Soeurs* produced for television and at Theatre London, London, Ontario. *Bonjour, là, bonjour* produced in Vancouver, Boston, and at the Saidye Bronfman Centre in Montreal.

Selected Bibliography

Primary Sources

"Au pays du dragon." Adaptation of a play by Tennessee Williams. MS, Montreal: Théâtre de Quat' sous, 1972.
Les Belles-Soeurs. Vancouver: Talonbooks, 1974.

Bonjour, là, bonjour. Vancouver: Talonbooks, 1975.

"Damned Manon and Sacred Sandra." MS, 1976.

"Demain matin, Montréal m'attend." Music composed by François Dompierre. MS, Montreal, 1970.

La Duchesse de Langeais and Other Plays. Vancouver: Talonbooks, 1976.

"The Effect of Gamma Rays on Man-in-the-Moon Marigolds." Adaptation of Paul Zindel's play. MS, Montreal, Théâtre de Quat' Sous, 1970.

En pièces détachées. Vancouver: Talonbooks, 1975. Translated as *Like Death Warmed Over*.

"Et Madamoiselle Roberge boit un peu." Adaptation of a play by Paul Zindel. MS, Montreal: Théâtre Maisonneuve, 1972.

Forever Yours, Marie-Lou. Vancouver: Talonbooks, 1975.

"Françoise Durocher, Waitress." TS, Montreal, Radio-Canada, 1972.

"Les Héros de mon enfance." Music by Sylvain Lelièvre. MS, Montreal, Théâtre de la Marjolaine, 1976.

Hosanna. Vancouver: Talonbooks, 1974.

"Lysistrata." Adaptation of Aristophanes' play. Ottawa, National Arts Centre, 1969.

"Messe noire." Collaboration with 15 authors. MS, Montreal, Gésu, 1965.

"Mistero Buffo." Adaptation of a play by Dario Fo. MS, Montreal, Théâtre du Nouveau Monde, 1973.

Ste-Carmen de la Main. Montreal: Théâtre Port-Royal, 1976.

"Surprise, surprise." MS, Toronto, Toronto Arts Productions, 1975.

"Le Train." TS, Montreal, Radio-Canada, 1960.

Secondary Sources

"Celebration of Words." *Time*, January 29, 1973, p.7.

GERMAIN, JEAN-CLAUDE. "*Les Belles-Soeurs*, ou l'enfer des femmes." *Etudes françaises* 6, No. 1 (1970), pp. 96-103.

MCQUAID, CATHERINE. "Michel Tremblay's Seduction of the Other Solitude." *Canadian Drama/L'Art dramatique canadien* 2, No. 2 (1976), pp. 217-21.

MONAHAN, IONA. "Parisians Bow to *Les Belles-Soeurs*." *The Montreal Star*, November 23, 1973.

POPKIN, HENRY. "Canada's Best-Known, and Angriest Playwright Is Coming to Broadway." *New York Times*, October 13, 1974.

USMIANI, RENATE. "Michel Tremblay's *Sainte Carmen*: Synthesis and Orchestration." *Canadian Drama/L'Art dramatique canadien* 2, No. 2 (1976), PP. 206-18.

————— *Gratien Gélinas*. Profiles in Canadian Drama Series. Toronto: Gage Publishing Ltd., 1977. (Contains a chapter giving the history of theatre in Quebec.)

Twelve

MICHEL GARNEAU
(1939-   )

Preface

Michel Garneau started writing when he was very young. The son of a Montreal judge he was raised in a cultured environment. One of his two older brothers was a painter, the other, Sylvain, was a poet, though he made his living as a staff announcer for the CBC. Sylvain had a profound influence on Michel, listening to his younger brother's opinions of what he was writing and encouraging Michel's own early literary efforts.

When Michel was still in his early teens and Sylvain in his early twenties the older brother died. Michel became obsessed with his death, refusing to attend school and finally leaving both home and school. Friends took him in and he supported himself washing dishes in a Honeydew Restaurant and selling magazines door to door. At fifteen he was drinking heavily. Eventually his parents became reconciled to the fact that he was not living at home, and for awhile sent him some money.

At this time he went back to school, studying at L'Ecole du Théâtre du Nouveau Monde. He wanted to be an actor and to write plays. He went on to study at the Conservatoire d'Art Dramatique. If culture wasn't Parisian then, it wasn't culture in Quebec. At the Conservatory he was asked to recite poetry and he chose to recite Sylvain's poetry. The professor (of diction) refused to comment because the poetry was spoken with a Quebec accent.

After leaving the Conservatory he worked for a summer for a radio station in Trois Rivières. This was the beginning of what was to become a varied career in radio and television, working as an announcer, disc jockey and in many other aspects of the two media. He worked for ten years in Montreal, five years in

Rimouski, for a short time in Ottawa, and then again in Montreal. Throughout this period he continued to write poetry, short stories, and plays. (He had been writing regularly since he was seventeen.)

His first produced drama, a one-act play with six characters, "Les Grands Moments," was premièred in a prison by the acting company, Les Jeunes Canadiens de Nouveau Monde. They then toured Canada with this play. There followed two short plays, "Saperlipocrisse et Crisseporlipopette" about two characters each 140 years old, and the play, "Beu-meu," both produced by the Montreal theatre, Le Théâtre Populaire du Québec. Subsidized by the Ministry of Cultural Affairs, they toured the province with these two plays in 1968. One year later he wrote Sur le matelas *at L'Isle d'Orléans, followed by a production in Montreal. There followed a play, "Dix-Sept," written for seventeen students at the National Theatre School.*

Another play for the same school was an adaptation of Shakespeare's play, The Tempest, *written in "Québécois." (Garneau says that he writes in "Québécois" not* joual. Joual *is a spoken language incorporating many English words pronounced as though French, and sometimes imitating English syntax. "Québécois" is the pure French language of Quebec which has developed separately from the French spoken in France. Its vocabulary includes many archaic French words no longer in European French usage.)* Quatre à quatre *was created for college students, then translated into English and produced at the Tarragon Theatre in Toronto, before being produced in the original language at Le Théâtre de Quat' Sous in Montreal, directed by André Brassard. Another play, "Le Bonhomme sept-heures," reminds one of the bogeyman, that monstrous imaginary figure used to threaten children. Actually it is not a child's play but a play on culturally organized fears, accompanied by the beautiful music of André Angelini. Another one of his plays,* La Chanson d'amour de cul, *(The Dirty Love Song), is Garneau's attempt to satirize pornography.*

Garneau's deep interest in language has resulted in his use of The Epic of Gilgamesh *for an original play. This epic, written in the Sumerian language of Mesopotamia, 6,000 years ago, may* be the oldest written text, antedating Homer. Possibly the first poem ever written, it is about friendship and death, incredibly relevant to people today, according to Garneau. From this epic, Garneau wrote a play set in an ancient marketplace. Actors sing the epic of Gilgamesh with interludes of live scenes giving comic relief to the audience and an impression of realism. Possibly the best of all his plays, it is dedicated to Sylvain and it is a deeply sensitive re-evaluation of life and death in an effort to free himself of the spectre of death.

The rich quality of Michel Garneau's drama, his poetry and love of language, his sense of spirituality in life, his ability to infuse his characters with vivid reality while at the same time presenting them as symbolic, suggest that he has that indefinable combination of gifts that produces great plays.

Garneau treads the fine line between the comic and the tragic. His sense of humour is delightful. At the same time his writings have a spiritual quality hard to define. He is not simply recording Quebec life in its own language; he is composing a highly sensitive drama akin to poetry. Seeing a Garneau play is like reading a superb poem. The lyric qualities in both produce the same results —a kind of ecstasy from the mystical insights perceived. His plays become symbols of a whole race of people — Québécois. Strauss et Pesant is a perfect example. In this triangular love affair the woman who dies has been the object of an obsessive love by the policeman to whom she is married and by the bishop who never relinquished her. The confrontation by the two men after her death, with its series of poignant flashbacks, has the effect on the audience of a dream. One watches the characters but one is also watching Quebec as she is prostituted by the government and the Church. It is a powerful prose poem and a rich drama. Garneau has simultaneously created live characters and vivid symbols. His fine sense of theatre keeps him in control of his dramatic techniques. The play becomes a deeply moving spiritual experience.

As Garneau has said: "Theatre is that incredible place where poetry can be spoken."

did why did what

i is i am something with heart
a furry somehow   like
a mountain blissful sheep
wet nose in fresh milk

oh non   i did not begin writing drama ever
i write
poems and proses and songs as words began singing in
me
before my mind knew my mind
before i knew i was singing
as i know now as i write grocery lists and errand lists
and words and ideas and lines of ink linking words
for ideas and sounds of type like i play piano
and learn flute and use guitar and blow in 'an 'out
of harmonica once in a bluesharp moon and write
plays and a novel forever and essays on things
that i think others are not thinking about
and this i do just like that 'cause i aim to be
an always-just-born-lyrical-skeptic
and writing is a good tool
and
"a poet is a poet for such a tiny bit of his life,
for the rest he is a human being, one of whose
responsibilities is to know and feel,
as much as he can, all that is moving around and
within him, so that his poetry when he comes to write
it, can be his attempt at an expression of the summit
of man's experience, on this very peculiar, and in
1946, this apparently hell-bent earth."
Dylan Thomas
found this delightful way of saying
that the poet is a poet all the time
and that, some of the time, she works, he works, we work

on books, which are the result of our and his and her
work in and on life.

i write of course
        to be a somehow tree in present history
        to play with my sap
        to play with the sap of the tree in the paper
        to be a domestic phoenix
        to inherit the world and inherit the word
        to inherit language
        and to do something which will shoot the
        isolation of (my) self from others full
        of smiling holes
        knowing that at the moment i'm writing this
        somebody in Somewheria or two miles away
        to my left is inimitably writing the same thing

i write of course
        to achieve a total and tenderly enlightened sense
        of humour seeping out of a simple and constant
        consciousness of the perpetual happening of the world
        and that i man is being born and that i
        man is tortured and torturing that there is not a
        third of a thousandth of a second that i man is
        not making love in a sparkling happiness as well as
        in a sticky sorrow

i write
        to tell of my splendid hate for all hermetism
        all that hides the comicness of the void and throws
        cultures whole cultures in always untimely out of
        time but in lifeeverafter hopes and we much more need
        a big beautiful healthy despair from the acceptance
        of the mess we've done our sheer responsibility
        and we need to use that frank despair to go back or
        forward to the pleasures of breathing and in this no
        longer
        cheapened breathing find the harmony which could
        help

us clean the world of the unbearable pain
nourished by afterlife
pathetic hopping hopes.

i write
      because it is a juicy shareable vengeance
      as a recreation of one's part of the world
      or of some special sore spots
      and a recreation of the world as perception
      and the naming of disorders usually disguised
      as orders which clash anyway with one's own
      sense of order or an eternal one
      that the present always rapes anyway
      a vendetta a violence violence from
      the kind of coward who claims to be
      non-violent and is of course a violence-namer

      it's also the happy choice of that cowardice
      knowing that violence is spiritually intolerable.

to write
      is to play at gods' eyes
      to play at being a total sight of the total mess
      a sight burning with the action looked upon and
      participating while passively pretending to be
      part of the harmony of the origin and of the end
      which could join you know if the weather gets
      really good.
      god was in the grave and was looking at cain
      and victor hugo was in himself watching god
      looking at cain who was in himself looking
      at abel watching him and in abel was god
      looking at cain
            who entirely surrounded started writing
      and begat the anonymous who begat homer
      who begat all sorts of people who begat
      victor who begat james joyce who begat
      jacques ferron and

i write
> everything
> because i know that there is only poetry.
> language is poetry.
> "Language is fossilized poetry." (Emerson)

> the more one masturbates the less one sees
> the mystical union of man and woman

> the more we use language outside of the
> jubilation of the breathing gift
> the less we know that all words are
> chips of the poem
> the novel i'm probably writing
> will be named
> dans la jubilation du respir-cadeau
> in the jubilation of the breathing-gift
> i also want to write a play bearing that title
> and poems and songs and a life
> in fact i want using the whole vocabulary
> of gestures to write myself a life
> which will be called
> in the jubilation of the breathing-gift

yes
> in the marvelous chaos of the universe
> which might be a big maybe infinite
> sputtering structure
> to build small communication structures
> is one of the entertaining things to do
> and can always be used as hommage

to write
> anything but well built
> like a boat so that it floats
> on the pleasure of being the sea of seeing
> and writing to always jump on the occasion
> of saying that utopia is workable

we just have to work on it
and i guess (i know) ((i'm being polite))
that we can't do it with capitalism
so we have to work on that death too

everybody knows in moments of goodness
that sanctity (of being) is the beautiful
scandal through which anything can happen

     and saints
out of the religious manias they have to display
in order to justify their social status and income
are good shouters of utopia
good public reality dreamers
good public makers of reality

     we all
dream in the head and the head heavy with the dream
floats down to the heart and in the heart we create
and then quite early one century everything of love
     will happen   by capillarity
utopia will not be achieved by instant illumination
revelation or color live enlightenment
     or
the enlightenment of everyone and everybody including
the more mongoloid of the politicians will happen
through communication through the capillary
network dug in our ways by the thinking souls
it is damned important to know
what stops
the intelligence of solidarity

millions of people are cultural robots

i write
     to fight the cultural robots
     not to become one
     and to say that cultural robotry is
     the living death of humanity

     language is my field of deadly flowers
     and my field is all yours

     language has to be understood
     not submitted to

     i love language
     it is the best of the heritage

i write
     to do my part
     that all humans will have a chance
     of knowing that language is a communal
     construction
     and no possession
     language is a tool that only exists
     between people in the sharing of it

     and that language is the sharpest
     political strength and the more dangerous
     and very well full of the most nice virtualities

     knowledge of language fertilizes a
     sense of humour and humour cleans the eyes
     and for the moment should be absorbed
     in excessive quantity this being the winter
     of humanity and we must reach spring

i write
     mainly about life
     about the arrival in the innocence
             the first white suck is pure
             (whatever the devil-fools mutter)
     about the fast glide into corruption
     which starts with schools and blooms in business
     and the robotization that accompanies the corruption
     and i write about the consciousness of being
     corrupt and the evidence it shows that the only

way is the tragic crazy comical sublime natural
leap into un-naïve purity hinted at by the
buddhas and christs and bakounines and rilkes
and freuds and jungs and karls and jennys (the marxes)
and poethomases of all colours
all those that sang under the tragic sun
with their toes dancing in the cry-baby swamp
            'cause
either you get out of the shock of being born
(you don't come out you GET OUT)
and you learn to live/die/die/live
just like anybody in the obscure cosmological
fraternity or else you stay a stunned wrinkled
foetus all fucked up in the cowardly promiscuities
of "ain't we all a poor bunch of fallen marvels
    and let's go back to daddy"
            and you do feel derelict
    abandoned by all including god
and you can try to con Him with a religion
you'll just sink and sink in the cultural magma
as if THAT was life
incapable of facing your solitude
of feeling the brotherhood of solitude
of conspiring for utopia because utopia is
about here's future
incapable of being a glorious passage
because the passage is here

i am a glorious passage
outside of being glorious passages
we are not distinct from being

it's like life enables us to see
ourselves passing
            the rest of the time
            i'm sure we are

i in the cultural magma
am not working for the cultural robots

but the cultural robots will try
to eat me
i should be a pariah
maybe what the cultural robots call a genius
and don't worry i'm not hamming towards madness
everybody is privately an outcast genius
as it should be but we should all come out with it
and come down on the cultural robots who are fiddling
with the lists of cultural values and fixin'
the cultural hit-parades

no cultural robots: no outcast geniuses,
just humans breathing creatively
unseparated, consciously unseparated from
the being of all

until then one survives in this society
through the admiration of the cultural robots
like saints survive through religions
it's the dirty coat we have to wear
                aware of the dirty coat
you name the garbage you're wearing
                unaware of the dirty coat
you become the garbage you're wearing
                and so many
are just their clothes
                so many are just
their cars or the hobbies they slave upon

                out of respect for being
                i know myself as
                different from anyone

                out of respect for man
                i know myself to be
                not a hair different
i choose myself to be a poet
                to walk around the world i know

with my bouquet of paper flowers
    whose every fiber of trees
are chosen by me
    to sing utopia
as it sings in me when i listen to being
i also listen to the big fat farting trucks
and i also laugh and tickle myself terribly
rubbing against the wild madness which makes us
carry eggs from one end of the world to the other
while chickens are everywhere

i write
    simply in the blueberry delight of the heritage
of speech talk o wondrous words
only thing which in the heart of my love of life
gives me wonderment akin to the one which invades
me when i look smell eat think talk chive
    if i have a personal symbol for nature
    chive it is
from the use of language as chive
i get many marvels of memory and desires
and right now in eating words the jolly
and pertly preposterous-as-a-green-green-frog
intuition that there is somelsewhere a planet
covered with chive and millions of softblue
trees slowly standing on millions of velvethills
surrounded by softgreen rivers hardgreen lakes
and populated by all animals but all of the size
and temperament of cats and
by tender and often hilarious couples
    and there death is a suave apoplexy
given in the chance of an orgasm so vibrant
that the couples go up in flowers germinating

certain couples abolish themselves when
they're twelve years old
others when they're very very old
but all couples know that making love
they conquer the chance of dying together

i write

> to tell of my delighted amazed marvelling
> at the realizing tools that words are
> and of my respect for this collective soul
> bearing multiple edges as cutting as
> bull-rush leaves

i also write

> because in the game of trades
> those of carpenter and poet and singer of songs
> and music or just being any playful artist
> seem to me more amusing and to be better openers
> of freedom than the trades of priesthood
> tavern-ownerhood or cophood
> > in fact the most humble utopia
> wants that everyone talks-sings and plays sounds
> and plays colours and plays all manners of matters
> and jubilates gratuitously in a collectively
> insured freedom
> and that all the gross trades so important
> parts of the present disaster
> will become curios of the ancient tragic farce
> > i is very happy that by becoming a poet
> > there is a lawyer (or you can fill in
> > > with your favorite clown)
> > less in the world

and i write

> about that which is even beyond utopia
> that thing that gesture being
> which some call the gods
> being that inhabits in the great silence
> of the great original fun
> call it what you may
> god the great manitou the one or the four and a half
> or the little kitten or joe the eternal
> me i don't give a bless i don't sigh an amen
> i gurgle myself with all the names of being

as i gurgle with the milky way once every summer
and i don't congratulate you for calling names
on the unsayable, on old unnamable, on dear old
immutable who probably didn't do to you half
of the things you think he did
and it seems a conceited shame to clumsily
shove your epithets and nicknames around
       (god is atrociously like gus
       and reads dog reversed)
very improbably towards such a lovely
gesture-presence-inactive-absence
       that of this which has no name
       in any language
       the un-created that all the created
       or the crated if you can see it that way
the un-created that we the created creatures
pretend is the source accomplishing that small feat
with our voices
       in the work of our voices pleasantly
searching madly
       where the hell and heaven and hunting
       grounds
do we come from and go
       with our voices singing the songs of existence
       as if the breath came from the un-created
       but we can only tap the beat of the created

it is ourselves we are celebrating
when we invent our confidence in the intuition
that in ourselves
       all is not hiding
       but revealing

but then one must want to be all
and it's not exactly easy to start
one of these mornings
if you don't have the comical certainty
that the ALL to jump in is already started

has been before you without you
will go on after you without you
or with it
and that by jumping in the void
in a disinterested fashion
                maybe even courageously
you're jumping into glorious life
like a rabbit
a rabbit who would have the understanding
of being a rabbit
a rabbit who can't get over the luck
the luck of being a rabbit
while still gravely considering
not too gravely just enough
the risks involved
but so minimal when compared with
the amazing occasion of being
a rabbit in the world
why a rabbit?

       because its reputation is better
       than man's
       so one does not feel that the rabbits
       should be punished and are getting
       what's coming to them

       and the rabbit is less shmaltzy
       rarely complains
       is so much more gentle
       that we may very well
       understand better
       the amazing occasion of being
       a human in the world
       when i say rabbit

and also because apart from the sublime
imbecility of humans
and the sublime genius of humans
and our drama of knowing ourselves

i don't much see the difference

if i were not a man
i wouldn't mind at all being a rabbit.

Chronology

1939	Born April 25, in Montreal, son of Judge Antonio Garneau and Madame Garneau
1951-55	Attended the Jesuit schools, Collège Brébeuf, Collège Sainte-Marie, and Collège Saint-Denis.
1954-55	Comedien: Ecole du Théâtre du Nouveau Monde. Auditeur Libre at the Conservatory of Dramatic Art of Quebec in Montreal. Radio announcer at stations CHLN and CKTR at Trois Rivières, and at CKVL in Montreal.
1956-60	Radio announcer and scriptwriter at CJBR-TV in Rimouski. Wrote *Eau de pluie* (poetry).
1960-61	Announcer-animateur at Radio-Canada-TV (CBOFT) in Ottawa.
1961-68	Established a major career on radio and television as announcer and writer of "Images en tête" (1962-67), and hundreds of shows in Montreal and Toronto. Worked with the television group, "Les Cailloux," as animateur-chanteur (1966-67). Published *Le Pays*, an edition of collected poems.
1961-68	Full time occupation (1961-64) and part-time (1964-68) on various programs for different radio stations in which he gave informative talks on various diversions. Wrote and had produced his first stage play, "Les Grands Moments," premièred in a prison and then on tour across Canada with Les Jeunes Canadiens du Nouveau Monde. Entrevues et musique de *Gros Morne*, ONF, réal: Jacques Géraldeau, for cinema.
1967-68	Worked for Radio-Canada in Paris, France. Wrote in English the play, "Who's Afraid of James Wolfe," for CBC-TV in Toronto.

1968 Wrote two short plays "Saperlipocrisse et crisseporlipopette," and "Beu-meu," produced at Le Théâtre Populaire du Québec, Montreal. Subsidized by the Ministry of Cultural Affairs, it toured the province. Scénario et musique de *Valerie et l'aventure*, CBC-ORTF, réal: Claude Fournier (first episode).

1968-69 Wrote and presented "Parlures paroles poèmes," touring the province of Quebec with Michèle Rossignol who collaborated with him on this program.

1969-70 On tour throughout Quebec, in collaboration with Françoise Berd and Michèle Rossignol, presenting the program, "Rencontre-Animation-Théâtre," produced by the Ministry of Cultural Affairs.

1970-71 Two short plays, "Hostay de croum" (Saperlipocrisse et crisseporlipopette) and "Beu-meu," produced at Théâtre Populaire du Québec. Read his poetry at "La Nuit de la poésie" in Montreal. Participated as an author at the "manifestation/spectacle," "Poèmes et chants de la résistance," in Montreal. With the cast he wrote the play, "Des chevaux, des rois, des dames, et des fous," for Les Jeunes Comédiens du Théâtre du Nouveau Monde, Institut Leclerc, Montreal.

1972 Wrote the play, "Dix-sept," for students at the National Theatre School in Montreal. Wrote the play, *Sur le matelas* produced at Théâtre du Huitième Etage, Théâtre Le Galendor, Ile d'Orleans.

1973 *Sur le matelas* produced at Théâtre de Quat' Sous, Montreal. Adapted Shakespeare's *Tempest* in *joual* for the National Theatre School. Wrote the play, "Le Bonhomme sept heures," with music by André Angelini, produced at the National Theatre School in Montreal in 1974 and at Le Théâtre de Quat' Sous. Wrote the play, *Quatre à quatre*, produced at Option-Théâtre du CEGEP Lionel-Groulx Collège.

1974 Animator for many literary groups for Le Centre d'Essai des Auteurs Dramatiques, at the Festival du Jeune Théâtre, Rimouski. Wrote *La Chanson d'amour*, produced at Théâtre du Nouveau Monde. Wrote *Strauss et Pesant (et Rosa)*, produced at Le Théâtre d'Aujourd'hui, Montreal. *Quatre à quatre*, translated into English as *Four to Four* by Keith Turnbull and Christian Bédard, and produced at the Tarragon Theatre, Toronto. Then produced in the original *joual* at Le Théâtre de Quat' Sous, in Montreal, directed by André Brassard, music by André Angelini. (Produced successfully in Paris, France, in 1976 and 1977.) *Gilgamesh* presented on Radio-Canada by André Major.

1975   Wrote the play, "Le Groupe." Adapted Shakespeare's *Macbeth* in "Québécois." Produced in Montreal. Play based on the *Epic of Gilgamesh*, music by André Angelini, produced at the National Theatre School in Montreal. Wrote the play, "Abriés et désabriées," music by André Angelini, produced in Montreal. Composed the music as well as participating as a singer for the recording of the record, *Allô Toulmônd*, with Raoul Duguay (chanson *Le Voyage*) disques Capitol-Emi, Montreal. Tournée *Théâtre-Québec* in France, production du Centre d'Essai des Auteurs Dramatiques (Montreal); participant as well as comédien and auteur. *Quatre à quatre* is presented there. Received a Canada Council grant for his work in drama. Adaptation of a work by Frederico Garcia Lorca, "La Maison de Bernarda Alba."

1976   Presented a Writers' Workshop, "De la poussière d'étoiles dans les os" at Ste Thérèse. Wrote a new series of plays for a young theatre group in 1975. "Les Voyagements" and "Rien que la mémoire," which were produced at La Maison de la Sauvegarde. *Les Célébrations* was produced at the University of Montreal. For another group of young actors, Troupe la Rallonge, in 1975 he wrote the play, "L'Usage du coeur dans le domaine réel" (The Use of the Heart in the Domain of the Real) which is a defense of his optimistic view of life. Lecteur à l'émission Chers nous autres, at Radio-Canada, Montreal. Wrote scénario de "Chanson pour Julie," production C. Lamy, réal: Jacques Vallée. He has written five other scenarios (non réalisés) and was narrator for many film documentaries produced by ONF and independent companies. Animator at Théâtre-Action in Ontario.

1973-76	Dramaturge at the National Theatre School, Montreal, 1973-78, and at the Collège Lionel-Groulx, Option-Théâtre, at Ste Thérèse in 1973 and 1976.
1977	Wrote the play, "Adidou adidouce," for Troupe Voyagements, produced at Maison des Arts de la Sauvegarde, Montreal. "Les Célébrations" and "Rien que la mémoire" were presented on Radio-Canada, Montreal, by Jean-Pierre Saulnier. His children's play, "Sers-toi d'tes antennes" was presented by La Troupe Organisation Ô.

Selected Bibliography

Primary Sources

PLAYS

"Abriés desabriées." Music by André Angelini. MS, Montreal, National Theatre School, 1975.

Adidou adidouce. Montreal: Editions VLB, 1977.

"Beu-meu." MS, Montreal, Le Théâtre Populaire du Québec, 1968.

La Chanson d'amour de cul. Montreal: Editions de l'aurore, 1974.

"Le Bonhomme sept-heures." Music by André Angelini. MS, Montreal, National Theatre School, 1974.

Les Célébrations, Montreal: Editions VLB, 1977.

"De la poussière d'étoiles dans les os." MS, Ste. Thérèse, Option Théâtre du CEGEP Lionel-Groulx, 1976.

"Des chevaux, des rois, des dames, et des fous." MS, Montreal, Les Jeunes Comédiens du Théâtre du Nouveau Monde, 1970.

"Dix-sept." MS, Montreal, National Theatre School, 1972.

"Le Groupe." MS, Montreal, 1974.

Gilgamesh. Montreal: Editions VLB, 1976.

"Hostay de croum." (Saperlipocrisse et crisseporlipopette). MS, Montreal, Théâtre Populaire du Québec, 1971.

"Il n'y a rien de plus nouveau que le soleil." MS, Montreal, 1976.

"Josephine la pas fine et Itoff le toffe." MS, Montreal: La Nouvelle Compagnie Théâtrale, 1976. (For children.)

"Macbeth." Adaptation of Shakespeare's play. MS, Montreal, 1975.

"La Maison de Bernarda Alba." Adaptation of a work by Frederico Garcia Lorca. MS, Ottawa, National Theatre Centre of the Arts, 1975.

"Petit Petant et le monde." MS, Montreal, University of Montreal, 1975.

Quatre à quatre. Montreal: Editions de l'aurore, 1974.

"Le Ravi." MS, Montreal, CEAD Théâtre d'Aujourd'hui, 1969.

Rien que la mémoire. Montreal: Editions VLB, 1977.

"Sers-toi d'tes antennes." MS. Montreal, 1975. (For children.)

Strauss et Pesant (et Rosa). Montreal: Editions de l'aurore, 1974.

Sur le matelas. Montreal: Editions de l'aurore, 1974.

"La Tempête." Adaptation of Shakespeare's *Tempest*. MS, Montreal, National Theatre School, 1973.

"L'Usage du coeur dans le domaine réel." MS, Montreal, Troupe la Rallonge, 1975.

Les Voyagements. Montreal: Editions VLB, 1977.

"Who's Afraid of James Wolfe." MS, Montreal, 1967.

THEATRE ESSAY

Le Théâtre sur commande. Montreal: Entretien No. 1, Editions centre d'essai des auteurs dramatiques, 1975. An extract is also published in *Jeu*, No. 3 (1976).

POETRY

Eau de pluie. Rimouski: A compte d'auteur, 1958.

Elégie au génocide des nasopodes. Montreal: Editions de l'aurore, 1974.

Langage. Montreal: Editions à la page, 1962.

Langage I: Vous pouvez m'acheter pour 69¢. Montreal: A compte d'auteur, 1972.

Langage II: Blues des élections. Montreal: A compte d'auteur, 1972.

Langage III: L'Animalhumain. Montreal: A compte d'auteur, 1972.

Langage IV: J'aime la litterature, elle est utile. Montreal: Editions de l'aurore, 1974.

Langage V: Politique. Montreal: Editions de l'aurore, 1974.

Moments. Montreal: Editions Danielle Laliberté, 1973.

Le Pays. Montreal: Editions Déom, 1963.

Les Petits Chevals amoureux. Montreal: Editions VLB, 1977.

La Plus Belle Ile. Montreal: Editions Parti-Pris, 1975.

Appendix

Selected List of Drama Awards in Canada

The following list is not all-inclusive. There are many awards for playwrights given by provincial arts councils, writers' unions, film and theatre festivals, not included due to limitations of time and space. The following list includes only nationally known awards given in Canada.

ACTRA Awards.   First presented in 1973. The two awards available to playwrights are for the Best Writer in the Dramatic Mode in the Visual Media (TV or film) and the Best Writer in the Dramatic Mode in Radio.

Canadian Authors Association Award.   Awarded annually for a dramatic work produced in the preceding calendar year. It consists of a silver medal and $1,000.

Clifford E. Lee Award.   An annual award inaugurated by the University of Alberta and Theatre Network's Studio Theatre, for the best Canadian play of the year. It includes $3,000 and a production of the play at the Citadel Theatre, in Edmonton. As a National Playwriting Competition, it encourages contributions from all areas of Canada, and from new writers as well as the better known Canadian dramatists.

Dominion Drama Festival Awards.   This festival was replaced in 1971 by Theatre Canada which does not give awards. The past D.D.F. awards are listed in the General Introduction of this volume.

Diplôme d'Honneur.   Presented annually by the Canadian Conference of the Arts to persons who have made an extraordinary contribution to the arts in Canada. Although it is not specifically for theatre, among its recipients have been dramatists, actors, directors, and others very much involved in theatre.

The Edmonton Achievement Award.   Awarded annually by the City of Edmonton for outstanding contributions to theatre and other arts by someone identified with the city of Edmonton.

Floyd S. Chalmers Award.   Annual award of $5,000 for the best Canadian play produced in Toronto that year. Given by the Toronto Drama Bench.

Lorne Pierce Medal.   Gold medal and $1,000 awarded every two years for a literary achievement in English or French, preferably dealing with a Canadian subject.

Ottawa Little Theatre Award.   Annual Canadian Playwriting Competition conducted by the Ottawa Little Theatre, Ottawa, Ontario. There are three prizes of $500, $350, and $200.

The Order of Canada.   Although this honour is not given specifically for theatre, many people involved in the arts and in drama have been its recipients.

Prix Anik Award.   The annual CBC award for the best drama, documentary and musical programmes.

Prix Marie-Claire Daveluy.   Award of $500 given every two years by ASTED (Association pour l'avancement des sciences et techniques de la documentation) to encourage young authors to write for young people. Open to any French-speaking person between the ages of 14 and 20 for unpublished literary works and drama for the 12 to 15 years of age group.

Prix Victor-Morin.   Award of $500 given annually to a French Canadian for outstanding achievements in theatre, television, or film in serving the higher interests of the French Canadian people. (Given by La Société Saint-Jean-Baptiste de Montréal.)

The Province of Alberta Award for Excellence in the Arts.   Awarded annually by the Province of Alberta for excellence in theatre and other arts. Recipient must be a resident of Alberta.

University of Regina Playwriting Competition.   Given once every two years by the University of Regina, Regina, Saskatchewan. Includes $1,000 and a production of the play.

Canada Council Awards

Exploration Program.   Three annual competitions providing grants from $300 to $20,000. Average grant is between $3,000 and $5,000 providing these funds for:
   (1) Investigation of new forms of expression and participation in the arts.
   (2) Inquiry into things past that hold special meaning in the cultural development of Canada.
   (3) Introduction of the new or different in the sphere of social understanding, or in the means of fostering public enjoyment of cultural activities, or our Canadian heritage.

Governor General's Literary Awards.   Annual awards of $5,000 each for individual works published that year of fiction, non-fiction, and poetry and drama. Instituted in 1937 by the Canadian Authors Association with the agreement of the Governor General of Canada. Since 1959 administered by Canada Council through the Governor

General's Literary Awards Committee, composed of eighteen members appointed by Canada Council and divided into two nine-member juries, one for French and one for English.

Senior Arts Grants. Two competitions annually in the visual arts and writing for those beyond the basic level of training and who have produced a body of work or established a professional reputation. These artists must have made a significant contribution over a number of years and be still actively engaged in their profession. Playwrights and scriptwriters should have had their work professionally published or produced. Value up to $16,000 to cover living expenses, travel, and project costs.

Arts Grants. Two competitions annually in all arts disciplines except music, to artists who have produced a body of work or established a professional reputation. Playwrights should have had their work professionally published or produced. Value up to $8,000, pro-rated according to the length of tenure, plus an allowance for travel and project.

Short Term Grants. To enable an artist to carry out a project requiring up to three months to complete. For artists beyond the basic level of training, including those who have made a significant contribution over a number of years. Value—$550 per month for three months plus travel and project cost allowance not exceeding $700.

Project Cost Grants. For artists beyond the level of basic training, including those who have made a significant contribution over a number of years. To cover only actual costs of a project. Value up to $2,400.

Travel Grants. For artists beyond their basic training including those who have made a significant contribution over a number of years and who are taking an invitational active part at meetings or competitions, or performances of their work.

Long Term Grants for Writers. For Canadian citizens at the Senior Arts Grant level who have made and are continuing to make a significant contribution to creative writing in Canada. To assist in undertaking a major writing project. Value up to $16,000. One grant each year to an English- and one to a French-language writer.

Note: The above list includes only those grants and awards available to individual playwrights to further the practice of their craft. For a more complete list write to the Canada Council, P. O. Box 1047, Ottawa, Ontario, K1P 5V8.

Index